Ian,

Thank you for all your support

Rich

"This book won't leave you untouched. I love that we learn about the framework of habits and attitudes that have helped Buddy Bramble to be what he wants to be, with stories that were comforting and inspiring."

Paul Smedley, Director & Founder, The Forum.

"*Choose to Be Relentless* is funny, serious, and practical, recounting the story of an award-winning leader that has led teams of thousands. It is a powerful guide for anyone looking for motivation, inspiration, and practical advice on how to live a fulfilling life."

Chris Cope, father of two, Digital Innovation Manager, Gloucestershire.

"As a recent graduate and politically involved 23-year-old, I found *Choose to Be Relentless* to be both extraordinarily comforting and motivational. I urge every young person starting out in the world of work to give it a read. Buddy's journey will resonate with people of all ages, in all stages of life. His recollections of life, work and family are illuminating and insightful."

Isabelle Poulter, graduate, Anglesey, Wales.

"*Choose to Be Relentless* is a powerful, must-read book and story of what it takes to take control of your life. Buddy demonstrates an abundance of humour, sharing his own personal journey along with his failures, successes, and lessons learnt. An open and honest book about how to make healthy choices and habits and how to recover when things don't go as planned."

Anita Yandell Jones, mother of two, Chief Customer Officer, Somerset.

"Leadership is about people, and you learn and improve by feeling their experiences. *Choose to Be Relentless* is a refreshing alternative to the standard leadership book. You get to understand Buddy's journey as he lets you into his life and you feel part of his career and family. Buddy's failures and successes come to life so that it is easier to apply the lessons learned to your own future journey. Well done on a refreshing alternative."

Guy Chalkley, CEO, New South Wales, Australia.

"*Choose to Be Relentless* is a wonderful example of bringing real life experiences and the journey of building relationships into the business world. The behaviours for life are brilliant. A model to help set yourself real aspirational goals that drive growth and release your true potential."

Laura Gillson, mother of two, Digital Product Director, Hertfordshire.

"It's easy to feel disconnected from self-help and motivational books, but that is not the case with *Choose to Be Relentless*. The steps shared to help live a well-rounded and fulfilling life are grounded in so much humanity that it becomes impossible not to make connections to your own personal experiences and to identify areas of growth.

It's a truly personal account that is written with care, humility and honesty and is delivered without a hint of judgement or condescension. I can honestly say it's one of the best books I've ever had the pleasure of reading and one I'll definitely be re-reading for years to come."

Leanne Merrill, living with long term partner, Marketing Leader, Wales

"I loved reading *Choose to be Relentless*. It is a fantastic book with many moments that made me smile and countless opportunities for me to reflect and consider my own life."

Richard Bench, married, Technology Leader UK & Ireland, Warwickshire.

"Buddy´s life lessons are an inspiration to many. This book brings them to life, in a funny, jaw dropping and relentless manner. The life lessons provided me the opportunity and life journey that I am sure other readers can utilise to accelerate their careers, using the framework, habits and questions that are thought provoking and enabling us all to keep learning and become winners."

Kees Van Ek, coach to two boys, Director, Harrogate, UK.

"I loved *Choose to Be Relentless*. An inspirational read with laugh out loud stories and emotional anecdotes coupled with deeply engaging questions. It is this mix that left me refreshed and energised and kept me invigorated."

John Maddocks, Global Portfolio Director, Essex, UK

"Buddy is undoubtedly the most inspirational leader that I have worked with. He is also, despite his self-confessed flaws, a thoroughly decent human being.

Buddy genuinely cares about making the human connections, which puts him in a different class to most."

Kathryn Betts, mother of two, Lincolnshire, UK

HOW THIS BOOK CAN HELP YOU

Choose to Be Relentless is written to help you become the person you want to be. It offers a framework that will inspire you to develop yourself and improve all areas of your life.

This book will be a valuable resource for various groups of readers. Students and young adults starting out in the world of work or are contemplating their future can benefit from its insights. Parents who are juggling their family responsibilities while building their career can also find it helpful. Those who are approaching retirement or seeking purpose and direction in life will find practical guidance in this book. Whatever your age or circumstances this book will stimulate you to be a winner on your own terms.

Within this book there are countless opportunities for you to reflect, consider, and examine your own life. You can choose to take responsibility for your present situation, identify your sources of happiness, and make the most of your potential. You will be able to create a better, happier life for you and the people around you.

Choose to Be Relentless will help you to step out of the shade and into the sunshine of life.

In Buddy Bramble's work as a consultant, coach, mentor, and leader of high-performing teams, he has met some truly talented people, working very hard and looking for the chance to be noticed. Sometimes stuck in the shade of life and being held back.

There are millions of talented people stuck in the shade. Too many listen to conversations in their head where they are held back by their own limiting thoughts; previous failure or criticism has made them feel that they are not good enough or they do not have the talent to succeed. Some in the shade of life have set such high standards for themselves that when they fail, they allow negative self-talk and doubt to creep into their thoughts. Some are so busy comparing themselves to others around them that they can quickly feel that they are not good enough, rarely stopping to spot their own unique talent. In the shade, people fear making mistakes, so they very rarely stray into the unknown.

Buddy knows exactly how being in the shade feels. He has been in the shade many times.

In a world of uncertainty and constant change we can all slip into the shade, sometimes.

The questions that play on the mind, and maybe yours, are along these lines. How can I:

- Let go of my past and stop worrying?
- Stop comparing myself to others?
- Become more relaxed about mistakes?
- Manage the negativity around me?
- Build better relationships?
- Be healthier and happier in my life?
- Create a better future for myself?
- Make steady progress and improve things?
- Decide what I want out of life?

For many, inside their fearful mind is a talent looking to be released. Just looking for an opportunity.

Choosing to Be Relentless is that opportunity.

Buddy has been on this journey himself and talks candidly with humour about his life and work experiences in this book. The hope for something better always inspired Buddy. He shares his failures, disappointments, successes, and lessons learnt in the hope it will inspire readers to make the most of their potential.

He shares his habits framework, behaviour model, and some practical tools that can help you change your life. These have been applied in his work and home, enabling others to reflect and focus on making progress in their life.

The book will help you find a new perspective and the answers to questions such as, how can I:

- Consider my life opportunities and improve?
- Refine my approach to physical and mental health?
- Become happier, healthier, and more successful?
- Manage the drainers that sometimes sap my energy?
- Build better relationships with people around me?
- Build a career and a family life doing things I love?
- Build an ambitious mindset of achievement?
- Become more resilient, confident, and hopeful?
- Become a winner on my terms?
- Identify what I'm passionate about?
- Build love into everything I do?

Thousands have applied much of the learning in this book and through their own efforts found their own sunshine.

Choose to Be Relentless gives you the practical guidance and tools to make the most of your life.

Choose to Be Relentless

Choose to Be Relentless

*Step out of the shade
into the sunshine*

Richard Brimble

First published in April 2023 in the United Kingdom by Understanding and Learning Limited

Copyright © Richard Brimble 2023

Richard Brimble has asserted his right to be identified as the author of the work in accordance with the Copyright, Designs and Patents Act 1988

All rights reserved. No part of this publication may be reproduced, stored, in a retrieval system, or transmitted in any form or by any means, electronic, mechanical, audio, visual, or otherwise, without prior written permission of the copyright owner. Nor can it be circulated in any form without similar conditions, including this condition being imposed on the subsequent purchaser.

Choose to Be Relentless is a work of non-fiction. This is a true story of a life. Names and identifying details of certain individuals and locations mentioned in this book have been changed to protect their privacy.

A Spotify playlist has been created to accompany the book. Some of Buddy's favourite, most inspirational songs can be found by downloading the "Choose to Be Relentless" playlist. There is an extended playlist if you have sixteen hours to spare.

Front Cover designed by Hight Design, Haxby, York

Printed and bound in the UK by CPI Antony Rowe Limited

ISBN: 978-1-3999-4770-1

Copies are available at special rates for bulk orders.

Richard Brimble is a customer experience and change management practitioner and life coach applying his unique approach within companies looking to create a differentiating factor to sustain their success.

If you need more copies of this book or any advice and guidance, please contact Richard at richard.brimble@understanding.co.uk.

FOREWORD

Working with 'Buddy Bramble' for more than a decade, I've seen him help others learn and grow. I've seen his distinctive approach to success in business also be based on active learning. He's helped us with learning and transformation in the networks and communities I helped to found for customer operations professionals. What I hadn't seen was his personal backstory, until now. It turns out this is a great way to learn about learning.

The twenty-five habits that shape his life come alive with insightful stories that are at times witty, at times heart-rending. He writes honestly about experiences which we can relate to. This book won't leave you untouched. Buddy shares an emotional journey that was literally life changing. He uncovers the human realities that lay the foundations of success, build fulfilling relationships, and help us win at what we want from life. *Understanding and learning* are at their heart.

I share with Buddy a passionate belief that we can each shape the opportunities in the world around us if we focus relentlessly on active learning. When we define and achieve success in life, on our own terms, we become pioneers and innovators. We make the difference because we don't limit our thinking or our goals. Indeed, Buddy's life habits and experiences give us a framework that we can use to tap into the unlimited potential of our humanity. As he demonstrates, we need to do this individually, in relationships with others, and as part of a wider purpose that gives direction to everything we do.

You can read this book as Buddy's life story. You can take away ideas on work or relationships, health or happiness. You can reflect on stories in your own life that connect with Buddy's framework of habits. You can allow the book to feed your imagination and consider how your own life could be different. You may also go further, using his practical framework to take control of your own destiny, in our volatile and fast-changing world.

Choose to Be Relentless gives you tools that you can use to work out how you can become the person you want to be and how to build love into everything that you do.

I hope it arrives in your life at the right time.

Please share *Choose to Be Relentless* with others too. This is Buddy's gift to us.

Paul Smedley, Director, The Forum – March 2023

This book began life as a letter to Buddy's children.

As the letter was being written, a thought occurred that it might be possible to add in some interesting family stories.

As the stories were written, it was clear that there were more thought-provoking adventures of family and business life to be told.

As the stories unfolded, Buddy was able to add in a framework of the life-changing habits that influenced his life.

He then added a life behaviours section.

The original thought had become seriously out of hand.

This book was originally published as a family edition in December 2022.

THE LETTER TO BUDDY'S CHILDREN

December 2022

Dear Alex and Patrice,

Like so many parents, we are so, so proud of you.

You are fit, healthy, happy, kind, likeable, and intelligent. You have strong moral principles based on treating people as they expect to be treated. You have enriched our lives and others around you.

It is all a father and mother can hope for.

You benefitted from the love of an extended family that gave you security, confidence, support, time, and attention. This home background gave you the foundation to contribute to life, knowing that you were liked and valued at home. This gave you the confidence and freedom to speak, travel, learn, make the most of your talents and not be fearful of the future. It gave you a great start in life. Make the most of it. Remember, we love you no matter what.

You have both focused on improving your health and building your relationships. This gives you a foundation to attack the learning opportunities in life. You are now all set to learn and grow your talents and achieve success on your terms.

So, Patrice and Alex, do you know what you want out of life, now and in the future? What do you need to change to make it happen? Are you willing to accept change? When you look back on your life in, say, ten years, will you have made the most of it? Find your purpose and goal in life. Know why you want to do it. Have a plan you believe in. Have routines that sustain the habits. Consistently applying the habits in *Choose to Be Relentless* will help you achieve in life. Stand up. Be noticed. Step out of the shade and into the sunshine of life.

We offer this as advice and guidance to you and any of our future grandchildren.

- Be responsible for your own circumstances.
- Be the best you can, for as long as you can.
- Be loving, resilient and aim high.
- Be passionate about what you love.
- Be happy and recognise the power of a smile.
- Be confident and put your talents out there.
- Be a winner and surround yourself with achievers.
- Be a learner and bounce back from experiences.
- Believe you can and visualise the future.

You are the future now. Make the most of it.

Mum & Dad

CONTENTS

WHAT DO YOU CHOOSE TO BE?...1
TAKE CONTROL OF YOUR LIFE AND FIND HAPPINESS...........9
ARE YOU OPEN TO THE OPPORTUNITIES?...............................15
WHAT DO YOU WANT OUT OF YOUR LIFE?...............................23
THE BEHAVIOURS YOU MEET IN LIFE...31
EXPERIENCING CONDITIONAL LOVE..51
ENJOYING LIFE AND FINDING LOVE...67
EXPERIENCING UNCONDITIONAL LOVE...................................79
CHOOSE TO PRIORITISE PHYSICAL AND MENTAL HEALTH.93
    BE LOVING...97
    BE HEALTHY...108
    BE PURPOSEFUL...117
    BE CARING...126
    BE CONFIDENT..135
    BE RESPONSIBLE...145
    BE ORGANISED...154
CHOOSE TO PRIORITISE FULFILLING RELATIONSHIPS......169
    BE OPTIMISTIC..173
    BE HAPPY...187
    BE PROACTIVE..201
    BE RESPECTFUL...218
    BE COMMITTED...233
    BE EMPATHETIC..242

CHOOSE TO PRIORITISE EXPERIENTIAL LEARNING 259
- BE PASSIONATE 263
- BE INSPIRED 275
- BE ENCOURAGING 290
- BE MOTIVATED 306
- BE CHALLENGED 320
- BE ACTIVELY LEARNING 331

CHOOSE TO PRIORITISE PROGRESS & PROSPERITY 347
- BE DRIVEN 351
- BE BOLD 365
- BE FLEXIBLE 378
- BE CURIOUS 391
- BE RESILIENT 404
- BE HOPEFUL 418

CHOOSE TO BUILD LOVE INTO EVERYTHING YOU DO 433
- Build the healthy foundations – love yourself 437
- Build relationships – love your partner and family 438
- Build learning – love friends and networks 439
- Build your life – love your purpose and direction 439

LEARNING FROM THE LIFE STORIES 441
WHAT ARE THE STORIES THAT INSPIRED YOU? 455
HOW TO PLAN FOR SUCCESS 459
ACKNOWLEDGEMENTS 475
RECOMMENDATIONS 477
THE AUTHOR 483

WHAT DO YOU CHOOSE TO BE?

WHAT DO YOU CHOOSE TO BE?

Introduction

What do you choose to be? Buddy chose to be relentless.

Choose to Be Relentless is written to help you become the person you want to be and offers a framework that will inspire you to develop yourself and improve all areas of your life.

The book is packed with raw, emotional, and funny life stories of Buddy Bramble, a humble, working-class man, who started work in a factory and made it to the boardroom of some of the world's best companies. His journey is sprinkled with moments of achievement and happiness. Also, moments where he needed to dig deep and bounce back from difficult circumstances and experiences. He lost and found deep love in his personal life.

In this book, Buddy shares his specific life-changing habits, one hundred thought-provoking questions, and one hundred learnings from his experiences of life. There is learning for all. Some components in the book will resonate with you more than others, depending on your present circumstances.

Buddy also shares the *Choose to Be Relentless* habits framework, the styles of behaviour he has witnessed in life and how you can manage them. He also includes his method of

WHAT DO YOU CHOOSE TO BE?

how he transformed his life, and the lives of others, for the better. Buddy knows that building understanding, developing trust and inspiring belief has been in the centre of his life achievements.

Choose to Be Relentless gives you the opportunity to consider the changes you can make to become the person you want to be. Applying the habits in this book will help you have a happy, healthy and a successful life on your terms. Applying the habits and his method helped Buddy to:

- Find what he was passionate about and build a career doing things he loved.

- Become motivated and inspired to build an ambitious mindset of achievement.

- Become a winner on his terms by applying known habits consistently.

- Provide the stimulus to examine his life choices and instigate change in his circumstances.

- Refine his approach to personal, physical, and mental health and believe in better.

- Become resilient, bold, driven, and hopeful.

- Stimulate meaningful, open conversations, and harmony with his partner and family.

- Become a happy, confident, healthier and more successful contributor to life.

The key components for life success

Buddy took time to decide what he wanted to achieve, why he wanted to achieve it, and how he would measure his success.

He created a plan focused on actions based around the following four components.

1. Physical and Mental Health to build the foundations to grow his potential.
2. Fulfilling Relationships to build the confidence to release his untapped potential.
3. Experiential Learning to increase his potential beyond his thoughts.
4. Progress and Prosperity to have enough money to enjoy his life and be a winner.

These four components were continually worked on during the various aspects of his life.

WHAT DO YOU CHOOSE TO BE?

Choosing to be relentless required hard work, focus, and a slice of luck. With so many distractions and emotional situations to manage, Buddy found that choosing to be relentless, being a winner, was not easy. When he was most successful, he applied most of the habits discussed in this book. There was no easy route for him. He worked hard, did his best, and focused on taking actions and learning. He had a relentless intent to achieve.

A synopsis of Choose to Be Relentless

Choose to Be Relentless begins with an introduction to Buddy's life of love and learning and how he took control of his life and found happiness. This is followed by a chapter on the opportunities in the future for the curious and the brave.

The next chapter focuses on the approach he took to get what he wanted out of life and introduces the habits framework he applied as he built a better life for himself, his family, and the people he worked with. This is followed by a chapter showing in some detail how Buddy managed the emotions of working with people with fluctuating attitudes to life. This chapter will be enlightening to readers as you will identify yourself within the model. Buddy also offers his suggestions to improve your behaviour and that of those around you.

There are a couple of chapters giving the background to Buddy's early life of experiencing conditional love and his young adult life of finding unconditional love. These aspects of his life set Buddy on his journey of reframing his negative thoughts and applying good habits as he took on the challenges of personal change and achievement. He walked out of his shade and found sunshine in all aspects of his life.

There are then four chapters focusing on the habits that Buddy chooses to be as he contributes to life. Within these chapters are stories from Buddy's personal and professional life. The stories are emotional, relatable and reflect the challenges Buddy faced to transform his approach to life. Buddy shares openly his learning from those life experiences.

Buddy knows it was possible to be fit and healthy, have confidence, improve his relationships, and achieve success in his life despite the conditions of his upbringing. After each habit there are relevant questions that you might want to consider as you reflect on your own life today and how it could be improved.

After these four chapters, Buddy highlights the differentiating factor of how to put love into everything you do in your life. For Buddy, love is the essential ingredient of winners. In the closing chapters, Buddy explores his final thoughts and seeks

WHAT DO YOU CHOOSE TO BE?

to identify the learning from the life stories. He encourages you to reflect on your own stories that might drive your own actions and learning.

In the final chapter, you will be introduced to the groundbreaking goal technique. This has enabled thousands to aim high and still be happy when falling short of their goal. Buddy also shares a tool to enable you to plan your own success, whatever your aspect of life.

Buddy knows that prioritising the regular application of these chosen habits helped him to focus his energy on overcoming his challenges and setting a direction that inspired him. Buddy has been lucky enough to have met some truly talented people. He has coached many to improve their attitude and energy for life.

He remains hopeful for the children of the world as they connect meaningfully and grasp the future with both hands.

Buddy hopes that readers find this a useful guide as they determine their future success defined on their own terms.

TAKE CONTROL OF YOUR LIFE AND FIND HAPPINESS

TAKE CONTROL OF YOUR LIFE AND FIND HAPPINESS

CHOOSE TO BE RELENTLESS

Hopes and dreams well beyond the factory gates

Buddy Bramble is sixty-three. He has been a watcher, an achiever, a learner, and a winner in various aspects of his life. He′s been on quite a journey. Buddy knows there are millions like him, not any more special than others, but working hard, looking for a break to succeed in life. A chance encounter in a pub changed Buddy′s life.

This is his story. It is full of groundbreaking personal and business achievements and behaviour models to help you improve.

Buddy was born in a small Somerset town to a working-class family who gave him the basics of food and a house. The house was not a happy home. It was a home where unconditional love was in short supply. His mother, Doris, didn't love her children very much. She failed to provide the love, security, and emotional support the children needed to be confident and tackle life's challenges fully.

Buddy′s mother looked up nervously to authority and down upon others in her class. Buddy was born into a family that had low expectations of him. From a young age, he was ignored, unloved, locked in a bedroom, and made to feel completely worthless.

TAKE CONTROL OF YOUR LIFE AND FIND HAPPINESS

Buddy had all sorts of hang-ups and emotional distractions as he moved through his childhood. Buddy wasted time living life accidently and not focusing on his education. It is his biggest regret in life. Buddy's only goal was to do well enough at school to join the local factory where his father, Jack, worked.

When he left school and joined an apprenticeship at the local factory, the family were delighted. Buddy was sixteen and had achieved in his parents' eyes. Well done, Buddy.

Buddy had hopes and dreams well beyond the factory gates.

Early in his adult life, Buddy asked himself, *Where are you today with your life? Are you happy with your answer?* He was not happy. Buddy knew that if he was to make a success of his life, he would need to take control and change his approach. He also knew he could rely on no one to help him. If a change was going to occur, it was up to him. Buddy changed his attitude and started taking action to make the most of the opportunities ahead. Buddy continually challenged himself to achieve much more than his sixteen-year-old self could have imagined.

When he was twenty-three, he met Jess and decided what he wanted out of life.

He became mentally fit for the future. He stopped comparing himself to others and focused on improving and doing his best. Focusing on experiential learning was his salvation.

Buddy climbed several personal mountains from that point onwards, slipping occasionally. One slip-up nearly killed him. It lasted eighteen months, but more about that later. Another slip-up meant he was out of work for twelve months with a young family and a mortgage to pay. Buddy bounced back from both and carried on climbing. The adversity gave him strength. Buddy knows what failure feels like and uses the experience to get stronger.

Buddy has certainly achieved more than many thought he could. Indeed, he achieved more than he thought all those years ago. He became an author of two books, has led hundreds of people in his business life, and received industry recognition for his achievements.

His unique models, routines, and habits were applied in many companies and influenced thousands worldwide. He built productive, healthy relationships, and coached many, whatever their background, to give them the confidence to achieve more than they thought possible. He has learnt so much from people he has worked with. He is proud of all of them.

TAKE CONTROL OF YOUR LIFE AND FIND HAPPINESS

A new course full of love, hope, and ambition

None of this could have been achieved without substantial change and transformation in his personal life. He left the pain and influence from his past behind him as he chartered a new course full of love, humour, hope, and ambition. Buddy learnt unconditional love from Jess and her extended family.

Jess helped Buddy to be vulnerable. To be less afraid and to share more. She has always been there ready to listen. Whilst Buddy was often alone with his thoughts, like all of us, with Jess around he never felt lonely. With his wife, they brought up two children, Patrice and Alex, to do the right thing, care about people, be ambitious, and make the most of their potential.

Buddy learnt so much from so many on his journey. He learnt a little from theory but a lot more from practice and the joy of experiential learning.

Today, Buddy is still learning as he grapples with the demons that still get in the way of his closest relationships.

He is not the perfect specimen, and perhaps he never will be, but you will see that he will keep trying to be the best version of himself while inspiring others to reach their dream.

ARE YOU OPEN TO THE OPPORTUNITIES?

ARE YOU OPEN TO THE OPPORTUNITIES?

Buddy knows that the next ten years will surely be quite a ride for the ones that want to get on board the experiential learning bus and contribute to a digital, social, and technological life.

A life full of opportunities for the ones who choose to be organised, responsible, happy, educated, purposeful, hopeful, bold, and resilient. They decide to be the very best they can be. They attack the day with energy. They put passion and love into everything they do. Not just one day but every single day. They will choose to be relentless.

Vision, understanding, purpose, and agility

As the world is recovering from the chaos of the worldwide banking crisis of 2008, the shock of the Covid pandemic since 2020, and the ongoing Ukraine crisis, a new game of life is appearing in front of our very eyes.

In the UK, we have also had a period of political turmoil that has worsened our communities. The underfunding of our public services has left many of our education, health, and long-term care services in trouble.

Around us all, we see volatility, uncertainty, complexity, and ambiguity. This makes many fear the future and get stuck in

ARE YOU OPEN TO THE OPPORTUNITIES?

conversations that do not move things forward. Caught in the shade of life worrying about the future.

Winners are not held back by fear. They see change as an opportunity. They see the sunshine in all aspects of life. A future world where an inspiring vision, common understanding, clarity of purpose, and individual agility allow everyone to grow their potential and contribute their best to life in the digital age.

Governments of the world will need to be inspiring, forward-looking, and put local communities, people, data, and technology at the centre of their thoughts. They need to ensure that everyone has an equal opportunity to succeed, whatever their start in life. This present generation will need to elect politicians that can focus on education that provides knowledge and insightful, creative students fit for this new world. Students that are team players, experts at collaboration and able to progress when the destination is ambiguous. Creating policies that give everyone the equal chance to make the most of their potential.

Seizing the opportunities in the digital age

Where you are born has a significant impact on your life chances. A few people are lucky. They are born in a land of plenty, milk and honey, love, money, and the opportunity to make the most of their talents.

Many millions more, sadly, are born in a land where their life chances are restricted by their place of birth, their education, or the dire circumstances of their early life. Every gain for them is a huge victory.

If ever there was a time when an egalitarian approach was needed, then this is that time. It is a time when more can have the opportunities to develop their habits and routines to make the most of their talents because they are free to do so.

The last decade has seen phenomenal innovation led by the transition to mobile and the rise of data accelerating the growth of new industries. Creative and intuitive humans, showing initiative and critical thinking skills, will see opportunities around them. The ones that open their eyes, work collaboratively, and use their ingenuity will create new jobs in yet-to-exist industries.

In front of Patrice and Alex is a technological and digital future where virtual and augmented reality, advanced robotics, and artificial intelligence will increase productivity, efficiency, and economic growth. This technology could eliminate some knowledge work altogether. We live in interesting times.

ARE YOU OPEN TO THE OPPORTUNITIES?

Artificial intelligence is already at the forefront of sophisticated applications that can create human-like text from a large amount of text data. One example is Chat GPT, a language model developed by OpenAI. It is designed to generate text that is coherent and sounds natural to a human reader. Early trials suggest that this application can be fine-tuned for a variety of tasks, such as translation, summarisation, and conversation. Some believe that this approach will replace Google as a search engine of the future. Others have suggested that this could also see the end of call centres as we know them. Interesting times.

This future revolutionises how communities and countries work together. More and more are combining office with hybrid homeworking, leaving some office buildings empty. Manufacturing, e-commerce, healthcare, and customer services will be reimagined beyond our thoughts. Interesting times.

Making the most of the opportunities

In the next ten years, opportunities will be available for those brave enough to jump into the unknown and learn.

Are you choosing to be bold?

CHOOSE TO BE RELENTLESS

Buddy knows that fear has often kept him safe, but it has also held him back. The challenge is to quieten the fearful mind and the incorrect assumptions that often get in the way of progress.

The best reach out and push past their comfort zone by applying the habits in *Choose to Be Relentless.*

So, celebrate your difference, your uniqueness, and step forward, not back. The future is for the millions of learners brave enough to jump when understanding is not complete.

Buddy knows that applying the known habits and routines in his life helped shape the man he is today.

ARE YOU OPEN TO THE OPPORTUNITIES?

WHAT DO YOU WANT OUT OF YOUR LIFE?

WHAT DO YOU WANT OUT OF YOUR LIFE?

CHOOSE TO BE RELENTLESS

What do you want out of life?

Buddy took time to agree what he wanted out of life, why he wanted to achieve it, and how he would measure his success.

Buddy thought about the key components of happy and successful people.

These four components below were continually worked on during the various aspects of his life. At certain times his focus was more on one than the others.

Buddy kept his life on track by focusing on these four components.

1. **Physical and Mental Health** to build the foundations to grow his potential.

    Buddy decided that an excellent physical and mental health standard was essential to build his self-respect. This would be the foundation for his future success.

    What do you want out of life, now and in the future, regarding your physical and mental health?

WHAT DO YOU WANT OUT OF YOUR LIFE?

2. **Fulfilling Relationships** to build the confidence to release his untapped potential.

He knew that a trusted network of family and friends would help him to build his confidence and undoubtedly help him release his untapped potential.

What do you want out of life, now and in the future, regarding your relationships?

3. **Experiential Learning** to increase his potential beyond his thoughts.

As he developed his confidence, he began to focus on continual learning and growing his skills and knowledge.

This highly developed work-life network helped Buddy grow his potential beyond the limitations of his thoughts.

What do you want out of life, now and in the future, in terms of learning?

4. **Progress and Prosperity** to have enough money to enjoy his life on his terms.

   Buddy took time to explore progress and prosperity and what that meant to him.

   He knew he wanted to progress and improve his life. He decided that prosperity is happiness, a healthy mindset, and a way of living life on his own terms.

   Buddy knew that having enough money would play a massive part in giving him the freedom to choose the life he wanted. Success for Buddy would be to inspire others to take the opportunities and make the most of their life.

   What do you want out of life, now and in the future, in terms of the prosperity you need to enjoy your life?

These four questions enabled him to think clearly about what his success would look like and what steps he would need to take to achieve any of his goals in the future.

He began to believe in better and make progress.

WHAT DO YOU WANT OUT OF YOUR LIFE?

Choosing to apply known habits in day-to-day life

Buddy began to see the importance of choice in his life and how people can make the most of their potential by consistently applying known habits in their day-to-day life.

Buddy developed the components into a framework, including the habits that informed his choices and became part of his life routine. This framework is on the following page.

At this stage of your life, what do you choose to be?

In his professional and personal life, Buddy has seen these life habits from many people from all walks of life. He wishes he could be more consistent in how he applies them himself.

The winners with clear focus and intent are relentless in applying these habits.

The rest of us are either improving these habits or focusing on being more consistent in their application.

For some, like Buddy, this is a lifelong learning experience for them.

CHOOSE TO BE RELENTLESS

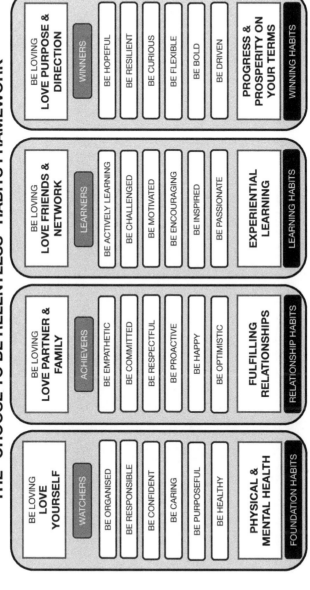

WHAT DO YOU WANT OUT OF YOUR LIFE?

As he developed his life, Buddy was able to understand the specific habits that supported his change efforts. These habits, highlighted through the Bramble life stories, are explored in the next few chapters.

Whilst reading, you may well stop and reflect as you consider the learning from your own life. What are your stories that inform your learning? Can you relate to the habits?

In the final chapter of this book there is a chapter on "how to plan for success" and apply the *Choose to Be Relentless* habits and be groundbreaking in your own personal and work life.

THE BEHAVIOURS YOU MEET IN LIFE

THE BEHAVIOURS YOU MEET IN LIFE

The styles of behaviour we meet in life

Buddy's journey was often interrupted as he sought to manage the emotions of working with people with fluctuating negative attitudes and energy levels.

Buddy found them hard work but coached many to improve their attitude and energy. He knows it helped them get a grip of their life. How does he know? They told him.

Through taking responsibility and applying the relentless habits, many today have a positive approach to life and are much happier. Buddy is proud of so many of them as they took control of their life. They are releasing their previously untapped potential.

During his professional and personal life, he was able to develop a good understanding of the types of behaviour that he enjoyed working with. He has needed to amend his behaviour lots of times as he coached others to find a better way.

Buddy's life is full of people who choose to be watchers, achievers, learners, and winners.

The gap between achievers, learners, and winners is so small. They all have a hopeful mind and a positive approach to life.

THE BEHAVIOURS YOU MEET IN LIFE

Buddy has worked with so many of these and knows he has inspired them to accomplish more in their life. The winners are just totally relentless.

The different styles of behaviour are easily identified as they present themselves in conversations and daily actions. Combined with their conditions of upbringing and their present circumstances, people easily slip into a style of behaviour that meets the current situation.

Buddy has seen people drop in and out of these styles depending on an event or individual choice. He has been in and out of many of these himself. Most people have a preferred style of behaviour.

There are also the drainers that most successful people avoid being with if they can. In his professional life, Buddy quickly realised that a lunch with a table of drainers would not be a good start to his afternoon.

The next few pages will make you stop and think about the behaviours you meet in your own life and their impact on you.

Buddy developed this model to help identify understand himself and others. It has helped him to improve his life relationships. Can you relate to these behaviours?

THE BEHAVIOURS YOU MEET IN LIFE

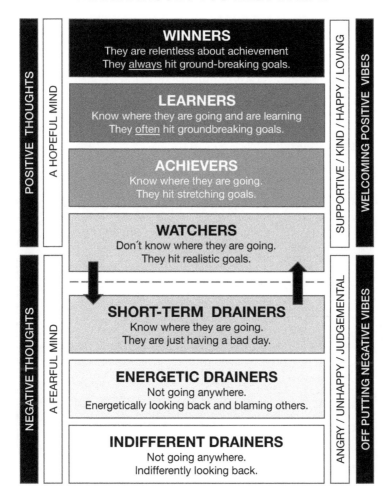

THE BEHAVIOURS YOU MEET IN LIFE

The Watchers – They are reliable performers

Watchers are busily avoiding mistakes. In most cases, they do just enough to get by. They do enough not to be noticed. They are always continually working on improving the six foundation health habits below. They master some but are not consistent in applying them in life. They don't always make the most of their potential.

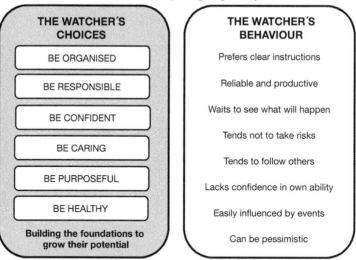

Watchers rarely make mistakes. They are steady, reliable performers. However, watchers often hold themselves back due to self-limiting thoughts. They prefer not to stand out and

CHOOSE TO BE RELENTLESS

they appear happy in the pack's centre. They would like that the light shines on others. Many watchers often have so much potential but need to believe in themselves. They often need someone to believe in them.

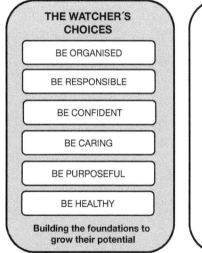

WATCHERS
Don't know where they are going. They watch.

THE WATCHER'S CHOICES	SUGGESTIONS FOR WATCHERS
BE ORGANISED	Share your plans with others
BE RESPONSIBLE	Reduce time on non-value activity
BE CONFIDENT	Recognise your own talents
	Identify today's five gone wells
BE CARING	Share your thoughts and feelings
BE PURPOSEFUL	Identify the positives in your life
	Take the initiative on your future
BE HEALTHY	Enjoy learning new experiences
Building the foundations to grow their potential	

Buddy has coached so many of these and helped them achieve more than they thought.

Watchers are talented but held back by their fearful mind putting doubt into their life. Buddy hopes he gave some of them opportunity and hope. In short, a platform to stand on.

37

THE BEHAVIOURS YOU MEET IN LIFE

The Achievers – They accomplish their goals and improve

Achievers know where they are going and focus on hitting their targets. They release their untapped potential. It is realistic for all to aim at being an achiever in life. Achievers build the habits and routines to help them quietly achieve their victories of continual improvement and achievement. They may not be well known in the wider world, but some learn more than they thought possible in their local communities and workplace. They are often doing great work and making significant contributions to life. Achievers are consistent performers.

ACHIEVERS
They know where they are going. They hit their targets.

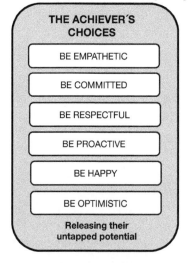

CHOOSE TO BE RELENTLESS

Applying the above twelve habits in daily life enables people to love themselves, succeed and build fulfilling relationships. Buddy knows that with these habits, achievers are dependable characters. Achievers are happy with where they are now and comfortable with their contributions to life. Could they achieve more? Probably.

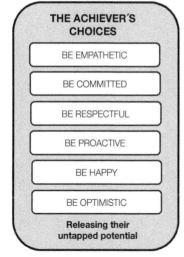

ACHIEVERS
They know where they are going. They hit their goals.

THE ACHIEVER'S CHOICES	SUGGESTIONS FOR ACHIEVERS
BE EMPATHETIC	Identify a stretching goal
BE COMMITTED	Mix with encouraging people
BE RESPECTFUL	Look outside your boundaries
BE PROACTIVE	Make NGW/GW a daily habit
BE HAPPY	Take action and learn daily
BE OPTIMISTIC	Use 'What, Need, How' in life
	Understand others' feelings
Releasing their untapped potential	Take considered risks

The Learners – They consistently learn new stuff

The previous twelve habits are the foundations of the learners. The learners are hopeful and decide to look beyond the health and relationship foundation habits and are more ambitious.

THE BEHAVIOURS YOU MEET IN LIFE

These learners understand what it is like to be an achiever but choose to push themselves to accomplish more. Daily.

LEARNERS
Know where they are going. They spot new opportunities.

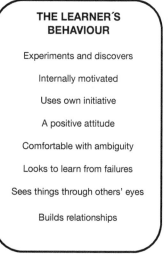

Learners are fit for the digital age. They know where they are going and are always looking for new opportunities. They focus on habits that drive continual improvement and active learning. These learners will push the boundaries into the unknown and ride the wave of uncertainty. With a facilitative style of leadership these people grow their potential and keep on learning. They are an energising force in all teams.

CHOOSE TO BE RELENTLESS

Growing and learning are essential skills when there is so much change occurring. Active learners who reach out and keep on experiencing the new will put themselves in an excellent position to take advantage of the opportunities ahead.

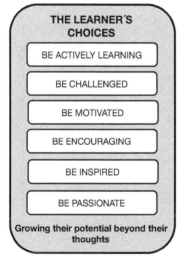

LEARNERS
Know where they are going. They spot new opportunities.

THE LEARNER'S CHOICES	SUGGESTIONS FOR LEARNERS
BE ACTIVELY LEARNING	Aim high – be groundbreaking
BE CHALLENGED	Decide what you want to do next
BE MOTIVATED	Surround yourself with winners
BE ENCOURAGING	Impress career decision-makers
BE INSPIRED	Share your own failures and learn
BE PASSIONATE	Identify when others need help
Growing their potential beyond their thoughts	Make time to listen to others
	Offer advice and guidance

Learners don't wait to be noticed or recognised. They put themselves out there. They are noticed. Some of Buddy's award winning teams have contained many learners who are still to this day aiming high. They believe in a future that they have already seen.

THE BEHAVIOURS YOU MEET IN LIFE

The Winners – They are relentless perfectionists

A few learners go further and become consistently relentless in their pursuit of perfection. These people become winners in the public space. Success for them isn't always about money, it can be the joy and satisfaction of knowing they have inspired others.

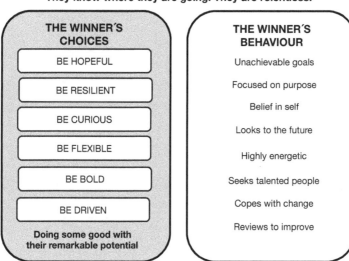

Winners are fired up with purpose, wanting to be the best compared to anybody else. They know where they are going. These are the groundbreakers. The winners consistently apply

CHOOSE TO BE RELENTLESS

the health, relationship and learning habits above and the winning habits. Therefore, being a winner takes hard work.

Winners are often up early, and away to hit their day with energy and passion. They avoid distractions and stand out in the crowd.

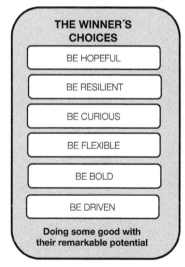

WINNERS
They know where they are going. They are relentless.

THE WINNER'S CHOICES	SUGGESTIONS FOR WINNERS
BE HOPEFUL	Motivate others to achieve
BE RESILIENT	Give back and help others
BE CURIOUS	Listen, build relationships
BE FLEXIBLE	Maintain focus on winning
	Keep on learning and improving
BE BOLD	Decide what is next for you
BE DRIVEN	Be open to other ideas
Doing some good with their remarkable potential	Surround yourself with winners

Winners are relentless and love what they do. Their love for their profession or work can sometimes damage their personal relationships. Achieving home/life/work balance is often a challenge for winners.

43

THE BEHAVIOURS YOU MEET IN LIFE

The Drainers – Breed negativity and pessimism

Drainers are not going anywhere. They concentrate on looking back, and some seem unable to move on from life events. They are just stuck in a loop of negativity.

There are three types of drainers—short-term, energetic, and pessimistic. Buddy has worked with a few of these, some he helped to improve, and some chose not to change their lives for the better.

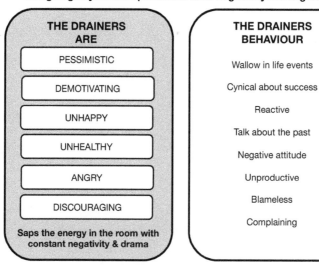

Short-term Drainers

There are many occasions when a negative response to a life event presents itself. When disappointment strikes, it can be upsetting and frustrating. It is very natural to respond negatively as people flush out their emotions about an event. For the short-term drainers, it is just for a moment.

Buddy has slipped into this style on a few occasions but used his habits to regain control. Most winners, learners, and achievers bounce back quickly from these moments. They take responsibility and don't let the event take over their life. They take control of the situation, make a decision, and move on. They look forward, hoping for a better future. Short-term drainers don't stay in the shade for long, they find the sunshine.

Energetic Drainers

Energetic drainers just can't let go of the irritation. They allow themselves to get sucked into a negative frame of mind that can quickly spin out of control. Unlike a mouse on an exercise wheel, they can't get off. This negativity can be topped up by gossiping with like-minded friends, who stoke the fire and add more oxygen to the situation. Energetic drainers seem to love the shade of life not the hope of a brighter future. Negative

THE BEHAVIOURS YOU MEET IN LIFE

energy can infect groups very quickly. It has a very powerful impact on people and their subsequent behaviour.

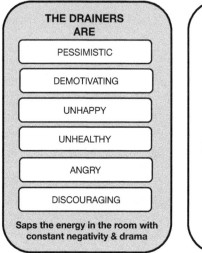

DRAINERS
Not going anywhere. Spend their time negatively looking back.

THE DRAINERS ARE
- PESSIMISTIC
- DEMOTIVATING
- UNHAPPY
- UNHEALTHY
- ANGRY
- DISCOURAGING

Saps the energy in the room with constant negativity & drama

SUGGESTIONS FOR DRAINERS
- Make changes to lifestyle
- Stop blaming others
- Understand your negative impact
- Take responsibility for feelings
- Identify reasons for own behaviour
- Avoid negative influencers
- Find someone who can help
- Talk to someone

The negativity of some social media feeds can influence energetic drainers, impacting on the mental health of so many. These energetic drainers actively go looking for negativity, impacting those around them.

Some can stay in this active negative mindset for months, sometimes years. They can quickly lose their hope to be able to change it and pessimism takes over.

This mindset is often a mask for other issues at work or home. These energetic drainers can be saved if we take the time to understand them. We should encourage them to take responsibility for moving their life forward positively. Energetic drainers need to focus on events they can control.

Watchers should avoid these active and toxic drainers. The watchers are clearly influenced and can easily be sucked into the negativity without realising it.

Pessimistic Drainers

If this toxic behaviour is not curtailed, the drainers can, over time, withdraw from social contact. They lose their energy and become indifferent and depressed as life circumstances and conditions fuel their negativity.

Pessimistic drainers fear the future, often lack any hope for anything better and seem stuck in a small, dark place. Society and governments should do all they can to help people in these situations. They may need professional help.

Choosing your style of behaviour

In any aspect of life, a human can choose to be a drainer, watcher, achiever, learner, or winner. These are just choices

THE BEHAVIOURS YOU MEET IN LIFE

that people can make. It is for people to decide what they want out of life and the style of behaviour they wish to be known for.

When Buddy didn't like how his life was going, he asked himself these two questions.

- Have you identified your preferred style of behaviour?
- What is the style of behaviour are you known for?

Buddy applied his habits throughout his life and on occasions he has felt like a winner. In his business life, Buddy worked with thousands of talented people who were looking for an opportunity to improve themselves. Some were watchers, who really have most to gain from applying the habits in this book.

Plenty of watchers are making regular contributions to life. They are delighted. They have decided what success is on their terms. Watchers tend to flock together, gaining comfort from the consistency of the people around them. They set easily achievable targets. They are reliable.

However, Buddy found that some watchers want to achieve more but may need more confidence to try. With good advice and guidance, watchers can become achievers. There are so many watchers held back by their fearful mind. With the proper support, they can achieve more than they could imagine.

Buddy is content that he gave people an opportunity to shine a little brighter. He is very proud of that.

Achievers, learners, and winners tend to surround themselves with people like them. In their own life, many people experience brief moments of success when they know what being a winner feels like.

Winners find the light in life.

Learners and winners have many more of these successful experiences than achievers and watchers. Learners and winners live on the edge and have many more moments when they fall. When they do fail, they quickly bounce back. They step forward not back.

Learners and winners have a resilience that is beyond the many. Some of the winner's habits are difficult to sustain for the many.

Learners and winners do not seem to let others define their achievements. Whatever the situation, learners and winners aim high and do their best every day. They make the most of their potential, regularly.

THE BEHAVIOURS YOU MEET IN LIFE

It is possible to slip in and out of styles of behaviour depending on an event or individual choice. Choices in life are often a question of your own attitude and energy levels.

Most people have a preferred style of behaviour. Might you consider:

- Where are you now?
- Where do you want to be?
- How are you going to get there?
- How do you want to be remembered?

EXPERIENCING CONDITIONAL LOVE

EXPERIENCING CONDITIONAL LOVE

"Controlling the house with a stick and fear"

Buddy lived in a blame-culture household; his mother, Doris, always looked for opportunities to criticise or demean any small achievement. This encouraged Buddy to fear failure and aim low during his early life.

He was conditioned from an early age not to look above being any better than his father, Jack. His father was a lovely, caring person. However, he was caught, like a rabbit in the headlights, by a domineering wife who controlled the house with fear, a stick, and inconsistent behaviour to maintain discipline. Doris didn't seem to enjoy her life.

Buddy saw teachers and other parents building children's confidence and potential outside his family home. Buddy decided early to surround himself with talented friends who were exciting and different from what he knew from his home life.

These school friends were encouraged to aim beyond low-level achievement, aiming high and being as groundbreaking as possible. They were continually improving. They were confident. They were not afraid to fail and seemed to love learning. They were not stuck in a small place; they were always aiming high.

EXPERIENCING CONDITIONAL LOVE

Buddy was always in the top sets at school, but the conditioning at home held him back from educational achievement. Concentration at school was affected by Buddy's mental reaction to how he was treated before school and his fear of what might happen when he got home.

A few years later, Buddy knew he needed to think differently. He decided his upbringing was not going to define him.

He wanted a different life for his unborn children. He wanted to give them a better start in life than he had.

"I'm going to ring the Samaritans"

Visits to people in authority always created anxiety in Buddy's home. Doris was always worried about what people would say if Buddy tarnished the family's reputation. It was a significant moment meeting an authority figure. Buddy had to look intelligent and respectable. Even today, Buddy looks in the mirror to check his appearance if he is visiting important people, like doctors or solicitors.

A visit from the local health worker, Nurse Dangerfield, was preceded by frantic rushing about to clean the front room. Ensuring that the front room was tidy, clean, and presentable was vital to the eyes of Doris. Buddy remembers a briefing

CHOOSE TO BE RELENTLESS

from Doris that told him to say very little if Nurse Dangerfield asked him questions about how he was.

In her responsible adult days, Doris was a chain smoker. She often left Buddy in his pram as she went to the next-door neighbour Helen's for a fag and a chat. She left the bedroom window open so that she could hear Buddy crying.

Buddy knew Nurse Dangerfield didn't need to know about Helen's fag and chat mornings. Buddy was often worried that a cat could quickly jump in and frighten him. Buddy doesn't like cats. Buddy's bedroom had bad memories for him.

On a visit to the doctor for Buddy's polio vaccination, he popped an awful-tasting sugar lump in his mouth as he jabbed a needle in Buddy's arm. As he left the surgery, Buddy spat the sugar lump on the ground outside, as he didn't like the taste. Buddy saw the lump of sugar as a reward for being so good in the surgery. He hadn't realised that it was, in fact, the polio vaccination. His mum went completely potty and told him to pick up what was left of the sugar lump, put it back in his mouth, and swallow it.

To this day, Buddy is still unsure if he is vaccinated against polio. Doris would have been too embarrassed to go back into the surgery and explain what had happened.

EXPERIENCING CONDITIONAL LOVE

Mealtimes with Doris and Jack were always a tense affair. Conversations at the table were always on the edge of a full-on row about something someone had done or had not done. That someone was usually Buddy. It was another opportunity for Doris to pick an argument with the wrath of her tongue. Meals were rushed down at double-quick speed to minimise the time with this toxic family. Often, Buddy would be sent to his room to reflect on his behaviour. Later in life, Buddy needed to reframe his thoughts about mealtimes within a family.

Buddy was often exhausted and sad. He developed an unapproachable face as he quietly cried himself to sleep after another evening of being sent to his bedroom. He woke up one night in January 1965 and thought he saw Winston Churchill's coffin at the bottom of the bed. It was terrifying for him. He put his head under the covers and waited for the morning light – what a relief when he realised it was a large ottoman. While Buddy was sleeping, Doris moved the coffin-shaped item to the bottom of the bed.

Buddy had sleepless nights and often woke up in his bedroom but not in his bed. On one occasion, Buddy woke up believing he was on the toilet, but he was in the corner and had made a dry but lumpy mess. He was disturbed. He quietly rushed about and cleared up the lot before Doris found out.

Buddy was a child that needed help, but he was too frightened to tell the inappropriately named Nurse Dangerfield. It was impossible anyway, as he was never alone with Nurse Dangerfield. After the nurse had gone, Buddy said, "I am going to ring the Samaritans and tell them how badly I am being treated in this home." A period of self-reflection followed in the bedroom. Buddy was only allowed out when he said he was sorry.

Buddy never felt good enough with put-downs, constant criticism, and ridicule. He found solace in a friendship with some great friends. At various stages of his life, they provided much emotional support as he plotted a way to escape his sad life at home. The friends rarely visited, but Doris always compared them with him when they did. Friends met Doris at various times. All of them were a class above Buddy. They looked better. They sounded better. They were just so much more superior than Buddy in so many ways. Buddy couldn't do right for doing wrong.

Buddy didn't want to be like his friends. He wanted to be valued for his uniqueness. Buddy had a few girlfriends, but very few met Doris; for sure, they would not have been good enough. Some were certainly not.

EXPERIENCING CONDITIONAL LOVE

"Go to the library; you are a growler"

Buddy loved music and particularly the lyrics and melody of songs of love and hope. The lyrics often expressed the feelings of happiness, comfort, and joy. Buddy could only dream of the security of being in a relationship full of unconditional love and commitment.

Music was his saviour, as the words inspired him to help him get through the daily challenges of his life. He found that song reduced his stress and uplifted his mood. He found the whole experience of lyrics to be highly therapeutic. What he likes most about music is the feeling that the person singing is beside him, living the emotion of his moment. Any song about hope or belief always inspires Buddy.

Music has been right by Buddy's side in happy and sad times.

He particularly likes singing and was delighted when he was selected to be in the school choir at primary school. On the day of the auditions, Buddy was ready for it. He sang loudly and proudly so that the teacher would spot him as one of the leading singers of the choir. As Mrs James played the "All Things Bright and Beautiful" opening bars, Buddy looked around at his nervous classmates. He saw his opportunity to shine as he broke into song. "Stop, stop," said Mrs James, standing up from behind the piano. "Buddy, you are a growler; go to the library." Buddy was shell-shocked that his technique was not good enough for the school choir. He was hoping for some coaching and advice to improve his vocal range. We will never know if he is a baritone or a tenor, as he spent most of school singing lessons in the library.

Buddy enjoyed school and very quickly made friends. He was well-liked as he was able to make people laugh and threw himself into school events. He had ambitions to be a journalist and wrote for the school magazine. He played in the school cricket and football teams. He didn't excel in either. He realised early that having a good left foot would separate him from all the right-footed players. He spent hours learning how to tackle, pass and control the ball with his left foot. This talent finally got him into the team.

Buddy went on to score forty goals a season in amateur football. He knew that he was fit and knew he could outrun others. He played for a pub team and managed another. He learnt his early management skills in the dressing rooms of West Country football.

He was in the top classes for English and Mathematics, but his concentration was inconsistent as he was distracted by his mental reaction to his home life full of conditional love. He had the potential and the opportunity to shine at school but didn't take it. He left at sixteen with five O levels.

"That's why you are there, and I am here"

It was no surprise when Buddy joined his dad at the local print factory. His life had been conditioned in that way. There was never any expectation that he might go to university. It never came into the conversation at home. The local factory was the target.

One of Buddy's roles at the print factory was to take the food orders from the rest of the qualified, competent workers – the journeymen. In those days, it was all men. It was a very dull job. Buddy became very good at taking the orders and money from the men, going to the canteen, picking up and delivering hot dogs, bacon sandwiches, and sausage sandwiches back to the men for their 10 am break.

Due to the controlling conditions of his home life Buddy threw himself into making a success of his apprenticeship. Doris had conditioned him to fear authority. He put his head down and avoided conversations with anyone in a position of power. On one occasion, Mr Butler, the department manager, an authority figure in Doris's eyes, appeared. He asked Buddy,

"What have you written on the paper attached to your clipboard?"

Buddy said, "It is the food order for the men."

Mr Butler asked Buddy, "Are the orders always the same?"

"Oh, yes," Buddy said. "Every day the same."

"You could save yourself some time. Try photocopying the sheet with all the orders and names and use the same sheet daily," said Mr Butler. Mr Butler was putting forward his years of experience to enlighten the seventeen-year-old Buddy on how to improve productivity in the workplace. Buddy felt small, holding his clipboard, pen, and a list of hot dog orders.

"Good idea, Mr Butler," said Buddy.

Mr Butler highlighted his importance and status by saying, "Buddy, that's why I am here, and you are there." Buddy never forgot that message and is proud that he never said that to any of his teams in the future.

As his apprenticeship finished, he applied for a typesetting job in another company and started a Monday – Friday, 6 am – 2 pm, 2 pm – 10 pm shift pattern of working. His work was a distraction from a home life lacking love but full of judgemental thoughts. Doris was an energetic drainer. She wasn't going anywhere. She loved looking back and reminding Buddy of his failures. Whatever potential he had, was being crushed.

A few months later Buddy became a manager at twenty-two years old. He then became editor of the local football club programme. Never did his family recognise his achievements. Not once.

Doris saw Buddy getting above his station in life. Buddy knows that she didn't much like this young driven, caring, and optimistic man. A man trying to find his way in a world beyond his bedroom. In his home life, Buddy learnt everything about how not to be as a person.

However, Buddy discovered the ability to be resilient. He knew that however harmful it might be in the future, surely nothing would be as wrong as not being loved by a mother. It was time for Buddy to find his happiness elsewhere.

"I wouldn't have had children"

Buddy, Jess, Alex, and Patrice were off to see Grandma Bramble. It was a lovely sunny day. The morning sun was lighting up the beautiful countryside, and the traffic on the M6 was behaving itself. Jess hated queues, so the Brambles were off to a good start.

The Brambles were progressing as Jess turned off onto the M32 north of Bristol. The atmosphere in the car was relaxed, fun, talkative, and always enjoyable as they shared views on solving the world's problems.

As the Brambles made their way to Middleton, a song on the radio encouraged them to sing along. One family favourite was the Bee Gees classic "How Deep is Your Love". The family were in full voice as they sang together, not quite in harmony but indeed high marks for effort from some of them.

Patrice always enjoyed the chorus "living in a world of fools" while pointing to his younger brother Alex, who smiled, knowing it was just brotherly banter.

As Jess drove through Temple Cloud, she asked Buddy if he was okay. Buddy hated these trips to see Doris and Jack. They always reminded him of a family life that differed from the one he enjoyed with his family up north.

Buddy was never too sure of the welcome he would receive; on this occasion, Grandma Bramble would not disappoint.

EXPERIENCING CONDITIONAL LOVE

The home that Buddy was brought up in was only a mile away. Memories of emotional manipulation, rejection, little stimulation from a young age, family ridicule and isolation from family life, and being hit with a stick and locked in a bedroom for hours.

The happy Bramble family were now on full alert as Buddy prepared himself for the unemotional meeting with his mother and father. As they parked outside, they looked at one another and prepared themselves for an unpredictable greeting. What mood would Grandma Bramble be in?

The door opened, and Alex and Patrice rushed forward to cuddle Grandma as all grandchildren would. As they got close, Grandma Bramble stepped back and thrust her hand somewhere near their lips, and they took turns kissing her hand. They wanted a cuddle. That was far too intimate for a mother that didn't even cuddle her children, let alone someone else's.

Jess was always able to come up with the right words and said, "Hello, Doris, how are you?"

"So pleased to see you and the children," said Grandma Bramble. That was a bit of a shock for the lads. They had the distinct impression that Grandma Bramble wasn't as pleased to see them as they recovered from learning to kiss the back of a hand while expecting a cuddle. So, three of the family received a welcome of sorts.

As Buddy appeared with the bags, Grandma Bramble said to Jess, "Next time, leave that bugger up North." Buddy was in hand-kissing distance but was already a third wheel. Unwanted with no purpose.

"Hello, Mum," said Buddy, "good to see you again." Grandad Bramble was in the background, oblivious to it all.

Not the best start to the weekend, but as they settled into a stilted conversation, Buddy pointed out that it wasn't a friendly welcome for him. His mum, doubling down on the welcome, said, "To be honest, if I could see my time again, I would not have had any children."

Buddy was never her favourite child. Buddy was reassured that had there been a fire at any time in his upbringing, she wouldn't have had the heart-breaking decision of whom to save. She wouldn't have saved any of them.

Buddy wanted not to believe what he had heard, but this emotional abuse was normalised in his brain. "I hope that when I am your age, I never feel that way about my children or, even worse, say that in front of my grandchildren," said Buddy.

Buddy was forty-three. He was reminded again of the cruel words that had peppered his upbringing. When Buddy was a child, when it mattered, Doris as a mother fell short. Years later, as a grandma, she still fell short.

Luckily, Buddy had left this emotional abuse behind twenty years earlier and rebuilt his life. He was now strong and in control of his emotions. Buddy and Jess were determined not to allow the tapes of Buddy's upbringing to affect Alex and Patrice.

Buddy learnt the importance of "doing the right thing" from Jess's mother, Pat. Pat was a much more loving mother and grandma, whom Alex and Patrice learnt so much from. She wasn't judgemental. She took time to understand.

Buddy still telephoned his mother and father weekly and visited them as often as he and his young family could cope. It was never a pleasant experience. He slept soundly at night, knowing he had done the right thing. It was right to keep the door open, despite the emotional trauma.

ENJOYING LIFE AND FINDING LOVE

ENJOYING LIFE AND FINDING LOVE

"I told her my parents voted Tory"

Buddy always had problems finding love. It didn't help that he didn't know what love was. He had a few schoolboy romances, but the lucky ones managed to avoid the dysfunctional Buddy. He thought he found it once or twice, but he was dumped just as it became interesting. It seemed like he didn't know about love at all. He put his energy into his first love – friends and football.

Buddy immersed himself in the camaraderie of a football dressing room. He became the manager of an amateur team, Red Lion Rovers, in the bottom half of the Middleton Football League, Division Three. He set about attracting the best young talent in the area to play in this team. He focused on building a culture where the team was more important than any one individual. Clive was a printer, Tim worked in the Ministry of Defence, Nick was an electrician, Ian was a printer, Martin was an artist, Micky was still at school, Pete was a plasterer, and Nigel worked in a post office. A collection of different people from different backgrounds. The Rovers were promoted in the first season, playing some of the most attractive football Middleton Division Three had ever seen. Spectators flocked to watch the home games. In one game, Buddy counted thirty-three spectators.

ENJOYING LIFE AND FINDING LOVE

Evenings were spent moving between the Red Lion, the Wagon and Horses, The Lamb Inn, and pubs in Middleton, chatting about football and enjoying the company of honest conversations. Buddy was popular. Thursday and Saturday nights Buddy would dance the night away at Tramps, the nightclub in Bath. It was the peak of the 70's disco movement. Buddy loved soul and Motown songs.

On one occasion, Buddy went to a Christmas disco in Tunley with many other football types. As he was leaving, Post Office Nigel, the team's centre half, asked if Buddy would give him and his girlfriend a lift home. As they squeezed into the back of Buddy's Mini, he could see that Post Office was punching well above his weight. Buddy was hoping for some banter but was disappointed as Post Office seemed occupied as his blonde-haired girlfriend was munching his face off, coming up for air infrequently. Buddy soon arrived at the girlfriend's house and dropped the lovers off. Buddy thought that Post Office was hoping for some extra time with the blue-eyed blonde, who certainly seemed keen. Post Office was disappointed as, on this occasion, he was not invited in for coffee or anything else for that matter. A few weeks later, Buddy found out that girlfriend had dumped him. "What went wrong?" Buddy asked.

"I told her my parents voted Tory."

"I have been looking for you all my life"

Buddy enjoyed his tenth pint of scrumpy at the Red Lion as a long New Year's Eve session ended. Lots of merriment and enjoyment with people coming and going. Buddy looked up, and in the smoke-filled haze of a 1980s pub, he could see what looked like the woman last seen in the back of Buddy's Mini. Although she wasn't someone's girlfriend this time. She looked across at Buddy, and their eyes met.

The room was crowded, but all they could see were one another. As the blonde-haired girl moved closer, Buddy reached for a mint to ensure his mouth felt fresh, just in case. He sucked long and hard and swallowed just in time as she arrived within touching distance. She was beautiful. Buddy looked around, assuming she must be looking over his shoulder at another bloke. She wasn't. As he looked back, she had locked onto his face and was munching away.

It was semi-darkness and noisy, and recollections may differ, but Buddy is pretty sure that she pulled away from his lips and said, "I've been looking for you all my life."

It was New Year's Eve, and they discussed that she remembered Buddy's Mini and that he had given her a lift home. Her friends said they were off to some other pub, and she was up and heading out.

She looked back again, "Hay, what is your name?" "My name is Jess, Buddy."

Buddy walked home that night with a spring in his step, hoping that he would meet Jess again sometime soon. On his way home, walking up Main Street Buddy felt he had found the one. Little did he know the emotional rollercoaster ahead of them both.

A few weeks later, Buddy entered the Red Lion and spotted Jess. Again, their eyes met across a room. They moved together and had a conversation to explore their views and interests. Their conversation was flowing and effortless. Buddy wasn't very good at small talk and even worse at having the confidence to ask Jess on a date. This wasn't any woman; this was Jess. Buddy took ages to get around to asking her out. Nervously, he asked if she had seen *E.T.* "No," she said.

"Would you like to see *E.T.* with me?" asked a hopeful Buddy.

"That would be great," said Jess, "love to." Buddy could relax. Jess was his girlfriend. She was only sixteen; Buddy was twenty-three. He had a car.

"You are going out with Buddy," said one of her friends.

"Yes, I am. Buddy makes me laugh. He is interesting. He is different," she told them.

"Tony Benn sent me a postcard"

Jess and Buddy slipped into meeting up on Tuesday and Saturday every week. Jess was so different from any other woman Buddy had met. They often went to quiet pubs and talked for hours about Thatcher's Tory Britain and the unfairness of her politics. They enjoyed the same music and discussed the countries they could visit in the summer. Buddy had found someone that talked about the future, six months away.

Jess had curly blonde hair and a welcoming smile. She was simply stunning. She was intelligent, thoughtful, kind, and spoke openly and honestly. They laughed a lot and enjoyed one another's company so much. Buddy was the happiest he had been in a long time. Buddy always had a buzz of excitement whenever he met Jess. Six weeks after they first met, Buddy surprised her on Valentine's Day. He bought a single red rose. A romantic moment. They became best friends, and they soon regularly met on Thursday nights as well.

ENJOYING LIFE AND FINDING LOVE

Buddy was full of surprises. On one occasion, he met Jess, drove into Bristol, and parked outside the GMB Union offices. As they climbed the steps to the conference centre, it was packed with beardy blokes, anti-war and passionate CND types excited to see their hero speak. Buddy had taken Jess to *an Evening with Tony Benn*. She was delighted as "Tony Benn sent me a postcard when I was twelve." She loved it so much. On another occasion, Buddy took Jess to an evening with the SDP leader David Owen. She didn't enjoy that much, but she was with Buddy, making it bearable. Often, Jess showed her empathetic side. When Buddy damaged his cassette of Roberta Flacks´ *Greatest Hits*, Jess recorded the album onto a new tape and gave it to him. She was so kind, empathetic and thoughtful. Buddy loved the company of Jess.

"He´s going to be thumped"

Buddy played Sunday morning football for Tunley. In one match playing left-back, he was wearing his glasses, and they fell off. Buddy couldn't see a thing as he looked around for his glasses in the mud. As he put them on, he looked up, and the opposition had scored. His teammates were furious.

Jess didn't like football but did come to a match once at the army base in Warminster. Tunley made a good start and was outplaying the army team. Buddy was up to his usual tricks of talking to the opposition right winger to put him off. It was having the desired effect as Wayne struggled to make an impact. As the second half was underway, Buddy tittered as Wayne ran past him, slipped, and messed up the cross. As Buddy made a killer pass to the super-quick forward Dennis, he heard someone say, "Take this". He looked round to see what "take this" was and found it was more a "take that" as Wayne whacked him and knocked him out cold.

The ref didn't see it. No one saw it coming, but it was painful. Jess saw it coming. During half-time, Jess was talking with Gail, the girlfriend of Wayne. Wayne had just come out of prison, and Gail told Jess, "Your number three better watch it; my Wayne has a short fuse. He's going to be thumped in the second half."

"If you are that unhappy, I'll take you home"

The romance wasn't always a happy one. Jess and Buddy had solid views and made their points with vigour and aplomb. They often spent Saturday nights in the Kings Arms and British Legion in Tunley.

One evening in the Kings Arms, Buddy was chatting to Brian, the local football bore. He wouldn't stop and just kept going for ninety minutes. He was discussing formations, style of play, individual players, backed up with stories of his playing career. Buddy could see that Jess was not enjoying being a spectator and decided the best way out of this was to leave the pub.

As they left to go to the British Legion, Jess made it clear how unhappy she was about having to sit and listen to Brian all night. Buddy wasn't that keen himself either, but one thing led to another, and Buddy said, "If you are that unhappy, I'll take you home."

It was an emotional response from Buddy. As he weaved his way through the Somerset lanes, he was about one hundred metres from her home. Jess was still angry about Brian, and Buddy's response to her views. Buddy had had enough of this ranting. He stopped the car and said, "You can get out here and walk." No goodnight kisses that night as Jess got out of the car and looked in, "I will see you on Tuesday at 8.30 pm when you might have calmed down." Jess slammed the door shut and set off walking.

At that point, both were angry with one another.

Buddy returned to the Legion to finish his evening without Jess chirping in his ear. In those days, there was no mobile phone or messaging service to express regret if lovers had had a fallout. Buddy knew that he had allowed his emotions to get in the way. His rational brain kicked in and he knew that he could have handled it so much better. He loved Jess and was full of remorse and regret for his response that night. There was nothing he could do but sit tight and give time a chance to heal the situation.

A few days away from one another gave the lovers a chance to reflect and consider their actions. On this occasion, it didn't need an outsider to spot who was responsible for the fall out. Buddy considered blaming Brian, who, to be fair, was a contributing factor. The evening had started so well before Brian sat down to inform Jess his views on the offside rule. Buddy knew he was wrong but how was he to resolve this situation brought about by his own thoughts and emotions.

Tuesday could not come quickly enough for him. As he pulled up in his Mini cooper outside Jess's home, he knew he had some grovelling to do. He knocked on the door. He was not sure what sort of attitude Jess would have. Was she still angry?

Jess opened the door. She was smiling and enthusiastically said hello and kissed him on the cheek. They sat down in the front room. Buddy knew that blaming Brian would be a bad start to the conversation. He needed to take responsibility.

ENJOYING LIFE AND FINDING LOVE

Buddy knew he would need to be authentic and sincere. "Jess, I have something to say. I am so sorry about what happened on Saturday night. I was totally in the wrong and I apologise for my behaviour. I should have handled it better. I should have been more thoughtful. I'm sorry. I love you and hope you can forgive me."

Jess forgave Buddy. Not surprisingly, they never met Brian again.

That night Buddy learnt the importance of taking responsibility and saying sorry, with sincerity, when he is wrong.

EXPERIENCING UNCONDITIONAL LOVE

EXPERIENCING UNCONDITIONAL LOVE

"Never known love like this before"

As spring turned into summer, the romance developed into something extraordinary. Jess was sixteen, and Buddy wanted to respect her and ensure the relationship was solid before he took it to the next stage. Jess listened to Buddy's opinion, valued his happiness, and offered the unconditional love he had never felt. She wanted to be with him, and Buddy could see that this was an extraordinary friendship. With Jess, he could be vulnerable and share his private thoughts and feelings.

It was time to talk about the summer plans. They discussed how long the holiday should be. Jess, all excited and hopeful, said, "Two weeks would be good."

"Two weeks, twenty-four hours a day with you and seeing your first thing in the morning, sounds awful," said Buddy, half joking. They had only spent 8–10 hours weekly in one another's company. Two weeks away together would confirm if this relationship had any legs. Jess suggested going to Greece to understand more about the great architectural and historical significance of the ancient buildings, the Parthenon, and the Acropolis of Athens. Buddy loved the idea. The most he had ever seen that might be ancient was West Kennet Long Barrow and Stonehenge on a school trip years earlier. Jess was a traveller and an educator. Buddy loved the idea of learning about other cultures. He saw how travelling would broaden his mind and bring the world together. Buddy was educated by Doris to distrust people. The more he travelled, the more he realised that there was no need to fear people not like him.

They decided to book a campsite on the coast, south of Athens. It was a super-hot summer, and the small tent was just too hot to be in during the day. The tent was only bearable between 11.30 pm and 7 am, so they were often out at local restaurants. Buddy tasted his first moussaka and had many Greek salads washed down with a bottle of Domestica. They visited the islands just off the port of Piraeus, saw all the ancient buildings, and had a memorable time together. Conversations flowed, and the time together helped to cement the relationship. They both felt safe in one another's company. Six months after they met and after hours of conversation, Buddy for the first time, leant over, looked into Jess's eyes and said, "I love you." He had never known or felt love like this before. He had found someone whom he could rely on. Someone who would not let him down.

Soon after they returned to the UK, Jess went on an Interrail trip around Europe with her friends. It wasn't long, but Buddy realised how much he missed Jess and her egalitarian ways.

CHOOSE TO BE RELENTLESS

They both missed one another. They slipped into the Tuesday, Thursday, and Saturday routine, sprinkled with short UK holidays in their two-person tent. They spent the winter together with friends, socialising, playing pool, and going to music concerts and nightclubs. They still found time to talk about life and how to improve it. They were members of the Labour Party and were hopeful that the 1983 election would go Labour's way.

Like all lovers, they had moments with the odd falling out but always managed to get back together and strengthen their love.

"You show that you don't care about others"

Jess was never late. She hated lateness.

Buddy wasn't quite so disciplined about lateness and couldn't see all the fuss. Jess was pretty uptight about it. She explained that "When you are late, you show that you don't care about others." "It's a selfish act of a control freak." Buddy thought about it and realised, not for the first time, that Jess was right. From then on, he arrived at 8.30 pm or sometimes a few minutes earlier.

EXPERIENCING UNCONDITIONAL LOVE

"When it mattered, they mattered"

Buddy already knew Jess's mum and dad as teachers at the local comprehensive Jess and Buddy had both attended. Bob was his former head teacher, so there was added tension for Buddy as he only knew him as Mr Armstrong. It was early in their courtship and Buddy had not officially met Jess's parents. For Buddy, the whole thought of meeting his former head teacher was stressful, nerve-racking, and best avoided for as long as possible.

As always, Doris answered the phone at Buddy's house. Buddy was in his bedroom again, this time planning what items he might need in the terraced house he was moving into shortly. "Buddy, it's some girl Jess on the phone." Buddy jumped up excitedly and went to the phone.

Jess always had a sense of fun and mischief about her, but this call was different. "Buddy, my father wants a word with you, tonight, on your own," she said in a stern and serious voice. "Can you arrive thirty minutes earlier?" she asked. Buddy was thinking *Father wants a word with you*. Buddy's worst-case scenario thinking arrived. His fear of authority came to the front of his thoughts. He knew he could rely on Jess to calm his fearful mind. "Jess, why does he want to speak to me?" On this occasion, he could not rely on Jess to calm any of his fears. "Buddy, I can't say. He will talk to you when you get here. Don't be late."

Buddy went back to the security of his bedroom. Firstly, he knew not to be late. Secondly, he had no idea what the head teacher wanted him for. Perhaps he was going to talk to me about the age gap between these young lovers. Jess was sixteen and Buddy was twenty-three. It wasn't clear – shortly all would be revealed.

Buddy arrived at the head teacher house. He rang the doorbell. Nothing. Buddy waited. His breathing was becoming more erratic as the stress levels rose. Buddy's mind was racing ahead of the situation. He rang the doorbell again. *Would a hopeful reassuring smile welcome him?* Eventually, Jess came to the door. No smiling face or reassurance and still sounding stern said, "Hello Buddy, my father is in there," pointing to the front room. Buddy didn't know what to expect as he entered the room, but he thought best to be formal and courteous.

Buddy could see the head teacher across the room and walked towards him. Buddy thrust his shaking hand at the head teacher and said, "Hello Mr Armstrong, good to see you again." Buddy had no idea if it would be good to meet Mr Armstrong again, but decided to hope for the best.

EXPERIENCING UNCONDITIONAL LOVE

"Hi Buddy, really good to see you again. Please call me Bob. Would you like a beer?" *Good start* thought Buddy. He sounded very friendly and not like the head teacher Buddy remembered. "Thank you, Bob, I will take a beer." Northern-bloke Bob liked beer. Buddy was more of a lager man, especially with lime or a splash of lemonade, but to fit in with Bob he was now, oddly, drinking beer.

Buddy was now sat chewing the fat about his old school days with Bob and his beer. Bob remembered Buddy for his enthusiastic writing for the school magazine. Bob was a top cricketer and played for the local cricket club in a style not dissimilar to Geoffrey Boycott – he was impossible to dismiss. Buddy remembered his final days at school being the annual staff vs students cricket match. Buddy was fielding in silly mid-off. Bob was caught by Buddy and was out for no runs. It was a memorable catch. Bob hadn't forgotten about it.

All this time Buddy was locked up in his fearful mind as the scene in front of him did not match his thoughts. *Why did Bob want to speak to me? Why was Jess so stern?* Bob eventually said, "So, Buddy, I guess you want to know why I wanted to talk to you this evening." Before Buddy could respond Bob said that they were moving home. They had some items of furniture that they didn't need and wondered if Buddy would like them. It was a lovely hour-long conversation full of warmth, humour, and respect.

Eventually, Jess came in and the lovers were soon off to the local pub for a chat. Later that evening Buddy asked Jess why she sounded so stern on the phone call. "Knowing that you were nervous about meeting my dad, I thought it would be funny to make it sound more serious than it was." Jess liked a practical joke.

That night Bob made it easy for Buddy. Buddy had nothing to worry about. These were parents that showed compassion, empathy, and care. Bob and Pat were lovely and welcomed Buddy into the family unit.

Buddy visited many times and was always treated as one of the family. He attended many family occasions, including the sixtieth wedding anniversary celebrational meal of Bob's parents. There was some early laughter when the young waitress arrived and asked Bob's father if he would like a roll, and he replied, "It's a bit early for me. " He was a funny guy.

Buddy could see a close family unit where everyone in it knew, "When it mattered, they mattered."

EXPERIENCING UNCONDITIONAL LOVE

"He missed you so much on the 18–30 holiday"

Buddy and Jess had been together for a year. They celebrated their first anniversary at the local Football Club Christmas party. The following year was not going to be easy for these young lovers. Buddy knew Jess would leave Somerset, go to York for three years, and leave Buddy behind. Her life had been conditioned to attend university. Buddy knew it was fitting that Jess prioritised her education over him.

Buddy decided that he would enjoy the spring and summertime with Jess knowing that this moment in his life was ending. They both had plans to go away with friends in the summer. Jess went to the USA on a summer camp and extensive travel. Buddy joined his pub mates and went on an 18-30 holiday. As they went their separate ways, there was a tearful goodbye.

In no time, Buddy was in Ibiza Town en route to the all-action town of San Antonio. The weather was lovely. The nightlife began at 11 pm and finished early morning. Sex, sea and sangria were in plentiful supply. Everyone was going for it. Buddy witnessed a wet t-shirt competition, and couples who didn't know one another grappling with their bodies in the full glare of the watching partygoers. When the group jumped off the party bus at 3 am, Nigel, quite a lady's man, asked Cheryl from Newcastle, "Hay, Miss Newcastle, would you like to come up and watch me change my shirt?"

"Yes, please," she said.

One of the holiday representatives said to Buddy at the start of the second week, "Are you enjoying the holiday? How many shags have you had?" *None*, Buddy thought, but one of his mates, Nigel, was keeping a five-bar gate tally on his bedside wall. Buddy hated it. He often went to bed at 11 pm. He was first down for breakfast at 8 am. He spent the days by the pool listening to the only cassette tape he had. *"When I Lose My Way"* by Randy Crawford who was one of his favourites. Looking around the scene and his future, he felt he was about to lose his way.

Jess and Buddy returned from their trips and rekindled their romance. Absence had made the heart grow fonder. One of Buddy's mates, told Jess, "Buddy missed you so much on the 18–30 holiday." Buddy agreed.

"Farewell, my summer love"

The last few weeks of that summer were a challenge for Buddy. Buddy and Jess began closing down the love knowing that distance, time, and ambition would break the relationship.

EXPERIENCING UNCONDITIONAL LOVE

Buddy played it cool. He knew the only love of his life was going away forever. He didn't want her to know how much he was hurting inside. Her education was so important to her, and it was selfish for Buddy to get in the way.

As September came, they met numerous times and discussed how they could make it work. "We can meet up at Christmas," said Jess, leaving the door ajar. On their final day in Somerset, Buddy and Jess said their goodbyes. One last kiss and his best friend had gone. As Buddy drove away, he knew that he was alone again. Buddy felt empty. He had a feeling of deep sadness. He couldn't concentrate at work. He couldn't sleep. What could he do about the situation?

Within ten days, he decided to catch the train to York and meet Jess to tell her how he felt. She needed to know. As he walked to St Lawrence Court, he wasn't sure she would be there. She wasn't. Buddy waited a few hours until she arrived. Buddy was so excited to see her. To tell her, perhaps for the first time, how much he loved her in detail. He never got the chance. Jess seemed shocked to see him and had moved on and was enjoying university life. They stayed together that weekend. However, Buddy could tell the flames were dying. On the walk together to York station, Buddy knew that this stage of his life was over. They both knew. As they said goodbye, he didn't look back as Jess would have seen him crying.

CHOOSE TO BE RELENTLESS

It was an awful, depressing train journey home. Buddy stocked up with whisky and a packet of fags to keep him company. He was crushed. A feeling of hopelessness and emptiness surrounded his head as he thought about his future without Jess. He felt alone. Unloved again.

As he got off the platform at Temple Meads in Bristol, he looked up, and there was Doris offering a few words of support. "You look awful. You stink of smoke and whisky." How he looked and smelt was the least of Buddy's problems. There was no way he could show his honest private thoughts and feelings to a mother who would use them later to control him. He was still alone and felt unloved. He had loved and lost. He had never felt this low in his life.

Jess and Buddy met again the following Christmas and were together on New Year's Eve, 1984/85. They were still in love, but distance, time, and Buddy's mental state were in the way. Buddy gave Jess Michael Jackson's *Farewell My Summer Love* as a final gift. Emotional. Heart-breaking. Yes.

Buddy had learnt so much from Jess. Less than two years after they first met, Jess and Buddy were no longer together. She was out of Buddy's life. He was on his own, with all his vulnerabilities. He was alone with his thoughts and lonely. Again.

EXPERIENCING UNCONDITIONAL LOVE

CHOOSE TO PRIORITISE PHYSICAL AND MENTAL HEALTH

What do you want out of life, now and in the future, regarding your physical and mental health?

CHOOSE TO PRIORITISE PHYSICAL AND MENTAL HEALTH

The Foundation Habits of Health

These physical & mental health habits are the foundations of life achievement. Learning to love yourself gives you the self-respect to face the world.

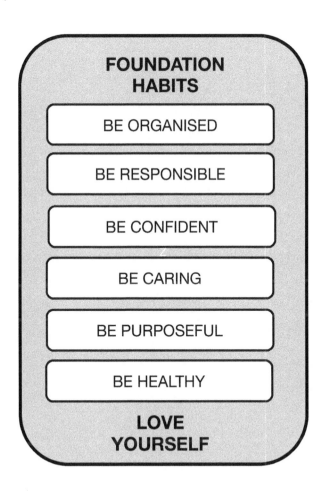

CHOOSE TO PRIORITISE PHYSICAL AND MENTAL HEALTH

These habits are often nurtured within the family environment at an early age. Parents' values, behaviour, and habits significantly impact their children.

These foundation habits focus on having a good mental and physical condition and having a purpose that gets you out of bed in the morning.

Building caring, kindness, and concern for others are also included within these habits. Showing confidence and feeling secure in your abilities, not in an arrogant way, but securely, helps to build the mental stability for achievement.

Finally, being organised and responsible for your actions and circumstances lays the foundations to release your potential.

Feeling good about yourself is vital for a successful life. Some watchers struggle as they can become distracted by their toxic relationships, the company they keep, and the emotion of these challenges.

BE LOVING

A deep and tender feeling of affection for or attachment or devotion to a cause, person or persons

CHOOSE TO PRIORITISE PHYSICAL AND MENTAL HEALTH

Be loving – it is not just a feeling, it's an action

Loving yourself and others is a key foundation for life achievement. The closeness, trust, and understanding helps to build strong and meaningful relationships with your partner, family, friends, and business network. It increases our sense of belonging and it has a positive impact on our physical and mental health.

By putting love into your life, including having a meaningful life purpose, you are creating a positive environment that nurtures your mind and allows you to achieve. As Buddy knows, only too well, it takes courage and vulnerability to love and be loved, but it's worth it.

Buddy has always thought that love is not just a feeling, it's an action. Make it a daily practice to show love and kindness to yourself and others. Put love into all aspects of your life. Buddy was amazed at how much love in his life changed his perspective. Love helped him make the most of his potential. It was the platform to be relentless.

Is "be loving" a foundation habit that you need to consider improving?

"You have got the job; when can you start?"

Buddy lost his way for a while after that train journey from York. He made some awful decisions. He lost his spirit. He lost his smile. He lost his drive. He lost his enthusiasm. He lost his job. He isolated himself from friends. Buddy was depressed. He was a walking car crash for eighteen months – a man with no purpose and direction.

It was a long road, but he knew that if he was to recover, he had to escape the circumstances of his home life and the memories that held him back. Now it was up to him to take control of the situation himself. So that is what he did. He set about reminding himself about his many talents. He knew he could manage a team of people and build out from there. There was no way he could truly love another while doubting himself. He knew he had to learn to love himself before he could love others.

Slowly, bit by bit, he regained his strength and realised that he would need to leave the family memories of Middleton. Buddy had some great friends in Middleton, but it was time to move on. If he was ever to be with Jess again, he needed to show her that he was strong, independent, level-headed, reasonable, and ambitious. The hope that Jess and Buddy could be together again inspired him to make the change and move to a different part of the country. He found a meaning and was motivated.

He had applied for two jobs. One in Cheltenham and the other in Carshalton in south London. He knew Jess wanted to be a lawyer. There was a law college in London. Buddy met Ray, the rotund operations manager of *Farmer's Weekly*, for the interview. A few days later, Ray phoned. "You have got the job; when can you start?" Buddy was on the road to recovery to be able to love another. He was on his way to Carshalton. He was hopeful, driven, and bold.

"Would you like an all-expenses paid trip to Jakarta?"

Buddy threw himself into his new job at *Farmer's Weekly*. It was new, and he had to learn quickly. He built a closeness with his work colleagues and soon realised that you had to build relationships with the key decision-makers to get ahead. He was a motivating manager and quickly built a reputation within the company. Buddy spent a year rebuilding his brain to believe in better for himself. As he challenged his doubts and fears and his negative thought patterns, he became a happier, more engaging person.

Buddy was becoming more assertive and building his confidence. Buddy bought a home in East Grinstead and took in a lodger, Scott. Scott was an entertaining person to live with. He was a passionate Scotsman. He enjoyed his drink, especially whisky. He was a good friend; he was just what Buddy needed at the time.

Together, they travelled to many places, and one weekend, Buddy was in Paris with Scott. They were at the top of the Eiffel Tower. It was twenty-one months since the "Farewell My Summer Love" moment. Buddy's life was different. It was time to test the waters with Jess. Jess loved travelling, and Buddy sent a postcard from Paris with the message, "Would you like an all-expenses paid trip to Jakarta?" He left his East Grinstead number and asked Jess to ring him if she wanted to chat.

"Now you have come this far; tell me it will be forever."

Buddy had a girlfriend of sorts. Worty was one of Scott's old flames. She was attractive and exciting but, most importantly, lived in Carshalton. It was so convenient as Buddy could walk to the office from her place. It was not loving, but she was available.

A few weeks went by. Buddy hadn't heard anything from Jess. Perhaps she had found a new, exciting bloke. It was never to be. Maybe he should work on making things work with Worty, who was keen.

The phone rang in East Grinstead. "Hello," said Buddy.

"Hi Buddy, it's Jess." Buddy had a tear in his eye and a lump in his throat. He hadn't heard Jess's voice for twenty-one months.

"So pleased you rang. It is so lovely to hear your voice after all this time." She explained that she was moving to London in September to attend Law college. Jess sounded so enthusiastic and happy to speak to Buddy again.

"I would love to come and see you the weekend after next," said Jess.

Buddy cried as he said, "I would love that too."

"I'll meet you at the information point at King's Cross Station." Buddy had hoped for this call for so long. When Jess left Buddy's world, he never stopped thinking about her. He now had a belief that it might be more than a call.

Buddy spotted beautiful Jess on the platform. She looked so happy, and so was Buddy. They were together again. They spent the weekend together in East Grinstead. They discussed so much as they rekindled a romance that had been interrupted. Buddy had so much to be sorry about. There were tears, laughter, and joy. She could see that Buddy was different too. He had ambition and confidence. A man going places.

As they reminisced about the past, Buddy and Jess built a commitment and belief that they might have a future together. Their romance journey had been so painful for both. If they were to make it, they had to commit to one another.

With *Still* from Lionel Richie playing in the background and knowing that they had let each other down and both had made mistakes along the way, they knew that they loved one another, still.

Holding back the tears, Buddy said, "Now you have come this far, we have been through so much pain together, tell me it will be forever," said Buddy.

With a beaming smile and tears in her eyes, Jess said, "I hoped you would say that. I never stopped loving you."

Buddy and Jess were together again, this time forever.

CHOOSE TO PRIORITISE PHYSICAL AND MENTAL HEALTH

"You've Got a Friend"

During the early summer of 1988, Jess and Buddy spent as much time together as they could. They made plans to move home to Crawley, so it was easier for Jess to get into London for her law studies.

Buddy found a new job in Brighton. Scott was still about, and they bought a Labrador puppy. A family was being built.

They visited Pat's mother, Jess's lovely grandma in Whitehaven, where Buddy learnt the importance of soaking rice in water to make the creamiest rice pudding. Buddy learnt about different Christmas traditions at Bob and Pat 's house. Opening presents after lunch, singing round the piano, playing games, and competitive league tables. It was a real family. Soon Jess and Buddy would be married and have children of their own. Buddy knew this family was where he belonged.

Buddy and Jess married in August 1989. Their wedding song, *"You've Got a Friend"* from James Taylor is still their favourite song. Honeymoon in Kenya.

Soon after, Bob and Pat moved with an eighty-eight-year-old nana to Cape Cod, Sandwich, on a USA adventure. They set up an English tea shop. Jess and Buddy visited as often as they were able. These were the beginnings of their financial problems.

In 1991, Buddy lost his job due to redundancy. Jess was so supportive. They agreed that they were happy to move anywhere. This time Jess and Buddy were off to West Yorkshire.

CHOOSE TO PRIORITISE PHYSICAL AND MENTAL HEALTH

Learning the lessons from life stories

Buddy's life stories contained so much learning for him. "Be loving" is a habit that Buddy always feels he could do much more. During his life he has learnt some of the skills to "be loving". He is consistent with this habit but is still learning.

The following actions helped Buddy to develop his "be loving" habits, his character, and build the foundations for a healthy and happy life. To apply "be loving" in his life, he told himself to:

- Concentrate on loving your uniqueness, be kind, and nurture the love you have around you.
- See things through the eyes of others and make a connection with the ones you love.
- Value the contribution of others and be supportive when they hit difficult times.
- Identify what you find meaningful and motivating. Find your passion and follow it.

Is the "be loving" habit important to you at this stage of your life? What actions might you be considering?

Learning to Be Loving

Consider your answers to these four questions below when learning to be loving. If being loving is important to you, then what actions might you consider and in what timescale?

- Am I focusing on feeling good about myself, so I can trust and love others?

- Am I building closeness, trust, and understanding with my partner, family, and friends?

- Am I building belief and commitment to the future with the people I care about?

- Am I energised by the experiences, goals, passions, and dreams that I have?

CHOOSE TO PRIORITISE PHYSICAL AND MENTAL HEALTH

BE HEALTHY

Having a good physical or mental condition

Be healthy – create a platform for achievement

The "be healthy" habit is a foundation for life achievement. Buddy knows that winners in life look after their health, making time in their busy schedule for physical and mental enrichment.

Maintaining a healthy mind and body allows you to chase your dreams, achieve your goals, and live a fulfilling and relentless life. By taking control of your health, you are taking control of your life.

Every day is a new opportunity to make better choices. Every step you take towards a healthier you, is a step closer to you being fit enough to make the most of your potential and of those around you.

Is "be healthy" a foundation habit that you need to consider improving?

CHOOSE TO PRIORITISE PHYSICAL AND MENTAL HEALTH

"Mosquitoes never bite me; I don't need a net"

Their first holiday after their emotional reunion was to Marmaris, Turkey. The Turkish rug they purchased has followed them to every one of their homes. Buddy had booked a low-budget place with no air conditioning. Even then, he was cutting back.

Buddy was this new confident character. He proudly explained that he would not need any mosquito spray. "Mosquitoes never bite me; I don't need a net." In fact, he would prove how his body was Teflon-coated. Buddy opened the window, put the net away, removed his clothing, and settled for the evening. Jess put on her pyjamas, carefully fixed the netting over her bed, and settled for her evening. We will see who was right. The following day, Jess hadn't been bitten at all. Buddy had been bitten possibly one hundred times over all areas of his body. Jess was right – again.

Early in Patrice's life, Jess identified that he had allergies. He either suffered from being stung by wasps, or he had to avoid grass pollen from West Yorkshire. Patrice was diving around in the long grass, enjoying catching a frisbee. He came rushing in, and his face was like a balloon. Jess sent him straight to shower as he washed every bit of pollen from his hair and skin. Eventually, the puffiness subsided.

On another occasion, Jess was shocked to learn from his teacher that Patrice was allergic to nuts. Patrice wasn't allergic to nuts. Patrice had to fabricate a nut allergy for years as the school cook removed every trace of nuts from any of Patrice's meals.

"Do you want extra fries with that?"

Buddy was a fit, mean machine when he was a young adult. He was thin but fit and could outrun many over a long distance. He rode a bike regularly, even cycling to Bath Recreation Ground on several occasions to watch the great Viv Richards and Ian Botham play for Somerset Cricket Club.

When he left Somerset, he focused on his career; later, his family and physical health took a back seat. When he first visited the USA in 1990, he was over-excited about the amount of food available. He loved the foot-long hot dogs and always had them with extra fries. This love affair with unhealthy food took over his life, and Buddy slowly put weight on him over several years. He reached 104kg and became very ill. He had problems walking, sleeping, and breathing. But more about that later.

CHOOSE TO PRIORITISE PHYSICAL AND MENTAL HEALTH

"Your scrambled egg is shite"

Scott was only happy when he was drinking and smoking. He often phoned Buddy from the Broadway pub in East Grinstead, encouraging Buddy to go drinking with him. It was often late and far past Buddy's bedtime.

He thought he was a good cook, even appearing on MasterChef, but he used too much pepper to Buddy's liking. On one occasion, Scott made vegetable soup for eight guests. As the soup was tasted, the guests were coughing, and their eyes were running. It had been over-seasoned. As Scott came out of the kitchen, Buddy said, "Scott, have you any more pepper for this soup?" Everybody laughed. Scott was oblivious and brought in the pepper grinder.

Buddy knew he was not the best cook, but he tried hard. One morning, he made some scrambled eggs and called Scott to say it was ready. He came down the stairs, and wasn't happy with the scrambled egg, and put it down for the dog. "That scrambled egg is shite," he said in his posh Edinburgh accent.

When the Brambles moved to West Yorkshire, Scott moved out. He married a lovely lady, Isla, and had three children. When Isla was pregnant, they found an au pair to lend a hand

CHOOSE TO BE RELENTLESS

as it was too much for them. While Isla was sleeping, the au pair and Scott had an affair. He split up with Isla soon after.

He still enjoyed drinking and smoking. Scott didn't live a healthy lifestyle and didn't prioritise his fitness. Sadly a few years later, the drink took him from his friends. It was sad. He was such a funny man.

"I don´t want you to catch Covid"

In 2020, the world was gripped by the fear of Covid. Undoubtedly, this was a worrying time for the world as the leaders grappled with this unknown virus and ever-changing situation.

Jess and Buddy were on a cruise. Soon after they left Singapore, countries were not keen on cruise ships docking near their shore. Cruise ships were seen as an ideal place for a Covid outbreak to spread quickly. It was supposed to be a seven-day cruise. It was extended to twenty days as the captain circled the South China Sea looking for any country that might be interested in allowing six hundred, potentially Covid-ridden, cruise passengers from various countries to land on their soil. In this uncertain time, not one government was keen.

CHOOSE TO PRIORITISE PHYSICAL AND MENTAL HEALTH

They were temperature tested every day. Jess was always stressed when she joined the temperature check queue. She was going through menopause, so her temperature fluctuated daily. Everyone passed the checks.

They hadn't been off the boat for twelve days. It was likely that no one on board this cruise had Covid. Eventually, the Australian government allowed the ship to dock at Darwin. Buddy and Jess caught one of the last flights out of Australia and landed at Heathrow. The Brambles were fortunate.

Jess watched the news regularly, and it became clear that people with certain conditions were struck down with Covid, and some died within days. It was a concerning time for everyone. Buddy had low platelets, was also overweight and medically obese.

Jess didn't want to lose Buddy to Covid and was always very serious about washing hands and taking medical advice. Walking became a habit. Jess and Buddy started to think about their health and what actions they could take. Jess was on permanent health alert. When Covid struck Derek Draper, the husband of Kate Garraway the ITV morning show host, Jess more than once told Buddy, "Wear a mask; I don't want you catching Covid and dying."

Learning the lessons from life stories

The "be healthy" habit was one that Buddy has not always treated seriously. He eventually decided to prioritise and improve his health. He is now dependable with this habit but is still learning.

The following actions helped Buddy to develop his healthy habits, character, and build the foundations for a healthy and happy life. To apply "be healthy" in his life, he told himself to:

- Exercise regularly, eat healthily, and rest your mind and body with sufficient sleep.
- Cultivate an enthusiastic and energising group of friends to maintain your mental health.
- Relax and enjoy your hobbies such as walking, reading, listening to music, or travelling.
- Focus on improving daily, avoiding the negative impact of comparison with others.

Is the "be healthy" habit important to you at this stage of your life? What actions might you be considering?

CHOOSE TO PRIORITISE PHYSICAL AND MENTAL HEALTH

Learning to Be Healthy

Consider your answers to these four questions below when learning to be healthy. If being healthy is important to you, then what actions might you consider and in what timescale?

- Am I caring for myself and being open about my thoughts and feelings?

- Am I prioritising fitness, consuming nutritious food, and living a healthy lifestyle?

- Am I concentrating on breathing, sleeping soundly, being calm, and hydrated?

- Am I connecting with family, friends, and community, feeling like I belong?

-

BE PURPOSEFUL

Having or showing determination or resolve

CHOOSE TO PRIORITISE PHYSICAL AND MENTAL HEALTH

Be purposeful – create a sense of direction

The "be purposeful" habit is a foundation habit for happiness in a healthy life. Having a sense of purpose gives our lives meaning and direction. It helps us set and achieve our potentially groundbreaking goals, and it gives us a sense of accomplishment.

When we have a clear purpose, we are more motivated, resilient, and engaged in our lives. Pursuing our passions allows us to contribute to our community and the world in a positive way.

Remember, your purpose is unique to you, so there is little positive benefit in comparing yourself to others. Take the time to reflect on what truly matters, why it matters to you, and make a plan to make it happen.

Don't hang around being a watcher, start today and make your life purposeful. Buddy knows that when he is fired up with purpose it brings him a sense of satisfaction and feeling of achievement.

Is "be purposeful" a foundation habit that you need to consider improving?

"If no one else knows how to do it, why not me?"

Buddy was working for *Farmer's Weekly*. He was energised and a motivated manager, living away from his place of birth and building his new life. An opportunity appeared for him to take up a new position in a new industry that very few knew much about. He was in the right place at the right time. The director responsible for the start-up spotted his talent and invited him to become the operations director for a brand-new start-up in Brighton. His home in Crawley was perfect for the commute. It was 1988. He was twenty-eight.

This role gave Buddy the purpose and direction he needed. *If no one else knew how to do it, why not me,* he thought. He took the job. He created a plan to succeed and was determined to make a success of it. The job involved long hours, and Buddy desperately accelerated his learning so that he could shine in this new industry. In three years, Buddy developed the skills to become an expert in telephone sales and service contact centre management. He was able to build an enjoyable life in this new growth industry. For Buddy, this achievement was groundbreaking. He was lucky to have Jess, who supported him throughout every moment.

CHOOSE TO PRIORITISE PHYSICAL AND MENTAL HEALTH

"The sea is too rough; only you can save him"

Buddy wanted to offer a better life to his children than he had. Buddy and Jess knew that travel would broaden their minds and help them appreciate different cultures. So travelling was essential to the Brambles. If they could, the Brambles always went away for a sunshine break. Buddy is not a great swimmer, but on three occasions, he has been the person to save Alex from certain death in the water.

The Brambles were on an island in Seychelles, enjoying the coolness of the sea and topping up their vitamin D. Alex was in the water, and a huge wave was building out at sea. Buddy could see it building up steam and force. He very quickly grabbed hold of Alex. "Breathe in, hold your breath and don't open your mouth," said Buddy. Alex inhaled just as the wave hit them full on. Buddy held Alex close to his chest as the power of the tide pushed them around in the water. No way Buddy was going to let go of Alex. He might have lost him under the water if he had let go. Eventually, the sea calmed, and Alex was safe.

The Brambles were enjoying the water park black hole in Fuengirola, Andalucía. Jess looked after Patrice, and non-swimmer Buddy looked after the non-swimmer Alex. Jess and Patrice set off down the black hole. Alex and Buddy were about to enter together. Alex missed his moment and slipped out of his ring into the circular holding pen full of people bobbing up and down in the water. It was a scary moment as the ring, Alex, and Buddy were separated and not in touching distance. Buddy was about to be sucked into the black hole. He had to use all his determination and energy to stop himself from being next to go down the slide. He grabbed the ring and could see Alex in the distance. He shouted, "That's my boy. Can someone grab him?" A young guy, Frederic, reached out and grabbed Alex. Another near-death experience was avoided. Buddy doesn't like water parks, slides, or black holes. Or heights, but that's another story.

The Brambles were at the Taba Heights on the Sinai Peninsula. The hotel brochure said there was good snorkelling at the end of the jetty. The Brambles loved snorkelling and collected their snorkel gear from their bags. They set off along the white sand en route to the jetty.

As they walked on the jetty, they could see up ahead. No one else was in the water. They could snorkel alone. One by one, they climbed down the steps and into the water. Jess and Patrice went first and said there was a strong undercurrent, but they should be okay. Alex and Buddy joined them. Quickly the current swept them away from the jetty. The current was too strong for Buddy and Alex. The strength of the sea was knocking them about. "It's too rough for Alex," shouted Jess "you will have to save him." The best way back to the shore was to swim and walk through the water.

Alex and Buddy started well, but Buddy had not seen the bank of coral under the water. He held Alex above his head as he waded on through the coral. With nearly every step, Buddy felt the coral cut him. After a few metres, Buddy and Alex were out of the coral and soon onto the beach's safety.

Buddy's bloodied legs looked like a deranged man with a knife had attacked him. Lots of blood dripped onto the white sand. Luckily, a few significant cuts healed quickly; the rest were only superficial scratches. The Brambles didn't snorkel there again.

"I am going to publish a book"

At the turn of the millennium, Buddy set up his consultancy business focused on providing advice and guidance to customer-focused organisations. He worked with directors to help them change their businesses by putting customer and people first and helping them release their potential. He identified that the key to organisational engagement was to build a culture where people took the time to understand others and not judge situations. Creating teams of purposeful intent was his strength. Alongside this was a need to act on and learn from day-to-day events.

Buddy was in the top set for English at school. He enjoyed writing and thought a business book was needed to capture all this learning. In 2005, he told Jess, "I am going to publish a book." He was determined, focused and not distracted. He became very purposeful as he set up the book's structure and thought about the key chapters to inspire managers. It wasn't an easy task, as Buddy could only write in the evenings as he was busy with his consultancy business.

Over the next six months, Buddy finished "keeping the human factor alive," made the final edits, and published it. Within days, it had appeared on Amazon. Buddy was now an Author.

"Let's talk about how we are feeling"

The Covid lockdown was not easy for many. The Bramble sons were living on their own. Jess and Buddy spoke to them regularly. Alex showed empathy and encouraged the family to say how they were all feeling, using marks out of ten. It allowed everyone to be vulnerable and helped the Brambles get through the months of lockdown. The Brambles still ask this question whenever they are together. It has helped everyone to be open about their thoughts and feelings.

CHOOSE TO PRIORITISE PHYSICAL AND MENTAL HEALTH

Learning the lessons from life stories

Buddy's greatest achievements have been when he has had a clear purpose. He jumps out of bed and attacks the day with gusto. "Be purposeful" is one of Buddy's dependable habits.

The following actions helped Buddy to develop his character, be purposeful, and build the foundations for a healthy and happy life. To apply "be purposeful" in his life, he told himself to:

- Know what you want to achieve, what it looks like, and set specific, measurable goals.
- Create a plan to achieve, identifying the important steps to take, and make a start.
- Know why you want to achieve, take responsibility and avoid any distractions.
- Identify the inspiring people who will encourage and guide you through any setbacks.

Is the "be purposeful" habit important to you at this stage of your life? What actions might you be considering?

Learning to Be Purposeful

Consider your answers to these four questions below when learning to be purposeful. If being purposeful is important to you, what actions might you consider and in what timescale?

- Am I leading a life to the full, with a clear purpose and direction?

- Am I defining what groundbreaking success on my terms looks like?

- Do I know what I need to do to make success on my terms happen?

- Am I performing a reality check to ensure that I can achieve success?

CHOOSE TO PRIORITISE PHYSICAL AND MENTAL HEALTH

BE CARING

Displaying kindness, concern and warm feelings for others

CHOOSE TO BE RELENTLESS

Be caring – show kindness and compassion for others

The "be caring" habit is a foundation habit for success in life. It is one of the most important habits you can do for yourself and for others. Buddy knows that to "be caring" has helped him to build strong and meaningful relationships. It increased his sense of belonging and purpose, and had a positive impact on his mental and physical health.

Caring for others also helps us to develop empathy, compassion, and a sense of community, which is essential for a fulfilling and relentless life. By showing care and concern for others, we also learn to be kinder and more understanding of ourselves.

Like love, caring is not just a feeling, it's an action. Despite his background, Buddy tried hard to show caring and kindness to himself and others as he improved his behaviour. Buddy saw for himself how much it changed his life and the lives of those around him for the better.

Is "be caring" a foundation habit that you need to consider improving?

CHOOSE TO PRIORITISE PHYSICAL AND MENTAL HEALTH

"Why do other dog walkers always talk to you?"

Jess has many talents that make her an attractive wife. She is loyal, thoughtful, caring, and forgiving. She is understanding and a good friend. She is always present in everyday life. Alex and Patrice know that Jess is an empathetic ear whenever they have worries or concerns. They know that they are cared for. Jess and Buddy are always there for their children.

Jess also has a resting face that shows warmth, friendliness, and approachability. Buddy has a resting face that shows annoyance, irritation, and unapproachability. When walking their dog in the countryside, Buddy often asks, "Why do other dog walkers always talk to you?" Often, other walkers will avoid conversation with the unapproachable Buddy. On the other hand, just behind, Jess can quickly start a conversation and build a relationship.

It's odd, as Buddy loves conversation with people and group activities but his face doesn't seem to join in.

"I still miss him, even after all these years"

Politics has always been a massive part of the Brambles' life. They know the importance of social justice, aspiration and allowing everyone to make the most of their talents. The lives of Buddy and Jess have been full of a few moments of Labour victories. The famous Neil Kinnock speech best articulated this in 1983. "If Margaret Thatcher wins on Thursday, I warn you not to be ordinary. I warn you not to be young. I warn you not to fall ill. And I warn you not to grow old." The Labour Party had to wait another fourteen years before they could change Britain.

Short conversations in their family can quickly turn into a dialogue about the best way forward for the betterment of their community. Alex graduated from the University of Exeter and became heavily involved in the local party there. He worked hard delivering leaflets, listening to voters, and building relationships with the members. He began to think about his political ambitions. He knocked on doors and ensured that the voters in his ward knew him and how much he cared about their lives. It was no surprise when he became a councillor. He was young and slowly built his reputation as someone that got things done. A few years later, Alex became the youngest member of the Exeter cabinet. The Brambles were very proud of him.

Later Alex found a job in private business and had to resign his seat as his new career was in Newcastle. Four years later, an Exeter Labour Party member said, "I still miss him, even after all these years."

CHOOSE TO PRIORITISE PHYSICAL AND MENTAL HEALTH

"You are not going to get involved"

Patrice has always been a very kind and caring person. Often, if he sees a homeless person, he will go into a food shop and buy food and a drink to help them through their day.

At a Bristol Rovers football match, a ten-year-old Patrice saw injustice as the police restored order on the terraces. The police were heavy-handed with one of the fans, and Patrice had none of it. Patrice set off and pushed past Buddy to let the police know they were being unfair and wrong. Buddy held him back. "Patrice, you are not going to get involved with the police."

The police were very wrong that day, but this was not the time for Patrice to be a peacemaker.

Buddy has always been kind but could be more consistent in every day situations. Over the last few years, he has noticed the power of random acts of kindness. He was in Salzburg, and an elderly American tourist with a walking stick was struggling to buy a water bottle from a vendor. They would not accept dollars as payment. Buddy stepped forward and said, "It's okay; I'll buy it for you."

Recently in Malaga, Buddy helped a young family carry a heavy bag down some steps. This is happening more frequently. As Buddy is helping people, they are happy, and in turn, Buddy feels good about his contribution to the lives of others.

Patrice has been caring and helpful for years.

"I don't like how people look at us"

Only a few years ago, the Brambles were travelling from Washington to New Orleans to understand more about the history of the deep south of the USA. They went to former slave plantations, coastal cities, and towns to understand more about Black history and to see in detail the unfairness of racism and prejudice.

Driving through South Carolina, they pulled off the freeway and stopped at a McDonald's between Savannah and Charleston for a break from history. Everything started well as the family bought their lunchtime snack. It was hectic. The restaurant was packed. However, there was an area that no one was sitting in, so the Brambles grabbed the space. They were happily sucking on their milkshakes and chomping away at their Big Mac and fries. They were talking about stopping off at Daytona Beach later for a swim.

CHOOSE TO PRIORITISE PHYSICAL AND MENTAL HEALTH

Halfway through the meal, Patrice spotted finger-pointing and unhappy faces looking at them. "I don't like how people look at us," said Patrice. Jess looked over. Patrice was right; the angry-looking white people were undoubtedly looking at the Brambles, as no one else was near them. Buddy quickly realised that the Brambles had sat in the wrong part of the restaurant. They were seated in the unofficial black-only area of the restaurant.

As local law enforcement police arrived, the Brambles made a hasty departure and jumped in their car. They understood then how black lives matter. The Brambles also understood what it was like to be stared at. For a moment back there, they could imagine standing in a black person's shoes. History was happening before the Brambles' very eyes.

Jess then spent a few minutes explaining the importance of education to improve the attitude of the racists that the Brambles saw that day. Shocking.

Learning the lessons from life stories

Buddy has worked hard to "be caring" and has become consistent in applying this habit. It was often one that Buddy needed to prioritise and improve. During his life he has learnt some of the skills to "be caring". He is still learning.

The following actions helped Buddy to develop his character, be caring, and build the foundations for a healthy and happy life. To apply "be caring" in his life, he told himself to:

- Be there for the people that matter to you, building a solid, fruitful, and strong relationship.
- Be kind, understanding, and empathetic in your words and emotional reaction to events.
- Become an active listener giving people undivided attention when they talk to you.
- Forgive and forget some life situations. Learn, take responsibility, and move on with life.

Is the "be caring" habit important to you at this stage of your life? What actions might you be considering?

CHOOSE TO PRIORITISE PHYSICAL AND MENTAL HEALTH

Learning to Be Caring

Consider your answers to the four questions below when learning to be caring. If being caring is important to you, then what actions might you consider and in what timescale?

- Am I acknowledging and present in everyday moments, conversations, and life?

- Am I showing kindness, so people feel valued and know they are cared for?

- Am I always looking to add random acts of kindness into my day?

- Am I noticing out-of-character behaviour and asking how they are feeling?

BE CONFIDENT

Feeling sure of yourself and your abilities – not in an arrogant way, but in a realistic, secure way

Be confident – minimise the impact of the fearful mind

The "be confident" habit is the foundation for success in life. It allows us to achieve our goals and live a happy and fulfilling life. It helps us to overcome obstacles, take risks, and pursue our passions.

When we are confident in ourselves, we do not allow the fearful mind to reduce our ambition. We are more likely to step out of our comfort zone, try new things, and reach our full potential. Self-confidence also helps us to build stronger relationships and improve our communication skills. Celebrate your difference and step forward.

Confidence is not something we are born with, it's something we build over time by learning from our experiences. Be kind to yourself, celebrate, and become aware of your successes. Don't be afraid to make mistakes as you learn new things in this digital, artificially intelligent world. Every step you take towards building confidence is a step towards releasing the untapped potential in yourself.

Is "be confident" a foundation habit that you need to consider improving?

"Jay will take your place"

Patrice loved his football. When he was a boy in short trousers, he was also the youngest in his year group. If only he had started pushing forty minutes later, he would have been the oldest in the class. This physically underdeveloped laddie would not be stopped. He worked hard on his skills and found himself selected for the school team at a very young age.

Eventually, Patrice joined the local village junior team. He was a fit and skilful player and had no problems dribbling and creating problems for the opposition. Buddy spotted that Patrice had developed a way of playing that avoided tackling. He was very good at running alongside players and keeping up with them. He always looked like he might tackle but never did. Buddy discussed this inability to tackle with Patrice, but in the next game, there was no change. He had a negative mindset block.

Buddy gave Patrice his standard motivational messages on the way to the next match. At one point, Buddy said, "I'm sorry, but you tackle like a softie; if you don't sort yourself out, Jay will take your place." Patrice was bothered and agitated about that possibility quickly responded, "Jay! There is no way Jay will take my place. I'm not having it. I'll show you." Patrice was angry and jumped out of the car with purpose and determination.

Patrice had his best game ever. He ran, dribbled, crossed, and headed, but most of all, he tackled. He won the ball many times and set up numerous chances for his team. At one point, the referee pulled him up when one of his tackles was late, and some poor laddie was on the floor holding his ankle and crying. Patrice won the Man of the Match, and when he got in the car to go home, he was still angry with Buddy. With emotion on his face, Patrice blurted out, "I said I would show you, and I did."

Buddy, to calm down the feeling, said, "Yes, you were great. Very proud of you. But can you do the same next week?"

Patrice became confident and very sure of his ability and believed in his talent. At the end of the season, Patrice won a Player of the Tournament award because he tackled like Roy Keane. Some praise for the laddie. Like his father Buddy, Patrice scored forty goals a season with many more assists.

"She loved representing the underdog"

Jess and Buddy were at a crossroads in their careers. It was 1998. Jess was unhappy where she worked, and Buddy was unemployed again. They were both sure of their ability and had the self-confidence to aim high.

Jess decided to break out on her own and start her own company. Buddy also decided to set up his own company. With two young children, it was never a good time. They also had a lovely home at Brig Royd in Ripponden, West Yorkshire, with a big mortgage that needed paying off.

Jess came from an ambitious family that made the most of their potential. Her father, Bob, was a head teacher at thirty-five. She was building a good reputation in Halifax as a top criminal lawyer that clients valued. Jess was thirty-three. She loved representing the underdog. Her clients knew that she cared. When she arrived in Huddersfield nine years earlier, she was the only woman. She took on the men and ran them out of town. Her mum and dad were so proud of her. She started her business, built a loyal base, and made a huge success. She sold the business in 2012. She was also around to be with the children every evening.

Buddy had been conditioned, at a young age, to allow people to erode his confidence and distract him from his achievements. He spent too much of his early life overly concerned with what people thought about him. He allowed their negativity to affect his natural enthusiasm for life. He had rebuilt his brain to think differently, and now he was realistically confident.

Buddy set up his business, was employed by some big companies and managed to get a reputation in his industry. At one, the CEO at the time said, "Understanding and Learning was the last remaining differentiator." Buddy left it late to make the most of his talents. He was the director of his own company in 2000 and became a board director of another in 2007.

However, he was away nearly every week and missed many parents´ evenings and school events. He wasn't always at home to see Alex and Patrice through their early years. He regrets that he wasn't. Buddy was always around at weekends and holidays adding banter and a different view to family life. He more than achieved in his career, but it came with a sacrifice. *Could he have been a better father?* For sure. Buddy is working hard now to be one.

"You are driving like a madman"

Buddy and Jess loved their family holidays. It was the one time they could all be together without the distractions of their careers. It gave them a chance to experience new activities, locations, and cultures. Patrice and Jess loved Formula One.

When an opportunity came to be in a go-kart at the Fuengirola racing circuit, Patrice jumped at the chance. So, after the safety briefing, Patrice, Buddy, and Alex put on their helmets and lined up alongside the instructor.

The first lap was fine as they all became used to the track and the cars. Buddy saw his role as a senior supervisor to ensure that the young Schumachers followed the rules. Patrice was confident, a natural and was in total control. There were problems with Alex, who had been spotted by the instructor going too fast and not being in control. He was driving so dangerously that the instructor told Buddy that he would be disqualified if he didn't drive within the rules. It was time to grip Alex. Buddy caught up with Alex and said, "You are driving like a madman. If you don't slow down and drive sensibly, the instructor said you would be disqualified." Alex calmed down, and soon the race was over. The Bramble's didn't try go-karting again.

"A good start in life"

Jess and Buddy are proud of their children. Buddy and Jess were always keen that Alex & Patrice should have a university education if they were academically gifted. The Brambles knew it gave them the best chance of a good start in life.

CHOOSE TO PRIORITISE PHYSICAL AND MENTAL HEALTH

Buddy always encouraged them to be the best they could be and not waste the talents they had been gifted with. Patrice went to Liverpool, and Alex went to Exeter. They were surrounded by some of the winners in life. Both have graduated and are building their careers, building confidence in their abilities. Patrice is a top salesperson, often appearing near the top of national league tables, with a talent for leading teams. Alex is making his way in the finance world, managing large budgets, and building his reputation as a commercial whizz-kid.

Jess and Buddy look forward to seeing how they take advantage of the opportunities ahead.

Learning the lessons from life stories

Buddy was lucky that he found people that believed in him. They helped him to prioritise and improve this confidence habit. He is still learning and improving.

The following actions helped Buddy to develop his confidence, character, and build the foundations for a healthy and happy life. To apply "be confident" in his life, he told himself to:

- Build relationships with achievers and winners. Find a coach to build your confidence.
- Recognise when your negative thoughts and self-talk are reframing the facts in front of you.
- Believe in your abilities, reminding yourself of your achievements and unique strengths.
- Build your capability and knowledge knowing that experiences are, in fact, the best learning.

Is the "be confident" habit important to you at this stage of your life? What actions might you be considering?

CHOOSE TO PRIORITISE PHYSICAL AND MENTAL HEALTH

Learning to Be Confident

Consider your answers to the four questions below when learning to be confident. If being confident is important to you, then what actions might you consider and in what timescale?

- Am I being kind to myself by affirming my self-worth and believing in myself?

- Am I conscious of the people that distract me and erode my confidence?

- Am I taking time to build my self-confidence by reviewing my achievements?

- Am I consistently making the most of my strengths, talents, and potential?

BE RESPONSIBLE

Being accountable for your actions and circumstances

CHOOSE TO PRIORITISE PHYSICAL AND MENTAL HEALTH

Be responsible– take control of choices and actions

The "be responsible" habit is the foundation for success in life. It allows us to take control of our actions and choices, and to be accountable for our decisions. Being responsible, stops us blaming our present situation on anyone else.

Being responsible also helps us to build understanding, trust, and respect with others. It allows us to be reliable and dependable in our relationships and in our work life.

Taking responsibility for the consequences of our actions helps us to learn from our experiences and to grow as individuals. Being responsible is not just about fulfilling promises, it's also about making conscious choices and being responsible for your own happiness. Being responsible helps the mental health of people.

Buddy took that first step, years ago. He could have blamed his circumstance. He didn´t. Buddy took responsibility for his life and was amazed at how much it changed his life, and others, for the better.

Is "be responsible" a foundation habit that you need to consider improving?

"I don't know who did it, but it wasn't me"

Brig Royd was a lovely family home with land that allowed the Bramble boys to run and run. It was a beautiful location, alongside a river and incredibly relaxing. The house was warm and welcoming, with an AGA cooker. Both Bramble boys took responsibility for getting coal from the outside coal bunker when Buddy was away. Jess was very appreciative of that on many cold, wintery evenings.

One Saturday, Buddy was on the way upstairs and noticed that "Alexander" had been written on the wall in large letters. Someone in the Bramble family was responsible. Jess and Buddy called the boys in from outside for a chat in the conservatory. Buddy sucked them in with, "Hello, we have a problem, and we need your help. I would like to show you something," as Buddy moved towards the door to the upstairs area.

As the boys looked at "Alexander" on the wall, they said, "I don't know who did it, but it wasn't me." Buddy pointed out that it was clear that the culprit was in that room.

Buddy continued. "I think we can be pretty sure that it wasn't mum or me. It's not our sort of thing. So that leaves just the two of you." So, who did it? Patrice was clear it wasn't him, and more so pointed the finger at his brother Alexander. Calmly, Buddy said, "I would like you both to go upstairs and chat about it. Only come down when you know who did it." Off they went. Buddy and Jess could hear the conversation upstairs, with Alex saying he didn't do it and Patrice saying he knew it was him.

"This is silly, Alex, it's you. Why would I write Alexander on a wall? It's your name, not mine." After fifteen minutes, Alex came downstairs and said he was sorry. He was responsible. He did it. The Brambles took time to understand why he did it, and then Alex spent much longer cleaning the mess from the wall. It was an early lesson on being responsible for your actions in life.

"Don't worry about breakfast; I've sorted it"

Buddy was always cutting back and keeping a firm grip on the family finances. The Brambles were in Dubrovnik and were planning to set off early to drive along the Dalmatia coastline. Buddy had checked out the hotel breakfast. It was too expensive. He took responsibility and said, "Don't worry about breakfast; I've sorted it. We will have breakfast on the route at a suitable picnic spot." Buddy found the spot and poured out orange juice drinks for all. So far, so good.

CHOOSE TO BE RELENTLESS

Happy Cow cheese with paprika and croissants would be lovely for breakfast. As Buddy prepared the snack, he felt proud of his efforts and delivered them to the family. As they all bit into the croissants, Jess said, "These are awful; what is in them?" "Just paprika cheese," Buddy said. He hadn't noticed that the croissants had been made with copious chunks of honey, and the combination did, in fact, taste awful. The Buddy breakfast was thrown away. Buddy was constantly reminded about his inability to make a good breakfast on the move. Buddy learnt not to be responsible for breakfast in the future.

"What are you crying about?"

The Brambles were in a Chinese restaurant in Wales, and Alex didn't like the rice as it was too yellow. He was making too much of a fuss. It was another tantrum. Buddy took him outside. Buddy explained that he was treating him as a grown-up. Grown-ups don't cry about yellow rice. He was three years old. The Bramble boys knew that tantrums were not the way to get things they wanted.

Alex had a choice: sit in the car alone in the dark or come back inside and act like a responsible grown-up. If he chose to be in the car, then he would not be allowed to be involved with the grown-ups in the future until he was much older. "Patrice is not crying about yellow rice, is he? The choice is yours." Alex chose to come back in. No more tantrums from Alex.

If the young Bramble boys were crying because they wanted something, Buddy always said, "Well, you have two choices; if you cry, you absolutely will not get what you are crying about. If you stop crying, you might, but only might. I can say that the only possible way you can get that item is if you stop crying about it. It's your choice."

This seemed to work for years whenever tantrums arrived. Once, it didn't work. Alex came out of the sea and was crying. Buddy thought it was a tantrum. The method kicked in, but it wasn't working. He had already got what he was crying about – he had been stung by a jellyfish.

In their life the Brambles have experienced many moments when emotion of the situation has led to tears. Both Alex and Patrice have experienced situations where they have shed tears.

Jess and Buddy have always been there for them when they have needed a shoulder to cry on. Showing your emotions is encouraged within this supportive family.

"You've been mugged off by that bus there, Dad"

Buddy had far too many car accidents and didn't seem to learn. He was always keen to contribute as if he would die tomorrow, but sometimes it seemed that the car was an integral part of his death plan. Buddy wrote off two lorries and drove through a hedge and into a field while distracted. He rolled a Mini down a hill and failed to overtake a car properly while looking for an apple. He drove on the wrong side of the road and hit a car in France. Once in Manchester Airport, Buddy picked up his car from a parking area. It was a tight space. The business owner moved one of the cars to make it easier for Buddy. All good, except Buddy, then drove his car up the parking lot to another tight spot and amazingly reversed straight into the car that had been moved to make his life easier. "Oh dear," said Buddy as Patrice laughed his socks off. There were other accidents – too many to mention.

The Brambles were travelling through Oldham, and Buddy was overtaken by a bus. Patrice said, "You have been mugged off by that bus there, Dad."

Buddy was having none of it and immediately overtook the bus, picked up speed, looked back and said, "I've not been mugged now, laddie." Then there was a flash. Buddy had been caught speeding again; how they laughed.

CHOOSE TO PRIORITISE PHYSICAL AND MENTAL HEALTH

Learning the lessons from life stories

Buddy realised very early in life that if he was to have an impact, he would need to "be responsible". He knew he was on his own. He needed to prioritise this habit over all others. This is one of Buddy's dependable habits that he can rely on.

The following actions helped Buddy to develop his character, be responsible, and build the foundations for a healthy and happy life. To apply "be responsible" in his life, he told himself to:

- Take ownership of your actions and their consequences. Admit when you are wrong.
- Be trustworthy, reliable, and dependable. Follow through and do what you say you will.
- Minimise the time spent discussing issues and distractions outside of your direct control.
- Respect others by being considerate and understanding in all conversations.

Is the "be responsible" habit important to you at this stage of your life? What actions might you be considering?

Learning to Be Responsible

When learning to be responsible, consider your answers to these four questions below. If being responsible is important to you, then what actions might you consider and in what timescale?

- Am I 100% responsible for the consequences, whatever the outcome?

- Am I a meaningful human being to someone else?

- Am I showing up, taking action, and contributing as if I would die tomorrow?

- Am I a dependable friend that people around me can trust to keep my word?

CHOOSE TO PRIORITISE PHYSICAL AND MENTAL HEALTH

BE ORGANISED

Having the ability to plan carefully and keep things tidy

Be organised – don't live life accidently

The "be organised" habit is a foundation for life achievement. Being organised helps us to manage our time, prioritise our tasks and goals, and reduce stress and anxiety. Watchers in life rarely take control, seeming to live life accidently as they scramble to react to day-to-day events.

Being organised also allows us to be more productive in our work, it improves our ability to focus and concentrate, and it makes it easier to achieve our goals.

Being organised is not a one-time thing, it's a habit that needs to be developed and nurtured. Start small and make a plan, you'll be amazed at how much more in control and productive you will feel.

Is "be organised" a foundation habit that you need to consider improving?

CHOOSE TO PRIORITISE PHYSICAL AND MENTAL HEALTH

"You have a healthy, beautiful baby boy"

Being organised and planning is essential for a relaxing childbirth.

As usual, Buddy was up early. He had taken Jimmy, their Labrador, for a walk and was preparing himself for his thirty-minute drive into Bradford, where he worked. He was just about to set off when Jess popped her beautiful head around the corner and said she could feel an attraction. "Not now, Jess; I'm off to work." "No, I said a contraction. I don't think you will be going to work today." It was an early indication of a Buddy hearing problem.

Buddy had been waiting for this day and was all prepared. Patrice was born fifteen months earlier, so he knew what needed to be done. He packed his bag with all the essential items he needed to get through the ordeal. He quickly buttered some rolls and threw in some fillings and snacks in the bag so that he wouldn't become hungry during the next few hours. "Jess, did you want a roll?"

"No. I feel sick at the thought. Can you take me to the hospital? Now." she said in an agitated voice. Buddy jumped into gear and helped Jess into the front seat. He quickly clocked on to the emotions required in this situation with his best understanding; he said, "Are you counting the contractions?"

"Yes, can you concentrate on driving?" Buddy sensed that the stress levels were high, and he was not helping.

Buddy found his way to the Halifax hospital. It was only ten minutes away. In no time, Jess was flat on her back. The midwife was looking to see what she could see. It seemed like Jess was 4cm dilated. She needed to be 10cm for the baby to pass through. "Oh good," said Buddy, "that gives me time to go and pay the car park fees and get my bag of vital food." The midwife looked oddly at Buddy.

She turned to Jess and said, "You will need an enema to facilitate this birth." It was a good time for Buddy to leave as a large syringe was inserted into Jess's rectum to facilitate a dump. Super organised Buddy returned ten minutes later with his bag. Jess was now a few pounds lighter and was breathing happily. "Jess, you seem much more relaxed now that I have returned."

"No, Buddy, I am under the influence of laughing gas and air. I'm so much happier now that these experts here surround me." Not sure Buddy was helping.

CHOOSE TO PRIORITISE PHYSICAL AND MENTAL HEALTH

"I'm not down the pub like some would be," snapped Buddy.

Every so often, the midwife came in and checked the dilation. Buddy and Jess discussed baby names again. They still hadn't decided. Things seemed very quiet and calm. It was so relaxed that the midwife came in and said, "We are off to lunch now. Any problems, Buddy, please press the button at the end of this cable."

Buddy saw their lunch break as a chance to enjoy his lunch. He had been on his feet all morning. Tiring stuff this childbirth. He reached into his bag for his cheese and pickle roll. He was next to Jess. About the same time as Buddy was thinking of biting, Jess was thinking of pushing. He looked where all the action was and could see a head. He had one hand on the head of the unborn child and the other on his half-eaten roll. He had to press the button. What could he do with the bread roll? Buddy put the roll in his mouth. He pressed the button with one hand and had the other hand on this head. He looked up and could see Jess breathing heavily. He had the best view in the house.

Buddy could feel the head moving forward. Just as the midwife came, the action started. In what seemed like seconds, the child's head was out, "Breathe, Jess, don't push quite yet," said the midwife looking in. "okay, Jess, push." In moments the rest of the body was out. The afterbirth was on its way. It was a messy affair. The cheese pickle taste mixed with the sight of the afterbirth was too much for Buddy. He had to sit in the corner on the visitor's chair. He felt sick. "Are you okay, Buddy?" said the Midwife. "You have a healthy, beautiful boy."

"What are you doing over there?" said Jess. Buddy went over to see this beautiful boy. He looked all purple. His head was shaped like a potato. He wasn't crying, but the Brambles were reassured he was healthy. Buddy looked at Jess and said, "He looks like an Alex to me." That was the name Jess wanted. He smiled, and Buddy said, "Are you okay, Jess? I love you. I'll go and ring Grandma and let her know you and Alex are okay."

A day later, Buddy and Patrice went to the teddy bear shop to buy his little brother a gift. Patrice was fifteen months old and selected a cuddly teddy bear. As they walked into the maternity ward, Buddy held Patrice's hand as he stumbled towards his baby brother. Jess had a tear in her eye as she saw them walking down the corridor. Patrice was holding the bear. He looked at his new brother, who was less purple now. Patrice blurted out, "Baby!" and chucked the bear at Alex.

Patrice then cuddled Jess.

CHOOSE TO PRIORITISE PHYSICAL AND MENTAL HEALTH

"There needed to be cutbacks"

In 1991, Jess and Buddy moved to West Yorkshire and settled into the lovely village of Stainland, high above Halifax. The Conservatives were still in power. Again. Jess and Buddy were hopeful that with Mrs Thatcher gone, a Labour government would soon be in control. Buddy loved the inspiring speeches of Neil Kinnock. The 1988 Conservative recession was behind the UK, and Prime Minister John Major was promising a bright future and jam tomorrow as he hoped for a victory in the 1992 election. Labour lost again on the 9th of April 1992.

Neil Kinnock resigned as the Labour leader with a speech highlighting how the incoming Conservatives did not have and would not develop the policies necessary to strengthen the British economy; they would not try to address the injustices in British society. He regretted that he failed to ensure that enough people understood that and the implications it had for the future. His sorrow is that millions, particularly those who do not have the strength to defend themselves, will suffer because of the election of another Conservative government. "Success will therefore have to wait," Kinnock said. "But it will come, and I will work for it." The Brambles had to wait for another five years for the incoming Labour government of 1997.

The Brambles could not sell their house in Crawley but could rent it to cover the mortgage. With new jobs for both, two mortgages and inconsistent payments from the managing agent in Crawley, times were tough for Jess and Buddy. Their first real family home was filled with second-hand furniture from the Sell-It Centre in Pellon, Halifax and car-boot items.

They had a debt of 25k on credit cards and 14k on Jess's student loan. This loan was attached to Jess following their marriage in 1989. Regular flights to Boston and the bed and breakfast business in Sandwich to see Bob and Pat often didn't help their finances.

The Brambles were very happy together but were living beyond their means, and not for the first time, there needed to be cutbacks in their way of life. To use a phrase from Doris, they needed to "cut their cloth to suit their loins." Buddy came up with a new set of questions they needed to ask before purchasing anything. Do we want it? Do we need it? Jess and Buddy had to both agree. If not, then the item could not be purchased. This routine became a habit and was very successful in helping them to reduce their debt. Slowly over the next few years, they increased their income and could reduce their debts further.

Buddy worked at a financial services company and built his leadership reputation. He was always obsessed with something. It was just the way he was. His latest obsession was pensions and investments. They had no money for either, but it didn't stop Buddy from contributing his thoughts about stocks, shares, and gilts to the family conversations. Luckily, Buddy did have a plan and over time built up a habit of investing in a pension for Jess and Buddy. Over many years, they built up a pension fund that hopefully will give the senior Brambles sufficient income to enjoy a comfortable retirement.

"He is an independent learner"

Alex is just super organised. Even from a young age, he would get his clothes out the night before so that his morning routine was calm. Even today, he has his habits and a schedule that he sticks with. His grandad Bob was the same. Before a holiday, Bob would always write down where he was going and what he was doing. He would photocopy the itinerary and give it to the family.

Buddy has a holiday packing list, built up over the years, that he uses to ensure that items are not left behind. He has a bag full of essential things whenever he is on holiday. He guards this bag with his life.

CHOOSE TO BE RELENTLESS

Another job move again for Buddy. Buddy and Jess moved to Hertfordshire in 2008, and Alex joined them. He was sixteen. He left a northern village and the local comprehensive with little ambition for their students. The school had set a low bar for them. He landed at a Hertfordshire comprehensive sixth form which had a different learning attitude. Students were sharp and wanted to learn, the teachers could be contacted at weekends, and the parents set high bars for their youngsters. On the first day of his new school, with new friends and surroundings, he came home and said, "The students are very bright. They have different conversations than I am used to. I will need to up my game." He did.

Buddy was now a director of a utility company. Alex was in his second year of the sixth form and was organised and focused on doing well in his A levels. Buddy took a call from a teacher from Alex's sixth form. There were some after-school revision sessions that Alex was not attending. Even worse, this teenager was seen walking down the hill laughing and joking with a bunch of girls. The stroppy teacher was furious and let Buddy know about it. Buddy could feel the steam coming out of the teacher's ears. Stroppy was going to have a stern word with Alex on Monday. Buddy let stroppy calm down, and eventually, the angry teacher said, "What do you think about it?"

CHOOSE TO PRIORITISE PHYSICAL AND MENTAL HEALTH

Buddy started the conversation well with, "I can see you are unhappy about it. Thank you for ringing me. I've no idea why Alex is not attending the group after-school revision sessions. I will chat with him tonight. I need to understand a little more about his reasoning as to why he prefers the company of girls to your revision sessions."

Stroppy jumped in with, "Mr Bramble, the revision sessions are very important."

"Yes, I appreciate that. What I can tell you is that Alex is an independent learner. On his bedroom wall, he has a wall chart, post-it notes and a complete timetable of exactly what he needs to do and when. He seems incredibly organised, focused, and determined to do well in his A levels."

"Well, that might be so," said Stroppy. "I will still have a strong word with him on Monday."

"That approach will not work with Alex. It will be counter-productive," said Buddy. "I feel that you are still agitated. What I would like you to do, is calm down. Let me speak with Alex over the weekend. We need to keep the dialogue open with Alex. I would like you to arrive on Monday with an understanding approach. Please don't judge Alex. Listen to him. You will find he is energised to do well in his A levels."

Alex was delighted in August when the painter Simon opened Alex's results letter and phoned Alex, who was on his holiday, to say that he had two A's and a B.

"I feel much more alert now"

Over the last fifteen years, mobile and social media communication, on balance, has been a force for good in sharing information and educating the world. However, social media has taken over the lives of many. In late 2022, Buddy realised that mobile notifications had taken over his life. He was no longer in control of life events. He was constantly distracted by the buzz of a message. He could not focus. His levels of concentration were poor. Even in conversations with others, his phone was always with him. The continual buzzing of a message was always pulling him to his phone. Something had to change.

He switched off his notifications and became more present in daily conversations. He was talking with Jess about it, "I feel much more alert now that I don't get any notifications on my mobile."

CHOOSE TO PRIORITISE PHYSICAL AND MENTAL HEALTH

Learning the lessons from life stories

Buddy's focus has often been on the destination, preferring to be clear about what he wants to achieve in life. The "be organised" habit was often one that Buddy has often needed to prioritise and improve. During his life he has learnt some of the skills to "be organised". He is still learning.

The following actions helped Buddy develop his character to become organised and build the foundations for a healthy and happy life. To apply "be organised" in his life, he told himself to:

- Create a weekly routine that builds chosen habits into daily life and action them.
- Focus on your purpose, prioritising actions using the "could, should and must" do it approach.
- Choose the use of social media selectively. Switch off phone notifications and enjoy life around you.
- Be relentless when contributing. Give it your all for an hour then take a five-minute break.

Is the "be organised" habit important to you at this stage of your life? What actions might you be considering?

Learning to Be Organised

Consider your answers to these four questions below when learning to be organised. If being organised is important to you, what actions might you consider and in what timescale?

- Am I valuing myself by managing how much time I spend on my purpose?

- Am I organised and have a plan with milestones to achieve high performance?

- Am I focusing on building good daily habits and routines to help me be creative?

- Am I ensuring I have sufficient income to enjoy today and invest in my future?

CHOOSE TO PRIORITISE PHYSICAL AND MENTAL HEALTH

CHOOSE TO PRIORITISE FULFILLING RELATIONSHIPS

What do you want out of life, now and in the future, regarding your relationships?

CHOOSE TO PRIORITISE FULFILLING RELATIONSHIPS

The Fulfilling Relationship Habits

Mastering these six relationship habits is essential to release untapped potential.

CHOOSE TO PRIORITISE FULFILLING RELATIONSHIPS

Having an inner confidence helps so many to connect meaningfully and respectfully with others and have a life of achievement. Having a loving family and supportive partner helps to grow the confidence to attack the opportunities in life. Buddy was lucky to find such a partner. He was in the right place at the right time when Jess fell into his arms.

These relationship habits focus on having a hopeful and confident approach to the future and taking control of a situation, not just responding to it.

Ensuring contentment, joy, and fulfilment in your relationships is the platform for making the emotional connection to broader opportunities.

Increasingly, sensing emotions and imagining what people are thinking, combined with showing consideration for others, are vital components.

A loving family network gives everyone a solid foundation to learn and grow. People naturally build good relationships with those around them and achieve plenty to be proud of in their lives.

BE OPTIMISTIC

Being hopeful and confident about the future

CHOOSE TO PRIORITISE FULFILLING RELATIONSHIPS

Be optimistic – focus on the possibilities in life

The "be optimistic" habit is a key relationship habit and vital as we navigate through life's challenges and difficult times. Winners have this habit in abundance and regularly release their full potential. It allows them to maintain a positive outlook, even when things don't go as planned. People are attracted to optimistic people and their natural energy and zest for life.

Being optimistic helps us to focus on the possibilities rather than the problems that the drainers in life easily find. Optimism can boost our immune system, improve our mood, and reduce stress and anxiety.

Having an optimistic mindset can also help us be more resilient and bounce back from setbacks more quickly. Buddy has always been an optimistic guy making a conscious effort to look for the positive in every situation. It has proved to be useful as he bounced back from the challenges in his life.

Is "be optimistic" a relationship habit that you need to consider improving?

"I think I am pregnant"

Before meeting Jess, Buddy had a few girlfriends. He wasn't very good at extending beyond a few dates. He was a confident and enthusiastic boy but didn't seem to have the patter that the selected ones were looking for. For example, he took one date to a Bath nightclub, and the only seats were near a toilet. Buddy pointed out, "I don't like the waft coming out of the toilet." They didn't meet again.

He visited the local library to read books about love, as he didn't have it in his life. He met one girl and was with her for a year or so. She worked in the bookbinding department in the local print factory. She was on the contraceptive pill. One evening she told Buddy, "I might be pregnant as I am late with my period."

Buddy gave her the emotional support she needed at the time, but on his drive home, he was mortified about what he had become involved with. Was this girl someone he wanted children with? Buddy was optimistic that Miss Bookbinding would be wrong in her assumption of a pregnancy. Buddy waited to see the outcome of the pregnancy test. When they met up, Buddy heard that it was a false alarm. His girlfriend wasn't pregnant. Buddy was lucky. The situation made Buddy think about his future and the social connections he was making. What might his future be like? Was Miss Bookbinding going to be part of it? A few weeks later, Buddy cooled the relationship. He was cautious in the future.

"I´m out of work again"

The more Buddy was away from his Somerset family, the better he was. With his Somerset friends, he was confident, humorous, and great company. He was well liked and well known in the town. Buddy was always looking for opportunities to better himself and made steady progress in his career.

As Buddy developed his reputation in the call centre industry in Bradford, Brighton and Leeds, his team won awards for innovation, quality of service, and teamwork. He was respected and was head-hunted many times for roles in the industry. He was very happy in his current role with a great team of talented people but had an opportunity to work in Sheffield. The position offered more money. After meeting the inspiring director Simon, he decided he would take it. With a young family and a hefty mortgage, it seemed very sensible.

Buddy took the job and optimistically made a good start. Unfortunately, within a few months, the director, with so much confidence in him, lost his job. Buddy was at the beginning of

CHOOSE TO BE RELENTLESS

a change programme and had lost his sponsor. It was an awful time for Buddy as the people above him withdrew their support for him. One by one, they undermined Buddy, making his work life uncomfortable and not enjoyable. One lived in Sheffield and was responsible for the Glasgow call centre. He was keen on Buddy leaving so he could run the Sheffield centre close to his family. Some of the Sheffield team of managers didn't see the best of Buddy during this time. It became clear that there needed to be a change.

Just before Christmas 1988, after only eight months in the role Buddy negotiated a perfect financial package to leave. He had enough money to see him through the next eighteen months. Buddy was thirty-nine. "I'm out of work again; what am I going to do?" he asked Jess. He knew that negativity, irrational thoughts, looking back, and destructive self-talk would not help him bounce back from this. He had been in much worse situations, which inspired him to be optimistic about the future.

Buddy learnt so much from this experience, probably more than the ones who conspired to remove him. He knew one thing, that never again would he chase money. Although he was out of work, he knew the New Year would begin with him chasing money.

CHOOSE TO PRIORITISE FULFILLING RELATIONSHIPS

Buddy decided to be optimistic about the future but firstly he put energy into his family activities that Christmas. The Brambles had a lovely family Christmas at Brig Royd that year. The laddies helped buy the tree and decorate it with Jess. The conservatory was decorated with red berry lights and red baubles. Unique stockings had been hung around the conservatory, with presents added by each family member during the preceding seven days. Grandma Pat's mince pies were so good that there weren't many left. As always, Jess worked hard in the kitchen to make the holiday season memorable. Turkey had been stuffed. The "cut and come again" piece of beef was ready for anyone who was peckish during the Christmas period to actually "cut and come again" whenever they felt like it. The family had their traditional fondue in the conservatory. Bottles of Alsace Gewurztraminer were already being consumed. Alex and Patrice were having their baths as part of their routine for bedtime. They settled into their beds, cuddling their Winnie the Pooh and Dennis the Menace water bottles for comfort and warmth.

Buddy read them the early 19th-century poem *Twas The Night Before Christmas* to calm the excitement. They knew all the words and would spot immediately if a line was missing. Buddy set off, "All through the house... not even a mouse...

sugar-plums dancing..." he read all the words as their eyes began to shut as the story ended. It was time for sleep.

Not for Buddy and Jess though, who now had the task of bringing presents in from the hiding place and placing them in the laddies' Santa sacks. The Brambles were now ready again for a Christmas with their extended family adding to the atmosphere. Jess always worked so hard buying presents for everyone; she needed a good night's sleep to prepare herself for Christmas Day's festivities.

"If they don't want you, give me a ring"

In the New Year, Buddy reminded himself of his achievements and looked forward to the future. He asked many contacts for advice and guidance on improving his CV and their views on his plans. He knew that the best jobs were often not advertised. He knew that whom you knew, and your social community were important when looking to make the best use of the opportunities out there.

As the year progressed, he began having serious conversations with Simon, the inspiring director that first appointed him in Sheffield. Simon was now at a brand-new mobile company who were expanding quickly. He wanted Buddy to join him to help them differentiate their brand within their call centres. Simon set about making that happen for Buddy. Buddy worked in the UK for the next three years, building a team learning culture that enabled the company to win awards and be the best mobile operator for five consecutive years. He met some incredibly inspiring people in the business who gave him so much personal support. It was an achievement for 5,500 people.

Buddy built a good relationship with one of the UK senior managers, Jim. He was very supportive of Jim. Jim was promoted within the group and secured a director of customer services role in The Netherlands. He phoned Buddy and said, "If they don't want you, give me a ring." As it happened, within weeks, inspiring Simon finished his role due to a takeover of the business. Buddy was so grateful to Simon for giving him the opportunity to make an impact. A new director arrived with different ideas for keeping the future bright.

The new director phoned Buddy on his holidays and said, "We are going our own way now without you. Rebecca from HR will ring you to agree on your departure and payoff. You will not need to come into the office anymore." It seemed like the future wasn't as bright for Buddy. Again.

The lights were not out long for Buddy. Within days Buddy had spoken to Jim, who had kept his promise, and they agreed on a long-term contract within hours. Buddy was going to be away during the week again. Up at three thirty every Monday morning. Flying from Liverpool to Schiphol, then by train to Duivendrecht and onto Arnhem. During the week, he worked with motivational and excited Piet, who was a biologist that loved bees and chimpanzees but worked in a call centre on change management. Buddy returned to the family in time for tea on Friday. This continued for three years. His contract was extended to include culture change at the head office in The Hague. For sure, the work helped them have great holidays and purchase their home in Spain. *Did this commitment come at a cost to his relationships?* Maybe it did.

"Don't put your hands in your pockets"

Buddy's role involved driving back and forth to various sites in the UK. It was emotionally difficult for Buddy being away from his family. The travelling meant that Buddy and the Bramble family didn't see much of each other during the week.

As he drove around the countryside of Britain, admiring so much history and the green and pleasant land, he would listen to his favourite music tracks to keep him company. He was often caught up in the moment of a song, distracted by the emotions and was caught speeding on a few occasions. He

CHOOSE TO PRIORITISE FULFILLING RELATIONSHIPS

had six points on his driving licence, so he knew he had to be careful, as twelve would lead to a ban.

He was driving to Newcastle on the A19. In his mirror, he could see a police car in the distance with blue lights flashing, clearly chasing a criminal up to no good. Buddy wasn't speeding, so when safe, he pulled to the middle lane to allow the coppers to pass. They pulled up behind him, indicating that Buddy should pull over. *Oh no, problems*, Buddy thought. "Hello, officer, how can I help?" Buddy cheerily said.

"Do you know why we have stopped you?" Buddy had been driving at 101.5 miles per hour a few miles back. Who knew? Well, certainly not Buddy, but the coppers had the evidence. Problems.

A few months later, Buddy was charged and had the summons to appear before the Sunderland magistrates to discuss the situation. If he were banned, his work would end. Luckily for Buddy, he had a top lawyer sleeping with him regularly, so he felt he could pull in a few favours. He felt optimistic and confident that Jess would take up the challenge of defending him.

On a bright, sunny morning, Jess and Buddy drove off to Sunderland. "Leave it to me, and I will do my best for you," said Jess. "My only advice is, don't put your hands in your pockets when you stand, as that annoys the magistrates."

Buddy adjusted his tie and entered the courtroom all suited and looking the part. It was only a traffic offence, but it was the most stressful moment in Buddy's life. A courtroom is imposing for the populace, and Buddy feels the pressure. He was optimistic though with Jess ready to mitigate.

"Please stand," said the lead magistrate. Buddy jumped up, keen to make a good early impression on the magistrate. Standing was easy, and Buddy's confidence was in a good place. Only a few seconds in, and all was good. Buddy was keen to give Jess a good start to work on.

As he looked over at the magistrates to agree on his name and address, Buddy was gripped by the lead magistrate. "Take your hands out of your pockets." Problems! Not a good start to work with, after all. Buddy knew he would get a load of grief later from Jess.

Jess then proceeded to defend Buddy with all her skills from years of defending criminals much worse than the bloke she married. It was the first time Buddy heard her in court, and he didn't look at her once, as agreed. She rolled out all sorts of mitigating circumstances that led to this speeding offence.

CHOOSE TO PRIORITISE FULFILLING RELATIONSHIPS

Jess passionately explained how very annoyed she was with Buddy. She assured the magistrates that Buddy was very sorry for what he had done and for wasting their valuable time.

The magistrates had heard enough and considered what the penalty would be. With relief in the Bramble family, the magistrates gave Buddy a £1000 fine and five points on his license. He was now on eleven points. One more point, and he would be banned. He could still drive.

Jess did the driving home, going on and on about hands in pockets.

Learning the lessons from life stories

Buddy is an optimistic character to have around, as he is always looking at the possibilities in life. This habit is one that he has always had in abundance. He can be depended on to provide optimism when all seems lost.

The following actions helped Buddy to develop his optimism, character, and build the foundations for a healthy and happy life. To apply "be optimistic" in his life, he told himself to:

- Write down your irrational, negative thoughts and review them with your rational brain.
- Avoid conversations with the drainers who will sap your energy within minutes.
- Remind yourself of your achievements and be open to new experiences in the future.
- Read and learn more about positive psychology and cognitive behaviour therapy.

Is the "be optimistic" habit important to you at this stage of your life? What actions might you be considering?

CHOOSE TO PRIORITISE FULFILLING RELATIONSHIPS

Learning to Be Optimistic

Consider your answers to these four questions below when learning to be optimistic. If being optimistic is important to you, then what actions might you consider and in what timescale?

- Am I making the best use of the opportunities that education has given me?

- Am I being optimistic, confident, and enthusiastic about the next year?

- Am I interested in other people and making social connections?

- Am I focused on avoiding negativity and any destructive self-talk?

BE HAPPY

Having an emotional state characterised by feelings of joy, satisfaction, contentment, and fulfillment

CHOOSE TO PRIORITISE FULFILLING RELATIONSHIPS

Be happy – make a conscious effort to be happy

Being happy is a key relationship habit and essential for a fulfilling and enjoyable life. It allows us to appreciate the present moment, enjoy our relationships, and make the most of our potential.

Happiness can boost our immune system, improve our mood, and reduce stress and anxiety. Having a positive attitude and being happy can also help us to be more productive, creative, and resilient. Buddy avoids the negative energy of worrying about the future. He finds that this thought process stops him making progress. He remains hopeful - a habit of winners.

Happiness is not something that happens to us; it's something we create for ourselves. Make a conscious effort to focus on the things that make you happy, surround yourself with positive people (winners and learners), and engage in activities that bring you joy. Who you mix with on your journey, is essential.

It is a choice that you make every day. Choosing to be happy changed Buddy's life for the better.

Is "be happy" a relationship habit that you need to consider improving?

"Watch out for the sharks"

Recharging, enjoying their leisure time, and having fun was always at the centre of the Brambles' life. Holidays were always important and happy occasions. For Jess, the travel section of the *Sunday Times* is a must read as it gives her thoughts about what holiday she could arrange next for her globetrotting family. Whether it was a city break, a walk in the countryside, a week away, or a more extended holiday in the summer, Jess took the responsibility very seriously. Patrice and Alex have some lovely memories of holidays of culture, entertainment, and fun. All were inspired and organised by Jess.

In 2001, Buddy took over the holiday plans. Buddy loved a bargain. He was always looking at opportunities to cut back their expenditure but not their fun. When the *Sunday Times* ran a series of articles on holidays on the cheap, Buddy couldn't resist making the arrangements. Jess took an uncomfortable back seat as Buddy led the travel plans. He had a very tight budget and set about spending it. First up was a cheap trip to Lithuania. Lithuania has been independent of Russia since 1990, so it would be an exciting learning experience for the young family. Vilnius, the spectacular and multicultural capital, was a beautiful city. It was a bitterly cold week, especially in the old unheated Russian hotel that Buddy had chosen for its cheapness. The boys learnt about Russian torture techniques in a Lithuanian prison and a country's culture, standing on its own two feet after years of oppression.

Jess took over for a while and arranged a train trip to memorable Kaunas so the family could feel and taste the old traditions and customs out of the capital. It was all delightful. There were increasing tensions within the family as some complained about the hotel in Vilnius. No one dared to complain to the owners, who were unapproachable and unhelpful. Fun-time Buddy got it in the neck as he was the one who chose the hotel. With two days to go before the end of the holiday, Jess put her foot down and said, "We are leaving this cold hotel." She booked the Radisson in Vilnius's town centre. It was welcoming and warm. Everybody was happy. It was a better hotel. It wasn't cheap, however.

Next up, a few months later, was a trip to Jordan. After a few days in Amman, the capital, we travelled in a cheap old taxi through the desert road to the archaeological site of Petra. Petra is accessed through a narrow canyon of pink sandstone cliffs. It was certainly worth admiring. We were distracted by the beauty, but blonde-haired Jess was grabbing the attention. A Jordanian with an attractive moustache and a welcoming smile said he would buy Jess for twenty-five camels. Jess was not for sale.

The following day, the family of adventurous travellers were still together. They set off in another cheap taxi to the coastal port city of Aqaba. They were booked into a budget hotel that came highly recommended by backpackers. They arrived early but could not check in to the hotel. The swimmers decided to check out the pool because it was a sticky and hot afternoon. The excitement turned to revulsion as they investigated an unhealthy discoloured pool full of fag ends and not much chlorine. Everybody looked at Buddy shaking their heads.

The next day, they jumped into a jeep and visited the desert of Wadi Rum. It was a memorable day travelling about and feeling the quietness and peacefulness of the desert. They enjoyed camel rides, a campfire meal under the stars, and other travellers' company. The highlight was sleeping overnight in a Bedouins-style tent, awaiting a sunrise – what a trip. Happy memories for sure.

Back at Aqaba, the Brambles kept well away from the hotel chosen by Buddy. It was only used for sleeping. They did enjoy their regular trips to the Movenpick hotel to swim and enjoy their ice creams.

CHOOSE TO PRIORITISE FULFILLING RELATIONSHIPS

Buddy knew that his summer holiday plans had to improve the situation. The family were in for a treat as Buddy felt he had left the best till last. It was still on the cheap but remains one of the family's favourite destinations. They were off to Malaysia to visit the Perhentian Islands off the east coast of Malaysia. Jess was responsible for organising the hotels and the route there. They visited Penang. They stopped for a coffee, where they heard, in the background for the first time, *"Springtime Laughter"* from Spyro Gyra, the American jazz band. They hired a car and drove from Kuala Lumpur down the west coast of Malaysia to Singapore. They enjoyed incredibly cheap but very tasty Nasi Goreng from a roadside café as they stopped to refuel. After leaving Singapore, they travelled up the east coast, stopping overnight in another cheap dive. They caught the early morning boat to Perhentian.

On Perhentian, the Brambles slept in a beach hut within fifty metres of some of the best snorkelling in the world. Sharks, clownfish, and turtles. The Brambles saw them all many times. Patrice and Alex had so much fun. Another young family nervously made their way into the water on one occasion. One of the very young children asked Patrice, "What is it like out there?"

They were looking for a few reassuring words but were left traumatised, as Patrice said, "It's great. Watch out for the sharks." Not sure that the family saw many sharks that holiday. The Brambles loved the evening meals overlooking the South China Sea. A walk around the island, stopping to enjoy the coconut milkshakes, was always popular.

This on-the-cheap year was great for family chat and relationship building. Despite the apparent success of the snorkelling holiday and the new experiences, it was agreed that Buddy should back off in the future and leave holiday plans to Jess.

"Gosh, is that the time?"

Some of the happiest Bramble memories were at home, enjoying the harmony of family life. Family meals together, especially at weekends, became a habit. The senior Brambles could bond with their children, talk about life events, and create a level of openness that helped them become good communicators in later life. Eating together enabled the Bramble boys to discuss anything that was troubling them. They did on many occasions. The conversations between them were often intense as strong characters shared their views. The lawyer Jess helped the boys hone their argument as they increasingly became vocal about their opinions on life situations. They were always happy occasions.

CHOOSE TO PRIORITISE FULFILLING RELATIONSHIPS

Music was always on around the home. The neighbours, the O'Shaughnessy family, became great friends and partying became a regular habit. The O'Shaughnessys, energising and happy, had two boys of similar ages, so there was always much to talk about. They were both teachers, and the families always enjoyed intelligent conversation during their parties' first few hours. As the drink flowed, the talks were louder and sometimes not so coherent. Very soon, conversations stopped, and the enthusiastic singing became increasingly louder. Later, they would sometimes have reflective discussions that made them all realise how thankful they were for what they had in life. Drink flowed, and often Buddy was the one to bring the party to an end, especially as his regular bedtime was 10 pm. Usually, saying, "Well, we have all had a good time," was his initial starter. This didn't usually work. "Is that the time? Gosh, it's late," would be better to move people on, especially if it was already after 2 am.

"Solid, as a rock"

Music and concerts were an integral part of the Brambles' life. The Brambles would be there if there was a live music event. They enjoyed any James Taylor event's dulcet tones, melody, and friendliness. The pure love and emotions that a Lionel Ritchie concert would evoke. No year would be complete without seeing a Motown or soul artist, Buddy's preferred genre. As he became refined in his music taste, he began to appreciate the soft rock artists of the 70s. What mattered to Buddy was the words of songs. The words had always been so influential to his mental health. A *"Choose to Be Relentless"* Spotify playlist accompanies this book.

Supermarkets are always good places to listen to Buddy's favourite music. On rare occasions he is shopping, Buddy often hears many of his favourite songs while putting his *Crunchy Nut Clusters* into his trolley. The Brambles rarely shopped together. On this one occasion, it would be memorable and not for the shopping. On came Ashford and Simpson's *"Solid as a Rock"*. Ashford was learning to trust and not run away. Simpson was getting to the thrill of hot, hot, and hot.

As they were both about to hit the famous "Solid", on the chorus of *"Solid as a Rock"*, Buddy thought he would liven up the activity. He noticed Patrice and Alex were walking together up an aisle adjacent to him and about to turn into where Buddy was. Buddy waited, and just as they turned into Buddy's path, he jumped out, and at the top of his voice, he sang "Solid!" right in their face. That was the planned vision. All was going well as Buddy double-checked; they were on their way. He waited out of sight and was ready to leap out. It was time. Buddy breathed in; the chorus was ready as he gave "Solid" his best emotion. He jumped out and shouted "Solid!" To his horror, a frail old lady with her shopping trolley and a walking stick was in the wrong place at the wrong time. She wasn't expecting anything solid at the time but got Buddy's "Solid" in her face. "I am so sorry. Are you okay? I'm so, so sorry. I didn't mean to startle you. It wasn't supposed to be you. I was having fun with my children." Buddy looked up; Alex and Patrice were laughing, having witnessed the scene. They ran off to tell Jess what had happened. Embarrassing stuff. Buddy left the shop and sat in the car.

"Hold it in and laugh later"

Buddy is thankful for what he already had and for taking responsibility for choosing his happiness all those years ago. Humour was in short supply in Buddy's early life as Doris didn't seem to enjoy intelligently crafted humour. She preferred slapstick stuff like a custard pie in your face or short stand-up jokes with an obvious punch line.

She could, however, tell a story. Her stories were often long and unintentionally funny. On one occasion, Doris told the Bramble family a story about a lad next door, Gregory. The long and the short of it is that Gregory had chucked in his promising and hugely successful corporate career and was now helping the poor people of the village and anyone else who needed it.

Joy didn't like Buddy doing well in corporate life and was, in a way, comparing him with this virtuous Gregory. "What is Gregory doing now to earn money?" said Buddy. Doris didn't answer but said how proud his family were of Gregory. Her descriptions became increasingly more expansive about the ever-so-talented Gregory. In Doris's eyes, Buddy should have been precisely like Gregory. She was so gushing about Gregory that they all assumed that he was now the CEO of Oxfam, Save the Children, or something like that. Indeed, what he was doing was worthwhile.

Alex looked across at Buddy and smiled. Buddy asked again, "What is Gregory doing now as a job?" Gregory cuts down trees, helps his family in the garden, and does shopping for people. Doris ramped up her comparison techniques to bring Jess, Patrice, and Alex unfairly and unwittingly into the story. He has a lovely caring wife who works in the NHS and children to die for. They are a delightful family.

This did seem an unlikely story. It was told to further show Buddy how he could have been. Poor Gregory was being used but didn't know about it. "Yes, but what is his job now?" Buddy

CHOOSE TO PRIORITISE FULFILLING RELATIONSHIPS

asked again. After twenty minutes of ebullient descriptions of this virtuous and very likeable Gregory, Doris blurted out that "He is now a milkman." It was such an unexpected finish to the story. Alex looked over at Buddy, who gave him an eye movement of looking up to the heavens. This didn't help Alex. He could not hold in his laughter anymore. He burst out laughing. This annoyed Doris, who told Alex that he had laughed on order after looking at Buddy. To put Alex down, she said, "You are just like your father."

Later, Buddy spoke to Jack, his dad, in the hallway. Jack said, "With Doris, it's better to hold the laughter in and laugh later." The Brambles left soon after and returned to their family home in Yorkshire. Our eight-hour round trips became fewer and fewer.

Learning the lessons from life stories

Buddy was fortunate to find love in his life and this gave him a good foundation to be happy. He can be relied upon to bring humour into his day-to-day conversations.

The following actions helped Buddy to develop his character, be happy, and build fulfilling relationships. To apply "be happy" in his life, he told himself to:

- Find the positives in life, live in the moment, and appreciate and recognise the good around you.
- Build career relationships with achievers and learners and gain from their positive vibes.
- Make time for loved ones as they can help to relieve stress and build your self-esteem.
- Prioritise your relationships with people who leave you feeling energised and happy.

Is the "be happy" habit important to you at this stage of your life? What actions might you be considering?

CHOOSE TO PRIORITISE FULFILLING RELATIONSHIPS

Learning to Be Happy

Consider your answers to these four questions below when learning to be happy. If being happy is important to you, then what actions might you consider and in what timescale?

- Am I thankful for what I already have in life?

- Am I having fun taking responsibility for choosing my happiness?

- Am I building harmony in my family, work, or community relationships?

- Am I recharging, enjoying my leisure time, hobbies, and entertainment?

BE PROACTIVE

Creating or controlling a situation rather than just responding to it after it has happened

CHOOSE TO PRIORITISE FULFILLING RELATIONSHIPS

Being proactive – take the initiative for your future

Being proactive is a key relationship habit and essential to release your potential. It means taking initiative and being in control of your actions, rather than simply reacting to events and circumstances.

Being proactive allows us to set groundbreaking goals, make plans, and take action to achieve them. It helps us to take control of our own lives and not blame others for our present circumstances.

Being proactive also helps us to be more resilient, as it allows us to anticipate and plan for potential challenges and difficulties. Being proactive is not just about taking action, it's about taking ownership of your life, your goals, and your future. It's what achievers do.

Years ago, Buddy took a step towards being more proactive in his life. Being proactive and taking control of his life was one of the best decisions he made.

Is "be proactive" a relationship habit that you need to consider improving?

"There is no baby born on that day"

Nana was ninety-two. She was now living with the Brambles in Stainland, West Yorkshire. She was not well and slowly losing interest in everyday life. Whenever she was in the UK, she never missed an episode of *Coronation Street*. Jess and her mum knew things must have been bad as Nana refused to leave bed to watch *Coronation Street*.

Nine months earlier, Jess and Buddy enjoyed an impromptu drinks party with their lodger Johannes. Buddy had purchased a bottle of 40% proof bourbon from Kentucky. They were all commenting on how easy *Wild Turkey* was to drink after the first glass had coated the throat lining. Jimmy, their dog, needed walking. It was a one-person job. For some reason, all these young adults were unexpectedly and noisily now outside in the park singing, with one wearing a Mickey Mouse dressing gown. It was 11.50 pm. Somehow the dog and the revellers managed to find their way home safely, waking the following morning with sore heads.

A few days later, Jess excitedly shared that she was pregnant. This was an emotional moment for Buddy and Jess. They embraced and talked about how their lives would change. They hadn't been planning this moment. They had not been focused on eating various foods to get the right balance of nutrients to ensure a trouble-free first pregnancy. They had only just finished detoxing from the *Wild Turkey* session. There was a health concern about the impact of *Wild Turkey* on a baby only a few cells old. As the cells doubled, the question was, *would Wild Turkey interfere with this baby's growth?* Jess was reassured by the doctor that there was nothing to worry about. The baby would be born in the last week of August. Buddy immediately spotted that if the baby was born in August, it would be the youngest in the school year. This was something to worry about.

Buddy and Jess looked at their savings account and saw they had just enough money to get through the month. There would need to be more cutting back. This baby would be a car-boot baby. It's all they could afford. Buddy and Jess kitted out the baby's bedroom with clothes and items from various Halifax families. It's incredible what good value you can obtain at car-boot sales. We were up very early every Sunday morning to ensure that the best quality items were snapped up. They only wanted the best car-boot items for this baby.

The last week of August arrived, and everybody was ready for the birth. As Nana's coughing became more laboured, there was increasing concern about her health. Could she hang around long enough to see this baby? Jess was also having some pains that were undoubtedly concerning enough to set the baby-being-born action plan in motion. Buddy was all set for a few hours of waiting before the big push. "It will be all right. I'm here and don't forget I love you," said a reassuring Buddy as they parked up at the hospital and rushed into the maternity ward. Jess was immediately prioritised as the experts had a look to see if they could see something. There was nothing to see. This baby was intelligent enough to know not to push today or anytime in the next week. It was still August. Jess was still in pain. The doctor suggested an enema to give the baby some room. Thirty minutes later, we were in the car on the way home. It was a false alarm.

Seven days passed. This baby was running late. Jess hated lateness, so she must have been fuming as she scooped in another spoonful of parsnip soup. There were a few more false alarms, none requiring desperate journeys to the hospital. It was only a matter of time, and Jess could not wait any longer. Eventually, it was the 31st of August, and Jess felt what she thought were contractions. She had awful backache. Buddy had proactively educated himself on contractions and confidently asked, "Is your womb tightening and relaxing?"

"I think so; it feels like extreme period pain," said an exhausted Jess, who by now was six days past the estimated birth date.

CHOOSE TO PRIORITISE FULFILLING RELATIONSHIPS

Thirty minutes later, Jess was lying in the hospital waiting, not so patiently, for the action to start. It was 9.25 am. The midwife explained that Jess's cervix was very soft and thin, and the baby's birth could happen anytime in the next twenty-four hours. It was a long day not helped by Mrs Shouty, a boisterous lady in another bed screaming out. Mrs Shouty occupied much of the day's entertainments, providing a cacophony of sounds to distract everyone. In her birth plan, Jess agreed to have an epidural, and in the early evening, the epidural team arrived, and within minutes, Jess was much more comfortable.

Buddy held Jess's hand and said how emotional he was. Jess said she was in pain. They had been through so much together, and their family were about to be three. The early evening soon became late evening, and Buddy was hopeful that the baby would be a September baby. It all seemed quiet down there, so it looked very promising. Buddy was counting down the minutes as the clock ticked to 11 pm. Jess had done so well; only an hour to go. Buddy used his underdeveloped management skills to motivate Jess to aim high at the target. The Brambles could see the target. A birth any time after 12 am would be an impressive effort from Jess. After nine months of hard work, it was now down to the last few minutes. Could Jess pull back from pushing?

At 11.05 pm, Jess said she felt like pushing. Buddy held her hand and said, "Could you wait a little longer, as it will be better for the baby if it arrives just after twelve." Jess squeezed Buddy's hand very tightly, dug in her nails and said, "I need to push now." Just as Buddy was thinking about anti-pushing techniques, the team of nurses arrived and pushed him out of the way. It did seem that baby was ready to push.

"Baby will come when baby is ready," the midwife said as they encouraged Jess to concentrate on breathing. *If this baby was to be a September birth, then this baby needs to stop pushing right now*, thought Buddy. This baby wasn't born yet and had no sense of time despite being inside Jess, who was obsessed with time. Jess settled down for a few minutes of pushing, puffing, and breathing. Keep calm.

Buddy looked at the clock. It was 11.20 pm. It didn't look good for hitting the target forty minutes away, as the baby's head was now engaged and ready to emerge. Out popped the head. "Stop pushing for a moment, Jess," said the midwife. *Could the head hang there and wait?* Buddy thought. *When does birth occur? When is it entirely out?* Too late to ponder. The baby started wriggling, Jess had a final push, and Patrice was born at 11.25 pm on the 31st of August.

CHOOSE TO PRIORITISE FULFILLING RELATIONSHIPS

Patrice had his bottom smacked by some nurse who was an expert on making new-born babies cry. Patrice cried. Jess cried. Buddy cried. What a happy occasion as Patrice was placed into Jess's arms. "Do you want a few moments to bond with Patrice?" said the midwife. Buddy was shattered.

It was well past his bedtime, so he said, "No, not really. It's past my bedtime. I'll do my bonding later." So Buddy set off home to let Grandma Pat and Nana know about the good news.

The next day, Buddy thought about what he could do to take control of the situation that Patrice had been born thirty-five minutes too early. He didn't speak to Jess about his plan. Buddy had his plan, was super proactive, and set off to the Halifax birth registration place. "Hello, I have come to register the birth of a baby." A series of straightforward questions followed: parents' name, date of birth of parents, mother's maiden name, parents' jobs, and date of marriage. All easy. No problems there. Name of the baby? Patrice. Place of birth? Halifax. No problems.

All is going well, thought Buddy. "What is the date of birth of Patrice?" said the registrar. Buddy puffed out a sigh of air as he started a long description to set the scene.

"It was a long day. It was a difficult birth. The birth went into the night. My wife and I were shattered. I arrived home at 3 am after bonding with Patrice, so it must have been just after 12 am."

The lady looked at her records and said, "There is no baby with that name born on that date. Did you give it a different name?"

"No"

"There is a baby Patrice, born at 11.25 pm on the 31st of August," Buddy had been rumbled. His plan had hit the buffers. "I can check with the hospital. Perhaps they have made a mistake," said the registrar. She had full confidence in Buddy as she knew that parents always knew the date and time of a baby's birth. Buddy could feel the confidence draining from him as his plan fell apart like one of his cheap suits. One thing he knew is the registrar didn't need to ring the hospital. That would have overcomplicated this simple plan. Buddy set about plan B.

"It was a long day. It might have been earlier. I'm happy to go with the 31st of August at 11.25." The first Bramble baby was in the world. Patrice was now destined to be the youngest in any school year.

CHOOSE TO PRIORITISE FULFILLING RELATIONSHIPS

Nana held Patrice, coughed, and smiled. She had waited for this moment. She died in her sleep a few hours later. She was ninety-two.

"I'll sit on the beach and look after security"

Buddy was a proactive chap. He always took responsibility for security in the family. He was always in control of looking after expensive or important items. Relaxing on holiday was always essential to Buddy's life, but he always had an eye on his bag of essential things. The beach was always an area to be on guard. Buddy didn't enjoy swimming, so that gave him a good excuse to say, "I'll sit on the beach and look after the security."

On the rare occasion he would enter the water to join in the family fun, he was always looking towards the sweaty bag, ready to run after any potential thief. Buddy running after a thief would have been an interesting sight, but in all the years on beaches, a running Buddy was never seen.

"Let me know the job you would like"

Buddy has always been aware of the importance of building good relationships. He surrounded himself with learners, achievers, and forward-looking characters. Many of his career opportunities have occurred because he was in the right place and, most importantly, knew the right people. He has often needed these people as he furthered his career.

In 2012, he received a phone call from the Director of HR, who explained that there had been a review of the business and his director role was about to be made redundant. He would receive a total redundancy pay-out but leave the firm once the business sale had been completed. It wasn't a shock to Buddy, but it was an odd phone call devoid of emotion.

A few hours later, Buddy received an unexpected but highly emotional call when David, the CEO, said, "I want you in my team. If you could give some thought about the role you would most enjoy, we can talk tomorrow. Let me know the role you would like to do, and you can have it."

Buddy had always enjoyed working with David and proactively made it a priority to build the relationship. David was a top leader who always supported Buddy and gave him many opportunities. Buddy's team of website, digital and social media pioneers led the industry as they developed an award-winning customer-focused social media presence. These people are some of the most talented in the industry. All of them have gone on to build successful careers with their huge talent.

CHOOSE TO PRIORITISE FULFILLING RELATIONSHIPS

"We need a chat about your future"

David continued to lead the business and was seen as a far-sighted and industry-leading character. Externally, he was the one that others spoke about and wanted to be with. Sadly, the new business owners also spoke about him. They decided they didn't want to be with him any longer. So, David talked to Max the chair and left the company. Buddy was distraught as he valued David's advice and support. He also knew that the owners didn't appreciate Buddy's unique talent and knew he was next to be going. But when?

Buddy has always been proactive and has taken responsibility. He spoke with Jess, and they decided to sell their house in Hertford and move to Exeter. They would be near their son Alex and a short drive from Doris, who now had dementia, and Jack, his father. Still, Buddy did the right thing to provide love and support to his family.

As the house sale went through, Buddy continued to work in Hertfordshire while living in Exeter. During the week, he lived in a campervan at a campsite and travelled back to Exeter to be with Jess. He didn't want anyone at his work to know that he was living in Exeter and had metaphorically started a new life.

The redundancy call came five months after they had moved to Exeter. Buddy had been building a relationship of sorts with the chair, Ferrari Max. Buddy named him Ferrari Max when Max spoke to him about needing insurance on his run-around while he was in London. "Could you arrange for this to be added to the company insurance to make it easier?" When Max said easier, he meant cheaper, as he wanted his son to be able to drive the car. His son was twenty-two. The company insurance wanted to know what the run-around vehicle was. It was a brand-new Ferrari.

"Hi Buddy, Max here; I am in the office on Thursday and would like to talk to you about your future." Buddy knew his time was up. His future was not likely to be with Ferrari Max.

Buddy prepared for the future meeting. Buddy had two sheets of paper to start the discussion about the future and any redundancy chat. He discussed both with Jess as she offered him legal advice.

Ferrari arrived on time for the meeting and asked if Buddy would like a coffee or tea. It all seemed very friendly as Ferrari began, "So Buddy, we are here to talk about your future."

Before Ferrari could get into his stride, Buddy jumped in. "Thanks, Max; I am excited to talk about the future and

CHOOSE TO PRIORITISE FULFILLING RELATIONSHIPS

delighted to have this opportunity to discuss my thoughts on how we move the company forward." Buddy explained that he wanted to discuss his ten-point plan for company success. Buddy started with his first point, "One – release the potential of the power of people…"

Before Buddy could explain his ideas, Ferrari jumped in and said, "Buddy, stop right there. We are here to discuss your future," and to get it over with, he blurted out, "and it is not going to be with this company. This meeting is about your redundancy."

Buddy put on his shocked, surprised, and sad face, and quickly put away his ten-point plan for happiness. Ferrari continued, "I can appreciate that this will shock you, and I can see you are upset." Buddy, prepared by Jess the night before, pulled out his set of redundancy questions. This was the most prepared that Buddy had ever been for any meeting with Ferrari as he set off.

"I have several questions for you, Max." Ferrari hadn't scheduled any time for questions and certainly didn't have any answers. Buddy gave him the written questions. He explained that he was distraught and would need time away from the business to assess his mental health as this news had broken him.

Ferrari said he could have as much time off as needed to deal with the situation. Within minutes, Buddy drove down the M3 to meet up with Jess at their home in Exeter. He was soon to be out of a job again, with another good payoff. There would be more time with Jess, who was now project managing the restoration of their home in Exeter.

CHOOSE TO PRIORITISE FULFILLING RELATIONSHIPS

Learning the lessons from life stories

Buddy chooses to "be proactive" as it helps him to be prepared for eventualities and be in control of his circumstances. Taking actions has helped him to be less stressful. This is one of Buddy's dependable habits.

The following actions helped Buddy to develop his character become proactive and build fulfilling relationships in his personal and work life. To apply "be proactive" in his life, he told himself to:

- Take responsibility for your circumstances and make the changes to improve your life.
- Take the initiative, identify the opportunities, and have an action plan to achieve your goals.
- Keep learning, be adaptable and open to the opportunities that the digital age brings.
- Avoid the watchers who can raise doubts in your mind and stop you taking the initiative.

Is the "be proactive" habit important to you at this stage of your life? What actions might you be considering?

Learning to be Proactive

Consider your answers to these four questions below when learning to be proactive. If being proactive is important to you, then what actions might you consider and in what timescale?

- Am I taking responsibility for my response to life events outside my control?

- Am I listening to what people say to me and not responding defensively?

- Am I surrounding myself with forward-looking winners and achievers?

- Am I making progress by choosing forgiveness and not division?

CHOOSE TO PRIORITISE FULFILLING RELATIONSHIPS

BE RESPECTFUL

Showing consideration and regard to someone or something

Be respectful – earn trust through your actions

Being respectful is a key relationship habit and essential for building strong and meaningful connections, both personally and professionally. It means treating others with understanding, kindness, and consideration. It helps to create a positive and inclusive environment that helps people to release their potential.

Showing respect also helps us to develop empathy, compassion, and a sense of community. Being respectful also helps us to earn trust and respect from others, which is essential for building successful relationships.

Respect is not something that is given, it's something that is earned through our actions and behaviour. Make it a daily practice to show respect to yourself and others, and you'll be surprised at how much more positive and inclusive your interactions will be.

Is "be respectful" a relationship habit that you need to consider improving?

CHOOSE TO PRIORITISE FULFILLING RELATIONSHIPS

"West Indians have thick lips, and I don't like them"

Doris had strong views. They were not born out of any facts. Jack read the workers' paper, the *Daily Mirror*, and Doris read the jumped-up *Daily Mail*. Doris's views were just opinions gained through her reading material or live conversations with other ill-informed characters that his mum knew.

Buddy would always question if he saw unfairness and a lack of empathy. The questions arrived daily. Doris had odd and, at times, racist views. There was a time when Doris said, "West Indians have thick lips, and I don't like them." She didn't know any West Indians.

Buddy couldn't believe it and confronted how this view could be obtained. Buddy was sent to his bedroom for daring to question. Buddy is still embarrassed and disgusted to this day, especially when this was repeated in front of his children.

This was a defining moment for Buddy in his relationship with his mother. It was 1999. Ten years after his marriage to Jess. The children were only six and seven years old. The Bramble family were sat around the kitchen table in Middleton having a cup of tea before their long drive home. They were discussing the achievements of the outgoing South African President Nelson Mandela.

CHOOSE TO BE RELENTLESS

As Buddy was extolling the virtues of a man who had gained international respect for his approach to peace and reconciliation, Doris interjected, "West Indians have thick lips, and I don't like them." Memories of a broken childhood flashed back to Buddy recalling the moment when years earlier, a young Buddy had been sent to his bedroom for daring to question an unfairness. This time, he was stronger and very quickly decided that he could not let this pass.

Buddy counted to ten knowing the young ears in the room had been taught to respect others, whatever their race, religion, or national origin. Buddy knew he had to call this out, knowing it would lead to an argument and not necessarily change the view of his mother.

There was a long silence as the family looked at Buddy to see if he would let this go or challenge his mother. As Buddy finished his counting, and with the anger subsiding, he said. "What do you mean when you say they have thick lips? Why do you say that?"

Doris doubled down, "I just don't like the look of them... all black" as she grimaced and shook her head.

Buddy had taken an understanding approach to the initial words knowing that seeing things through the eyes of others

CHOOSE TO PRIORITISE FULFILLING RELATIONSHIPS

is always a good place to start a conversation. He was hoping that Doris might choose some additional words to clarify and calm the atmosphere in the kitchen. She didn't.

It was clear that Buddy was talking to a racist. Doris had no idea of the impact her words were having on the children. Patrice was only seven and said, "Grandma, that's so unkind."

Perhaps Buddy should have waited and spoke to Doris on her own. His counting to ten process was overtaken by the confidence of his child to confront his grandma with the facts. Buddy wanted to show support for his brave son for standing up to a mother who had always told Buddy to sit down and be quiet.

With emotion taking over from the rationality of a few seconds earlier, Buddy looked his mother in the eye and knew a rant was going to be unleashed. If ever Buddy was going to stand up to his mother, then this was the moment.

Buddy breathed in and with the years of contained words he began, "Patrice is right. That is unkind. You just can't say that. Surely you don't believe that. It's not right. It's unfair." Buddy was in his stride as the room went silent. "To shake your head when saying the word 'black' is just so very wrong. It's an awful thing to say. I can't really believe what I have just seen and heard."

Everyone in the kitchen looked at an increasingly angry Doris. Doris never seemed to have a method for double-checking the words that came out of her mouth. On that front, she was not to disappoint on this occasion.

Doris rolled her eyes upwards, sipped her cup of tea, sighed, and shot back at Buddy. "Have you finished?"

Buddy thought it was a question that needed answering and began, "No, I have more to say."

Buddy soon realised her question was rhetorical as she took control of the situation. "I will not have you talking to me like that, in this home. It's what I think, and I will say what I like. I will not be told by you, *especially you*, or anyone else, what I can or can't say in my own house." Doris got up from her chair and Buddy said, "I just think you should think about how West Indian children would feel if they were here now. Why do you fear them so much?" Alex had been quietly listening to this short exchange and said in a quiet but clear voice, "Dad is right. I have lots of friends at school that don't look like me but in fact, are just like me."

CHOOSE TO PRIORITISE FULFILLING RELATIONSHIPS

Doris decided it was time to bring others into her orbit, "Even your children are speaking up, just like you did. Those children are just like you." Alex and Patrice were sat in the glow of knowing they were "just like their dad", not realising that this was not a compliment. For Doris, being like Buddy was not a good thing at all. Some may dislike Buddy, but none get close to the feelings that Doris had for him.

As the family were recovering from this exchange, Doris pushed back her chair and indicated that the Bramble visiting time was over. She said, "It's getting dark now. You have a long drive."

Doris went off to her bedroom to count to ten while Jack was left to clear up the table and say his goodbyes to the family. As the family were leaving, Jack spoke to Buddy on the drive, "I am so sorry about your mother and what she said. You were right. It was so wrong. I will go and talk to her. Have a safe trip home."

Buddy and Jess were proud of Alex and Patrice that day. Buddy knows he should have handled it better and maybe not in front of everyone. He might have been more persuasive if it had been privately handled. He was still learning, while Doris was certainly not.

Buddy thought long and hard about disclosing this but feels that everyday racism, in all its bigoted forms, should be confronted.

"She sounds in more pain than you"

The birth of Patrice was interrupted somewhat by Mrs Shouty. The Brambles had settled down for a long day. Buddy had made a few sandwiches to help keep the energy levels high. As the day progressed, the contractions became more prolonged and more frequent. The baby was pushing itself down towards the womb entrance, and the pain was unbearable for Jess. Her tension was not helped by Mrs Shouty whose contractions took over her voice box. She didn't seem to be coping very well. She certainly was not thinking much about any calming breathing techniques Jess had learnt at our antenatal classes.

The noise was not calming Jess, struggling to cope with the intermittent pain of this wriggly baby shuffling about inside her. Jess was becoming very agitated about Mrs Shouty down the corridor as it seemed that whoever shouted loudest was getting better treatment. The nurses were often popping in, adjusting pillows, checking progress, and leaving quickly as Mrs Shouty screamed in pain again. "Why is she getting all the attention just because she was shouting?" asked a tired Jess, who had been flat on her back for five hours.

Buddy launched into a speech about the principle that all people are equal and deserve equal rights and opportunities, showing consideration of others, dignity, and respect, finishing with, "Anyway, you are always thinking of others; she does sound in much more pain than you." Liberated by his words' integrity and pride in his little egalitarian speech that would have received a massive clap at a Labour Party rally, Buddy looked back at Jess, hoping for a similar response. Not even a hand movement, let alone a clap. Buddy's carefully crafted words had not had the desired effect. Jess blurted out, "I don't care; I want my epidural, and I want it now."

Buddy went outside into the corridor and talked with the nurse, who explained that the epidural could not be attached until Jess was three or four centimetres dilated and in active labour. It seemed that Jess would have to wait a little longer. Buddy knew this would be a difficult conversation as he entered the room. Jess was expecting an epidural catheter to be attached to help the pain subside. What she got was a newly informed, educated, and overconfident Buddy.

Buddy was like a junior midwife fresh out of medical school. He was blathering about dilation, centimetres, forceps, and the hospital policy as he explained the situation with a burst of energy that was not helping. "Stop right there. I want to talk to the midwife, not you. I know my body, and I need an epidural now," Jess said in a firm voice that suggested that Buddy was not the man to deliver the message. Just as Buddy started, "Well I think you are being a bit unreasonable and not respectful—" The midwife suddenly appeared with a bag of medical tools and a reassuring, reasonable, respectful and calm voice. She asked Jess to spread her legs as she pulled out a torch, a vaginal speculum to measure dilation, and a ruler to check the centimetres. Buddy slipped into the background realising an expert had arrived. Joy. Relief, Jess was 4cm dilated, and it was time for the epidural. Jess assumed the epidural team were just outside waiting for the call. The replacement would be delayed as, yet again, a Tory Britain had left the NHS in an underfunded state, and Jess was told she was third on the list.

Mrs Shouty wasn't shouting anymore, so a period of quiet seemed to calm everyone in the ward. The epidural team arrived, and Jess was much more comfortable within minutes.

"Will you be safe in a Traveller camp?"

In 2011, the Brambles purchased a camper van and enjoyed the freedom and many UK holidays and trips around Europe.

CHOOSE TO PRIORITISE FULFILLING RELATIONSHIPS

One year they were travelling through France, and all was not well with the vehicle. There was an obvious problem. Ten kilometres short of their campsite, they broke down within fifty metres of a Traveller site full of exciting Travellers settling down for the night.

Here was an opportunity to respect others and not discriminate or be disrespectful based on early judgement. In their best French, Buddy and Jess explained the situation, and a few Travellers came out to help push the camper off the road and into their camp. Buddy and Jess had become Travellers. The breakdown people said they could get someone out tomorrow morning. The Brambles explained they were in a Traveller site. "Will you be safe in a French Traveller camp overnight?" said the concerned advisor at the end of the phone.

"I think so," said Buddy. This was another lesson not to judge people before you meet them. The Travellers were one of the kindest communities the Brambles had met, ever. They allowed them to use their electricity and water, offered them food, and were very understanding and friendly. The Brambles slept very well. Although, when the Brambles were preparing to leave the following day, they heard a commotion outside. The gendarmerie arrived with flashing blue lights, arrested a couple of people, and took them away.

"That was a vital mistake"

Balancing family life and achievement was always a challenge in the life of the Brambles. If able, they would always have a long weekend away; sometimes, this would involve a quick weekend break in Europe with Alex and Patrice.

One Friday, the Brambles were late and rushing to fly out from Liverpool Airport. Patrice and Alex distracted Jess as she looked for a turnoff to get to the car park. Patrice took no notice of being asked to keep quiet, and at one point, Jess nearly hit an oncoming vehicle while turning. Buddy looked at Patrice and grabbed him by his lapels and told him to stop it. This was out of character. Buddy had overreacted. Before Buddy had time to say sorry for overreacting, Patrice, who was only eight said, "That was a vital mistake." Everybody laughed.

Indeed, it was a vital mistake. Buddy said sorry. He had lost it and was not respectful.

A reaction like that hasn't happened since.

Buddy is so proud that the family has maintained respect for one another through care, understanding, and conversation.

CHOOSE TO PRIORITISE FULFILLING RELATIONSHIPS

"Chicks and birds"

Buddy was brought up in a racist and disrespectful family. It was the 70s. Many families were just like Buddy's. The UK is now better with race relations than fifty years ago. There is still a long way to go. We must all be vigilant towards continually improving how we are as individuals and as a society.

Speaking up if people are discriminating or disrespectful starts with people looking at themselves. In his public life, Buddy has a good history of treating everyone with worth, dignity, fairness, and respect. He is a feminist believing in the equality of the sexes.

In his home, under the cover of family banter, he would often revert to 70s language, especially when bantering about women with other men. His language and habits have not always matched his thoughts. Regularly, he would talk about women as chicks or birds. For many years he thought that was not wrong; it was just banter. On reflection, this language and tone was wrong. Very wrong. This language did not treat women with worth, dignity, fairness, or respect. Buddy has stopped using this language and is now much more aware of the impact of language and behaviour.

Learning the lessons from life stories

Buddy has worked hard in his day-to-day life to make "be respectful" a consistent habit. On a basic level he values everyone he meets but knows that he has needed to prioritise and improve the application of this habit in his day-to-day life. He knows he could improve his active listening. He is still learning.

The following actions helped Buddy to develop his character, be respectful, and build the fulfilling relationships he now enjoys. Buddy was relentless and told himself to:

- Be considerate of others, treating them the way you would like to be treated. Be kind.
- Listen to understand others without judging them so the relationship develops.
- Consider language and tone, especially when reacting negatively to an emotional situation.
- Avoid gossip as it is very likely to be negative in tone and disrespectful to the person not there.

Is the "be respectful" habit important to you at this stage of your life? What actions might you be considering?

CHOOSE TO PRIORITISE FULFILLING RELATIONSHIPS

Learning to Be Respectful

Consider your answers to these four questions below when learning to be respectful. If being respectful is important to you, then what actions might you consider and in what timescale?

- Am I treating people I see with worth, dignity, fairness, and respect?

- Am I self-regulating and liberating myself by always showing integrity?

- Am I balancing work achievements and enjoyment of my personal life?

- Am I speaking up if people around me are discriminating or disrespectful?

BE COMMITTED

Making a pledge or course of action to someone or something

CHOOSE TO PRIORITISE FULFILLING RELATIONSHIPS

Be committed – focus and overcome the setbacks

Being committed is a key relationship habit and essential for achieving our goals and making the most of our potential. It means dedicating ourselves fully to our planned achievements and being persistent in the face of challenges and setbacks.

Being committed helps us to stay focused and motivated; it helps us to overcome obstacles and to reach our full potential. Being committed also helps us to be more resilient, as it allows us to learn from our experiences and to grow as individuals.

Commitment is not just about being dedicated to a cause, it's about being dedicated to ourselves, our partner, family, friends, and wider network.

Find what you really love doing and make a start. Make a commitment to your goals and aspirations. You will be amazed at how much more motivated and fulfilled you will feel.

Is "be committed" a foundation habit that you need to consider improving?

"You need to sort yourself out"

In 2016 Buddy had pain in his liver and spleen. He had spent many years enjoying life to excess. He enjoyed bread, baguettes, cottage pie, rice pudding, ice cream, custard slices, Belgian buns, sugary snacks, and cereals. He was a dream to any shop that thrust carbohydrates, cakes, biscuits, crisps, and chocolate bars at him. He was ballooning in weight and topped the scales at 104kg. He now had a pain in his stomach. Enough was enough. He had a problem and went to see the doctor.

Dr Timothy looked at him as he waddled through the door and sat on a chair that was slightly too small but was, in fact, a standard size. Unlike Buddy, who was now obese. Dr Timothy gave him some advice and basically said you are a fat boy. Sort yourself out. "If you carry on like this, you will die early." Buddy was fifty-six and not ready to die quite yet. She said Buddy needs to eat more fruit, fish, and vegetables, and cut back on carbohydrates and sugary snacks. Take action on what you can control. Stop talking and start doing. A bit of walking would help too. I'll set up an appointment with a consultant to check your pains, but in the meantime, here are some tablets to calm your stomach.

CHOOSE TO PRIORITISE FULFILLING RELATIONSHIPS

A stern message, but Buddy knew that Dr Timothy was right. Buddy needed to be committed to a new course of habits that would get him back on track. Later a consultant identified that he had a fatty liver, an enlarged spleen, gallstones, and an ulcer. Losing weight was now essential if Buddy was to regain control over his body. He chooses to be healthy.

Buddy made steady progress over two years and reduced his weight from 104kg to 92kg by eating sensibly and walking a little more. Good effort. His internal organs recovered and were now in a much better place. To celebrate, he started eating what he liked again and, not surprisingly, put on weight. In 2020, he was 98kg.

When Covid advice suggested that overweight people were highly likely to suffer complications, Buddy and Jess jumped into action. Buddy lost 20kg in a short period and is now a healthy 78kg and much better. He has days when he has a cheat-food day, but in the main, he is balancing exercise with nutritional food intake. Buddy recommends being committed.

"Hit his life with energy"

In the summer of 2022, Buddy began to think about writing his life story but wanted it to inspire his readers. This would be a highly personal book aimed at his children and his yet-to-be-born grandchildren – an opportunity for others to reflect and learn from events in the Brambles´ family life.

He had such an inspiring story and began thinking about the contents and the key messages. In the quietness of his family home in Alhaurín el Grande, Andalucía, he started thinking about his memories, the impact of Jess on his life, and the love he has for Alex and Patrice. So much had happened to Buddy. He had learnt so much from life events.

His vision for the rest of his life was to hit his life with energy and be relentless in pursuing his goals. Buddy wasn't ready to die, and while he still could, he would be relentless and committed in doing what he loved doing.

His 100-day plan and charter was developed using the main chapters of this book; a plan was created for Mental and Physical Heath, Fulfilling Relationships, Experiential Learning, and Prosperity on His Terms. A copy of this charter is at the back of this book.

His goal by January 2023 was to be personally fit and healthy, build upon his relationships, be the author of his second book, and have the finances to enjoy his life. He achieved this goal.

CHOOSE TO PRIORITISE FULFILLING RELATIONSHIPS

"Taking responsibility for life"

Buddy has been on quite a journey. His most significant commitment has been to change himself. He continues to be challenged as he removes the demons and habits in the way of his achievements.

He took control of his life in 1986. Moving to a new part of the country on his own was a brave decision but one he knew had to be made. He chose to take responsibility for himself and not blame others. He decided not to continually look back at the error of his ways or the mistakes of others. He knew that if he was going to be successful, however, it was to be measured; he knew it was up to him.

When he found Jess again, he was already strong and believed in himself. The emotional support and influence of Bob, Pat, and Jess helped him considerably as he chartered a new course in his life.

Buddy has had a lifetime of recovery. He hopes he has helped people to make the most of their potential.

"Don´t forget, I love you and who you are"

There have been many occasions when Buddy has fallen short, especially when out of work. During those low times and anytime in the last forty-three years, Jess has always been there, showing her love and commitment.

When Buddy needed a friend, he could always rely on Jess to say, "Don't forget, I love you and who you are, whatever happens."

This has given Buddy so much strength as he progresses through his life.

Buddy has been a fortunate boy to have found Jess, for sure.

CHOOSE TO PRIORITISE FULFILLING RELATIONSHIPS

Learning the lessons from life stories

When he has a clearly defined purpose and is surrounded by like-minded people, he puts everything into anything. He acts like a winner. He can be depended upon to "be committed".

The following actions helped Buddy to develop his character, be committed, and build the fulfilling relationships he now enjoys. To apply "be committed" in his life, he told himself to:

- Take time to understand why you want to be committed to your chosen action or goal.
- Check that you love what you are aiming for, as this will give you energy on the journey.
- Be resilient and persistent and follow your dreams, bouncing back from any challenges.
- Involve loved ones so they support you and understand the sacrifices to achieve the goal.

Is the "be committed" habit important to you at this stage of your life? What actions might you be considering?

Learning to Be Committed

Consider your answers to these four questions below when learning to be committed. If being committed is important to you, then what actions might you consider and in what timescale?

- Am I making personal commitments for the next 100 days?

- Am I taking action on situations I can control, avoiding procrastination?

- Am I a reliable, loyal team player, collaborating and contributing?

- Am I emotionally supported by the people close to me, keeping me on track?

CHOOSE TO PRIORITISE FULFILLING RELATIONSHIPS

BE EMPATHETIC

Having the ability to sense other people's emotions and imagine what someone else might be thinking

Be empathetic – relate to the feelings of others

Being empathetic is a key relationship habit. It is an essential aspect of building strong and meaningful relationships, both personally and professionally.

It means understanding and being able to relate to the feelings, thoughts, and experiences of others. Showing empathy also helps us to develop compassion, understanding, and a sense of community.

Being empathetic also helps us to be more effective in our communication and problem-solving skills. Empathy is not something that comes naturally to everyone, certainly not Buddy. It's a skill that can be developed and nurtured.

Make it a daily practice to put yourself in other people's shoes, and you'll be amazed at how much more positive and inclusive your interactions will be.

Is "be empathetic" a relationship habit that you need to consider improving?

CHOOSE TO PRIORITISE FULFILLING RELATIONSHIPS

"He's trapped his foreskin in his zip"

Brig Royd was a great place to live with so many happy memories. In 2003, so they were closer to the boys' comprehensive, the Brambles' moved into a converted chapel, in Luddenden Foot, near Halifax.

It was a typical Sunday for the Brambles as they set about their day. Buddy had taken Lucy the dog for a walk and collected the Sunday papers. Patrice was rushing about identifying where his football kit might be. Alex was contemplating what he might wear for school on Monday. Jess was planning to go shopping. Sundays were always hectic as the family were always rushing. If the family were rushing, it usually involved football. Like every Sunday during the season, there was a live TV match starting at four o'clock. There was a lot to do before then.

Patrice had found his boots and was ready for his morning football match. Alex often came along and always gave his brother support. Patrice was a fit, talented footballer, scoring many goals and providing many assists to help his team win matches. He was a popular team member and could always be relied upon to be in the correct position, avoiding the wrath of Joey, the manager.

CHOOSE TO BE RELENTLESS

Joey was an organised manager believing players needed to be in the right place at the right time to match the team's 4–4–2 formation. The formation was essential to Joey's success, especially when defending. Some of the players never seemed to get it.

The ungainly right-sided midfielder, Noah, was constantly shouted at for not being in his place. He was subbed off many times but never seemed to know his place. The highly skilful left-winger, Jonesy, often agitated Joey as he lost the ball again while setting off on one of his mesmerising dribbles. Northern-bloke Joey shouted, "Jonesy, ballet dancing's down the road." Buddy wasn't sure what that meant and thought it best not to ask. Jonesy looked up and was mesmerised. He was soon subbed off.

Some of the team struggled to always take responsibility. After a goal was conceded from a long ball through the centre of the defence, Freddie looked up and shouted, "Where's the defence?" That was a reasonable question, apart from the fact that he was the centre-half. He had failed to head the ball clear when he had the chance and was looking around to blame anyone. He, too, was subbed off. Patrice was never subbed off. He was always in the right position. He was a cool cat when it came to penalties. This game was over, and the Bramble family went home.

245

CHOOSE TO PRIORITISE FULFILLING RELATIONSHIPS

Weary footballer legs climbed the stairs. Buddy settled into reading the *Sunday Times* in the reading room. It was all quiet until Jess said, "Buddy, we have a problem here." Discreetly, Alex had informed Jess that he did, indeed, have a problem. It was unclear how it had happened, but Alex had trapped his foreskin in his zip. Jess hadn't seen a penis trapped in a zipper before. Patrice arrived to check on the commotion.

The four of us looked at Alex's foreskin trapped. It was funny for the three of us. Not amusing for Alex, who couldn't move without pain. Alex was lying on the sofa, unable to see the pink skin but could feel it. We looked at Lawyer Jess for inspiration. She may have had years of legal experience, but her medical advice was, on this occasion, questionable. Alex was looking for an empathetic ear and was alarmed when Jess, one step short of Buddy calling in the social services on the grounds of child abuse, suggested that we should pin him down. "You, Buddy, should quickly unzip his zipper. What do you think, Alex?"

"No!" he shouted, nearly as loudly as Mrs Shouty at the hospital. Jess calmly explained the plan. It will be over in seconds. The three with no penis problems were keen to go ahead. Penis boy, dressed in his popular orange Quiksilver t-shirt, looked horrified.

"Let's pin him down and get it over with," said Jess. Buddy wasn't sure but went along with the plan. As Patrice and Jess held little boy Alex down, Buddy went between Alex's legs to get ready to zip. Buddy looked up at Alex, who had a look of fear on his face, "No, Dad, don't do it!"

Imagining the emotions Alex was going through, Buddy decided that instead of pulling the zipper down, he pulled back from the scene and said, "Sorry, I can't do it."

Alex, Patrice and Buddy set off to the hospital. Alex carefully made it to the car. He usually jumps in, but on this occasion, he held back. Alex took ages getting into the car. Eventually, the Brambles set off. "Can you avoid bumps in the road?" suggested Alex. The Brambles arrived at the hospital, and Buddy went off to pay for parking. Alex somehow solved the problem when he returned to the car. His penis was now somehow back in the safety of his pants. Medical emergency over.

The Bramble boys got home just in time for Sunday live football. The family would sit with Grandad Bob and watch any game, debating decisions and discussing the match. It was particularly boisterous if Liverpool were on, as this was their team. Alex was a bit distracted. He had been given a pink mobile phone for Christmas, and he was investigating how

247

long it took for a damaged foreskin to repair. The Bramble men enjoyed watching football. It is what they did. It was suitable for male bonding. In the middle of the match, Grandad looked over and said, "What is pink and always in Alex's hand?" He was a funny man.

Jess would often be in the kitchen. She would be quietly peeling, mixing, basting, chopping, and grating anything that needed preparation for the post-match meal for hungry men. Sunday meals with the family were always special. What a memorable day.

"Why are you on the streets?"

Jess and Buddy always emphasised the importance of thinking of others and listening to understand the view of others deeply. Patrice has always been a laddie who shows empathy and emotion when he sees unfairness.

While many will judge a homeless person, there is a story behind each. They often have no family and no one that cares about them. They are alone. Patrice cannot walk past a homeless person without doing something.

A few weeks ago, Patrice was in Liverpool when he walked towards a homeless person and said, "How are you? Can I get you some food in Tesco?" Patrice got his phone out and noted the food he wanted. Patrice purchased ten pounds worth of good quality food. He gave it to Wayne. A smile lit up Wayne's face. Food may cost a little bit of money but kindness costs nothing.

"If you don't mind me asking, why are you on the streets?" asked Patrice. Patrice built trust by listening empathetically and creating conditions where Wayne could constructively express his thoughts. Just hearing him gave Wayne respect and value. Patrice was told he had come out of prison four weeks ago. There was nowhere for him to go but the streets.

That night Patrice made a difference in an individual's life. He cared. Wayne felt better. Patrice felt better.

"Ready to show his new friends he could party"

The Brambles knew Alex was a party animal years ago. At a New Year's Eve party in Prague 2001, an alcohol-free young Alex showed his moves as he strutted confidently across the dance floor. Only a few weeks ago he was caught on camera in Quito, Ecuador dancing the night away. He can sure party. Back in 2010 he was sixteen and ready to be an adult.

CHOOSE TO PRIORITISE FULFILLING RELATIONSHIPS

Living in Hertfordshire changed the trajectory of Alex's life. As he stood on his feet, he became a man and started a new life with a new circle of friends. He became popular and was soon ready to show his new friends he could party. He noticed Jess and Buddy were due to have a weekend away in Yorkshire in December. He saw his chance to throw a house party. Jess and Buddy knew nothing about it as the arrangements were discreetly made on social media.

With six days to go to party time, Buddy wandered into the front room and noticed that Alex had left the laptop open. It seemed Alex was off to a party this weekend. It was going to be in some parents' house in Hertford. They were going to be away for the weekend. Buddy was pleased that sensible Alex was making such good friends and settling into Hertford life. He was even more delighted that Alex showed he could be trusted. It was not him organising the party.

Buddy reflected on how grown-up Alex had become in such a few short months. Buddy should have left it there, but human curiosity took over, and he scrolled up to see any juicy gossip between the inbetweeners. He was pleased he did. It became suddenly apparent that not only was Alex going to the party, but he was in fact, the organiser, the host. The party was to be in the Brambles' house.

CHOOSE TO BE RELENTLESS

Buddy took Jess into Hertford for a coffee and cake to chat about this revelation. It was decided that Buddy couldn't let on that he had been snooping into personal social media. It was snowing, and there was a chance that the snow might close the roads to Yorkshire. "Perhaps we could suggest that we might now not go to Yorkshire because of the snow," put forward Jess.

Later that day, the family sat down to read the papers. Alex was all pumped up and super confident for some reason. He knew it was only a few days before "the party man" could enhance his credentials with his new group of highly intelligent inbetweeners. "Looks like the weather could be bad this weekend," forecasted Buddy, reaching the limits of his O-level Geography. This didn't worry Alex as he had party plans inside. "If it is snowing, then I'm not driving," said Buddy. Jess suggested that we could always go by train. So we checked out potential trains, but these were far too expensive. This charade continued for a few minutes.

Alex's face showed that thought was occurring, but his lips were not moving. After a while, his considerations and reflections turned into a set of carefully crafted questions aimed at Buddy. "You don't mind driving in the snow, Dad. Perhaps you could go earlier and avoid the snow. Have you checked out the coaches? If you don't go, you could spend a

251

weekend somewhere else." The questions and options came thick and fast as Alex moved at speed to ensure that Buddy and Jess were not anywhere near Hertford this Saturday. It was a funny moment. Jess and Buddy practised their *hold-in-their-laughter-and-laugh-later* skills.

Jess had had enough and said, "That's it. I don't want the stress of being caught in the snow. We won't go."

Alex's face looked like a little boy with his hand caught in the biscuit tin. No longer a confident up-and-coming Peter Stringfellow, but a boy with a problem. The trap had been laid. Buddy and Jess disappeared to have a good laugh outside. An hour later, young Stringfellow wandered around with the world on his shoulders and looked like he needed someone to talk to. "Mum, I've got a problem."

The last time Alex had a problem was when his penis was stuck in his zipper, so Jess listened. Alex explained the situation. It became clear that it was a small party of between five and ten people or maybe a few more. Jess explained that we could always sit quietly upstairs and not interfere. Not sure Alex liked that idea. Buddy knew that sixty had been invited, so Alex wasn't transparent about the numbers. Jess asked a few lawyer-type questions. Very quickly, all the details came gushing out of young Stringfellow. Party started at 8 pm, sixty had been invited but possibly more. The numbers had got out of hand, and Stringfellow was in trouble.

Buddy and Jess showed empathy about the situation and agreed that the party could go ahead. They didn't want to embarrass Alex in front of his new friends by cancelling the party. They were reassured that these were sensible inbetweeners. They trusted Alex not to let them down. Not entirely; one of the stipulations was that Patrice would need to be invited to ensure that nothing untoward was occurring at the party.

Patrice was in Liverpool at university and arrived at the party via train and a tricky snow-covered taxi from Stevenage. He was now the oldest in the room and quite a catch for the young women in the room, who drooled over his presence. The spotty-nosed teenagers had competition from Patrice, who was also the coolest guy in the room.

Buddy and Jess phoned a few times to check how things were progressing. Patrice said that the inbetweeners were behaving. He had to intervene to turn the music down. He also had to be on puppy control. Ten-week-old Millie, the Labrador, was the star attraction, with the women keen for puppy pictures. Puppy party socialisation completed. Tick.

CHOOSE TO PRIORITISE FULFILLING RELATIONSHIPS

When Buddy and Jess returned home, the home was spotless. The only evidence of a party was an empty bottle of Bud Light left downstairs. Alex could be trusted to use the house for parties again. He never did though.

"Dad, dad, don't come in"

Alex settled into Hertford's life and began building up a good group of friends he enjoyed being with. They helped him settle in, and he was doing very well as he focused on achieving good grades to get into Exeter, his chosen university.

Every so often, Alex made trips to the local park to meet with a fellow sixth former, Miss Bengeo, who enjoyed chatting with him. They played on the roundabouts, checked the swings, and enjoyed the slide. These innocent activities with Bengeo helped build trust between them, and they soon decided that it would be okay to sit on a bench and explore their interests a little further. Alex soon realised that Bengeo was talented with her fingers as she told him she was a grade seven on piano.

This sort of girl could be introduced to Buddy and Jess. So, one Saturday, Buddy and Jess met Bengeo. She was posh, dressed immaculately, and full of intelligent conversation. As she left, Buddy and Jess hoped to see her again. Alex had made a good connection, and it was great to see him so happy. Bengeo was keen to take it to the next stage as she wrapped her arms around this new guy who was so different from the rest.

Buddy was always flying off somewhere. He was off to Paris, had forgotten his passport, and rushed back to Hertford to get it from the upstairs office. It was 4.30 pm. He opened the back door, rushed in, and started running up the stairs calling for Alex as he set off from the ground floor. No answer; Buddy assumed that Alex was on the slide with Miss Bengeo as he started the climb the stairs to the office next to Alex's bedroom. He heard a bit of shuffling and a loud voice shouted, "Dad, don't come in!" Usually, Buddy would immediately see this as a reason to go in, but on this occasion, he very quickly thought not. He could feel the emotion in Alex's voice and quickly showed empathy about the situation. Whatever was in there, Buddy didn't want to see it. Alex also didn't wish for Buddy to see it. "I'm just getting my passport. I won't be coming in. Are you okay?" Alex said he was fine. "I will see you later," as Buddy quickly left the area.

As Buddy descended the stairs, he noticed a pair of shoes, a handbag, a jumper, and a short coat strewed across the stairs. None of these belonged to Alex. Whatever was going on in that room, the clothing removal appeared en route to the room.

CHOOSE TO PRIORITISE FULFILLING RELATIONSHIPS

How Buddy missed the obvious signs when he arrived home that day is still a mystery.

A few weeks later, Bengeo and Alex decided to call it a day. The Brambles thought she would never be seen again. A few years later, Patrice excitedly phoned people to say Miss Bengeo was on *The Voice*, the primetime ITV talent show. She was a talented lady, for sure.

Learning the lessons from life stories

Throughout his life, Buddy developed his empathetic skills knowing only too well that he has not always met his high standards. He reviews continually this aspect of his behaviour. It´s a habit that he is constantly improving.

The following actions helped Buddy to develop his character, empathy, and build the fulfilling relationships needed for a happy life. To apply "be empathetic" in his life, he told himself to:

- Care about people, listen and give them your full attention. Be there when they need you.
- Acknowledge their feelings. Show people that you understand where they are right now.
- Understand the thoughts and feelings of others while being self-aware of your own.
- Encourage openness in conversation by asking open questions and then really listen.

Is the "be empathetic" habit important to you at this stage of your life? What actions might you be considering?

CHOOSE TO PRIORITISE FULFILLING RELATIONSHIPS

Learning to Be Empathetic

Consider your answers to these four questions when learning to be empathetic. If being empathetic is important to you, then what actions might you consider and in what timescale?

- Am I listening (without judging) to deeply understand the views of others?

- Am I always looking for dialogue/agreement to help move things forward?

- Am I constructively expressing my thoughts and opinions?

- Am I building cooperation and managing my emotions in challenging situations?

CHOOSE TO PRIORITISE EXPERIENTIAL LEARNING

What do you want out of life, now and in the future, in terms of learning?

CHOOSE TO PRIORITISE EXPERIENTIAL LEARNING

The Experiential Learning Habits

Mastering these six learning habits help people to grow their potential beyond their initial thoughts.

CHOOSE TO PRIORITISE EXPERIENTIAL LEARNING

Having a great set of friends and a well-connected group of work colleagues separate these people from the others. This network has welcoming and positive vibes and helps people believe in themselves, continually learn, and seize opportunities. Buddy found that when he associated himself with winners, he became more successful.

These learning habits focus on people being passionate and inspired about their contributions in life. They are confident, and this gives them the freedom to value and encourage others. They are enthusiastic, determined and challenge themselves. They acquire new knowledge, behaviours, and skills because of action-learning experiential experiences. They learn much from the ongoing interactions and engagement with people around them. Environments that have understanding, trust and emotional connection help to foster this spirit at home and at work.

A solid group of aspirational, motivated, inspiring friends and a network of achievers enable these people to learn quickly. People learning have often worked incredibly hard. They make sure they are noticed in the crowd. Opportunities often present themselves through their well-connected network.

BE PASSIONATE

Having, showing, or caused by strong feelings or beliefs

CHOOSE TO PRIORITISE EXPERIENTIAL LEARNING

Be passionate – find what you love and keep improving

Being passionate is a key learning habit and essential for growing your potential beyond your initial thoughts. It means dedicating ourselves fully to our interests, being excited and enthusiastic about what we do. Passion helps us to achieve our stretching goals and sometimes even be groundbreaking.

Passion also helps us to stay motivated and engaged. It helps us to overcome obstacles, be more creative, productive, and resilient.

Passion is not something that we can force. We discover passion by exploring our interests and achieving our goals. Achievers and winners do this naturally. The very best find what they love and keep improving to be the best version of themselves.

When Buddy is passionate about his interests, he is so much more motivated, fulfilled, and happy in his professional and personal life.

Is "be passionate" a learning habit that you need to consider improving?

CHOOSE TO BE RELENTLESS

"We will need to film that again"

Buddy is a passionate guy. When Buddy is passionate and purposeful, he is fully engaged and committed to whatever he does. He puts all his energy and enthusiasm into the subject matter, aiming to be the best he can be. Authoring his first book, managing a football team, or discussing pensions, Buddy was all in. The subject matter always takes over his life. It's how he is. If it's something new, bright, and shiny, Buddy is at the front learning about it.

Early in his marriage to Jess, Buddy, out of the blue, became passionate about video-making. He purchased a subscription to *Camcorder Monthly* to obtain tips on becoming the next Steven Spielberg. Buddy was serious about producing a quality job, and often the first cut wasn't quite right. On location in Kenya, Buddy was very annoying as he explained to Jess, "We will need to film that again, as I am not happy with it." Thirty-three years later, he is probably still annoying.

Buddy bought all the mechanical gear to create home movies. Often, they would return from a holiday and spend a few hours creating a video of their experience. Buddy would select the items that would be visually appealing, while Jess would identify the best music to match the situation. It was before any children, so the Brambles had plenty of time to be creative.

CHOOSE TO PRIORITISE EXPERIENTIAL LEARNING

Sitting on the floor of their house in Crawley, surrounded by connectors, wires, and their thoughts, they could create good movies for family viewing. When complete, they would travel to Somerset for a video evening with Jess's family. Not sure when, but Buddy's passion for video-making suddenly stopped. Buddy was like that. He gives his all, and then something else takes its place. Buddy must be fired up with a purpose – he can't sit about and just relax.

The Brambles moved home nine times, and sadly, the video memories were lost in transit in one of these moves. Who threw them out? The Brambles do not know. They do know that Jess threw out Buddy's unique collection of football trophies.

"Grandma will bring tea and crumpets"

Grandma was passionate about cooking and baking. No Sunday would be complete without hanging around for a Grandma Sunday lunch with all the trimmings. The conversations around the table were always fun, as Grandad was a fun character with mannerisms and stories to entertain.

Grandma often made three different desserts. It was always challenging to choose which one to have. Grandad didn't need to choose. Grandma knew he would have a bit of each one.

After this gastronomic delight, the men would retire to another room to watch a live football match. The women were somewhere else, probably chatting about how lucky they were to be married to such wonderful human beings.

Near the end of the first half, Grandad would always say, "Grandma will be in shortly with afternoon tea and crumpets." As the first half ended, the women arrived with tea and crumpets. These were simpler, happy times for Grandad.

Buddy learnt the skills to contribute positively to family life. After the football, Jess and Buddy would travel back to Crawley. Buddy knows and feels the love of a family.

"I can't believe a daughter of mine"

Politics has always been a passion for the Brambles. They have left-of-centre opinions, with Jess believing she is more left-wing than Buddy. Jess is a *Guardian* reader with an intelligent, educated view of life's challenges. Buddy learnt his opinions from the unfairness of his upbringing and the shop floor of a factory.

They agree on many things that matter, wanting social justice and aspiration for the many. They have always supported the Labour Party. From the creation of the NHS to the minimum wage, the Labour Party makes a lasting difference in the lives of many. The thirteen years of the last Labour government were such happy times for so many.

During their married life, they have, very sadly, sat through too many electoral defeats allowing the Conservatives to gain power and put their influence on the country.

Buddy and Jess always enjoyed the political skill of the former prime minister Tony Blair. His ability to craft a message gave them so much learning in their life. This is a great example, "The only difference between compassionate conservatism and conservatism is that under compassionate conservatism they tell you they're not going to help you but they're really sorry about it." Jess loves this short collection of words.

Jess and Buddy have always encouraged conversations about politics within the family. The Brambles are a bunch of solid characters with slightly different views on how to bring about a better world. Many evenings have been spent in the family discussing minor areas of disagreement, often with no resolution; even more so when Grandad Bob was alive, as he had purist views about the way forward.

On one memorable occasion in Seville, Grandad and Jess discussed the Labour approach to education policy and specific academies as lifelong supporters of comprehensive education. Both had much to agree on. The former comprehensive school's head teacher's blood was up as Jess discussed the benefits of academies in inner-city London with her father. There was evidence that they were making a difference in communities. Conversations were getting very heated and increasing in volume and tone.

The Spanish people in the Plaza de España, were looking over aghast at this English family debating the minutiae of political strategy and implementation. It was forty-six degrees, and a perspiring and increasingly agitated Grandad said, "I can't believe a daughter of mine would be supporting academies." He was as angry as Buddy had ever seen him. What had Blairite Buddy done to his daughter?

As Jess and Buddy walked away from the table, it was left to Grandma to calm the waters again. She was very good at that. As Grandad aged, he became increasingly angry about politics and the country's direction. Meanwhile, Labour lost the 2010 election and moved away from the centre ground of politics. Grandad would not have enjoyed the thirteen years after 2010. Looking at the recent political polls it seems like many of the present voters feel the same.

CHOOSE TO PRIORITISE EXPERIENTIAL LEARNING

"Take an interest in politics"

After years of defeats at the ballot box, the Brambles thought it was such a joy to see Labour win in 1997. After eighteen years of Conservative rule Labour arrived to repair the damage.

Living through the Michael Foot, Neil Kinnock, and John Smith years was painful as Labour lost election after election. The 1st of May 1997 was a new day. It was also the day a horse was found severely injured on the field at Brig Royd. How it happened is anyone's guess. The police arrived and arranged for it to be taken away. Bad timing for the horse but perfect for the Bramble boys' education. They would be educated in a Labour Britain. Political implementation was going to get better for many. It did, much better. Jess's family politically educated Buddy. Buddy will never forget Grandma giving him the Tony Benn book, *Dare to be a Daniel*. This gift inspired Buddy and built his passion for politics. The book's title came from the famous American hymn based on the book of Daniel.

- Dare to be a Daniel,
- Dare to stand alone!
- Dare to have a purpose firm!
- Dare to make it known.

Buddy loved that book. These words have inspired Buddy to have a purpose in life.

If there was a political rally, then the Brambles would attend. They attended the Labour Party events, which helped inform the boys' political views. In 2004, the Bramble family were in Manchester, and Buddy noticed an ageing Tony Benn sitting on a seat outside the conference centre. The Brambles went over and spoke to him. Alex and Patrice were eleven and twelve, the same age Jess was when she received that postcard from Tony Benn. The boys enjoyed their conversation with Tony as he shared his wisdom. With Tony's permission, Buddy took a picture of them together. As Patrice and Alex were leaving, Tony said, "Take an interest in politics before politics takes an interest in you." Here we are, eighteen years later, and this statement has never been more true.

In 2013, Buddy and Jess attended Tony Benn's last public appearance. He was publicising his final book *The Blaze of Autumn Sunshine*. It was an emotional event as all could see that Tony was frail but still sharp as a button. Buddy was surrounded by ladies and blokes who probably read *the Guardian* or *the Morning Star* and were brought up on far-left ideology. Buddy was perhaps the only Blairite bloke in the room.

CHOOSE TO PRIORITISE EXPERIENTIAL LEARNING

"We have time for one more question," said Owen Jones, *the Guardian* columnist. Blairite Buddy was first up with his hand. Jess looked over, concerned about what Blairite fanboy would say. She tried to pull his hand down. Too late. Owen pointed to the man with the glasses at the back of the room. Buddy was selected. Buddy stood up.

"Tony, you have inspired so many people over the years. You have been an inspiration this evening." The crowd clapped. As the clapping subsided, Buddy continued, "May I ask, what inspires you now?"

Tony responded simply, "Young people."

Tony died five months later, peacefully at home.

Learning the lessons from life stories

There is no doubt that Buddy is a passionate guy. He puts all his energy into his dreams. This is a habit that Buddy could depend on as he found his way through a digital world where learning by doing became a key differential.

The following actions helped him to develop an experiential learning mindset, be passionate, and encourage others to make the most of their life. To apply "be passionate" in his life, he told himself to:

- Reflect on what you want to achieve, now and in the future. Are you passionate about it?
- Agree goals around health, relationships, learning, and prosperity on your terms.
- Create an action plan that helps you take the first step on your journey doing the stuff you love.
- Meet people who are passionate about your interests, who will support and inspire you.

Is the "be passionate" habit important to you at this stage of your life? What actions might you be considering?

CHOOSE TO PRIORITISE EXPERIENTIAL LEARNING

Learning to Be Passionate

Consider your answers to these four questions below when learning to be passionate. If being passionate is important to you, then what actions might you consider and in what timescale?

- Am I applying myself to what I really love and what I really want?
- Am I competing with myself to improve and get better, every day?
- Am I contributing in a way that positively impacts others?
- Am I concentrated on and ambitious about where I might be in five years' time?

BE INSPIRED

Having an extraordinary quality, as if arising from some external creative impulse

CHOOSE TO PRIORITISE EXPERIENTIAL LEARNING

Be inspired – be curious and explore the unknown

Being inspired is a key learning habit and essential for growing potential beyond initial thoughts. It means having the drive and motivation to pursue our goals, to learn new things, and to create positive change. Winners have this in abundance.

Inspiration helps us to tap into our creativity, to see new possibilities, and to push ourselves to look beyond our initial thoughts. Being inspired also helps us to stay motivated and engaged and to be more resilient in the face of adversity.

Buddy was inspired by experiential learning and kept an open mind. He was curious and was willing to explore new things. He became inspired, motivated, and fulfilled as he helped hundreds of people make the most of their potential.

Is "be inspired" a learning habit that you need to consider improving?

"Your energy, enthusiasm, and knowledge blew James away"

For seven years, Buddy worked away from the family during the week, returning at weekends. He developed his interim management business, working in different European industries. These locations enabled Jess and the family to join him for long weekends in Dublin, Amsterdam, and Rothesay on the Isle of Bute.

Buddy was working in Dublin. He took a call from a recruitment consultant in London. This call had the potential to change Buddy's life again. The consultant discussed an interim role as a director of a utility company in the south-east. As Buddy listened to the challenges this company had, he knew that he was the candidate that could solve the issues they faced. The interview would be in three days. "Would you be available, in London, for an interview?" said the consultant. Buddy flew back from Dublin and talked to Jess about the role. Buddy had worked with many top directors in his time but had never been approached to be one. He knew this was his opportunity to energise, aim high, and be what he wanted. Jess gave him confidence as Buddy explained, "If I am to get this job, I will need to prepare like never before."

CHOOSE TO PRIORITISE EXPERIENTIAL LEARNING

Buddy had two days to be ready. He focused on knowing as much as possible about the interviewer, the company, and the industry. He prepared his answer to the "tell me about yourself" question. Buddy was like a man possessed as he put all his focus into his preparation. He had eight prepared stories with firm business benefit conclusions. Buddy was ready. He knew what he was going to say.

Buddy sorted out what he would wear and booked the train. He stayed overnight in a local hotel and was ready for his 9 am interview. As he sat in reception, he knew he had worked hard on his preparation and felt confident. Buddy visualised the feeling of getting the role. His head space was free of any doubts, just belief. "Hi Buddy, I'm James; come on in."

As they sat down, James talked for ten minutes about the role and its challenges. He didn't pull any punches; he explained in detail how awful the customer service performance was. He had many problems that needed a tactical and strategic approach to resolve. Buddy felt energised, as while James didn't know the answers, Buddy knew how to fix his problems.

James made it easy for Buddy. "I have looked at your CV. I can see you have lots of experience working for top customer-focused companies. Perhaps you could start by telling me about yourself." Buddy smiled and, with passion and energy, began his short three-minute pitch. Buddy explained who he was, how he worked, the problems he had overcome, and the business results he had delivered. The three minutes flew by as James nodded in agreement. They were less than fifteen minutes into the interview, and Buddy had made a connection.

As James asked more questions, Buddy rolled out his prepared stories, peppering them with solutions to James ' problems. It was possibly the best interview that Buddy had ever delivered. The discussion concluded with James explaining that he had two more interviews today and would decide over the weekend. As Buddy travelled back to Luddenden Foot Chapel, he felt confident. He had done his best.

The recruitment consultant phoned Buddy and said that his interview had gone very well. He was by far the best candidate. His energy, enthusiasm, and knowledge blew James away. Was he prepared to join them? "Yes, of course," said Buddy. The printing apprentice from Somerset was going to be a customer service director.

Buddy took time to understand the dysfunctional group and soon realised that they could achieve more together than alone. Buddy didn't need to change any of the managers in the team. They just needed to be a team that could work together.

CHOOSE TO PRIORITISE EXPERIENTIAL LEARNING

He focused on coaching them to be better at what they did. Buddy is proud that the company moved from near the bottom of the industry league table to 2nd place in less than nine months. James was delighted.

Buddy met his good friend Charlton during this period. Charlton is a lifelong Charlton Athletic fan. Since then, Buddy and Jess have spent many hours with Charlton and his wife Sandy enjoying the banter between West Country Buddy and South London bloke Charlton. As a passionate Bristol Rovers supporter Buddy has always hoped that his team would at some point be above the Addicks in any league table. He has waited years for the moment. In December 2022 the moment arrived.

The couples enjoy traveling and have met in various places around the world, including Stansted Mountfitchet, Perth, Bristol and York. The marriage between Charlton and Sandy in San Francisco City Hall was a memorable day. The loving couple were surrounded by their closest friends all there to enjoy the moment. Prior to the wedding Jess and Buddy spent a week enjoying the delights of Portland and the Northwest coast of the USA. They enjoy the company of Charlton and Sandy very much.

"Always recruit people that are better than you"

Early in his management career, Buddy noticed that some junior managers worried about having talent in their teams. These managers would often recruit people into their teams that could be controlled and certainly didn't threaten their superiority. These teams were often devoid of ideas and creativity. They came in, did what was needed, and then went home. The manager had a monopoly on the ideas. Buddy had a different approach and wanted to learn from experts and successful people. He has always recruited people who are very different from him. This has challenged him as he learnt new ways of working. Early in his career a CEO gave him this advice, "Always recruit people that are better than you, as it's the way to build a great team."

Buddy is proud that in his business life, he never fears talent around him; he was inspired by them. He hopes he has encouraged people to aim high and achieve more than they thought possible.

"Would you consider being a non-executive director?"

From his complex background, Buddy climbed mountains and became a well-known character in his industry. He managed to influence the culture of many companies in the UK, USA and

CHOOSE TO PRIORITISE EXPERIENTIAL LEARNING

Europe. In his younger days, he travelled to West Bay in Dorset annually, but no further. His career took him to many parts of the world. On one occasion, he obtained a contract in Australia with the opportunity to contribute to a culture change. Buddy was able to travel and work and be paid for it.

In 2013, he was invited to an evening of celebration at the European Contact Centre and Customer Service Awards. It was a wonderful evening. Buddy sat with the chair of the awards and leading figures from the industry. Company after company were winning awards for the quality of their service and leadership.

Buddy continued to drink the free wine as the awards ended and enjoyed the fun. In the background, he heard Jimmy Carr, the comedian, talking about a lifetime achievement award for someone who had worked in a list of award-winning companies. Buddy was interested, as he had worked at these companies and was sure to know who it was. Then, Jimmy said, the winner is Buddy Bramble. It seemed like Buddy did know who it was. It was him. Everybody was standing and clapping. Buddy was a bit unsteady on his feet as the alcohol kicked in. He weaved through the exuberant audience. When he arrived on stage, he received the award and said to Jimmy, "Love your gags, Jimmy," hoping for a bit of banter. No banter from Jimmy, who said, "The camera is that way." Buddy looked away towards the camera. He hasn't looked at Jimmy since. As he walked back through the crowd, he saw the faces of people he knew offering congratulations. He was now one of the few to receive a lifetime achievement in an industry only twenty years old. Buddy had been on one hell of an inspiring journey with a focus on making a difference in the lives of others. The evening was emotional, for sure.

Buddy thought back to Christmas 1998. That was the year when Buddy was deciding how to best use his talents in the future; he recalled that he asked himself these five questions:

- Do I love what I am doing?
- Can I find what I love doing?
- Does the world need what I am offering?
- Can I be great at it?
- Can I make a living out of it?

Buddy's answers helped him to create the need for Understanding and Learning as a unique differentiator for progressive organisations. To this day, he continues to offer advice and guidance to organisations looking to design in active learning into their business, not as one-off interventions but built into everything the company does.

One of his recent clients increased their employee engagement levels substantially leading to increased sustainable revenue on the back of the culture change.

In 2022, the Chair of the Professional Planning Forum, the leading contact centre accreditation company, contacted Buddy. He said, "Would you consider being a non-executive director?" Of course, Buddy said, "Yes." It's been quite a journey for Buddy. Yet, Buddy is still learning from experts and successful people.

"Can you get me a drink of water?"

In 2008, Jess busily combined being a mother with leading a legal practice. Patrice and Alex were making good progress at the local comprehensive in Calderdale, West Yorkshire. Grandma and Grandad were using up their retirement savings travelling the countryside while squeezing in Halifax Town matches. This became a passion for Grandad. He was fixated on the Shaymen. Buddy was over a year into his director role in Hertfordshire, and it was clear that the Brambles would be on the move again.

Not Grandma though, who wasn't moving at all well. She needed to be in a wheelchair when on trips or visits. In November 2008, Buddy received a call from a tearful Jess explaining that Grandma was in hospital. She had suffered a heart attack an hour ago. Buddy dropped what he was doing in Hertfordshire. He travelled home to offer what support he could. Although the family knew that Grandma was ill of health, this was still a shock.

When Buddy arrived at the hospital, it was clear that Grandma had taken a turn for the worse. The doctors suggested that she might not make it through the night. She was lying there and not speaking. The doctors said they would ensure that she was comfortable, but there was nothing they could do. Her heart was not strong enough. All those years inspiring and looking after others and not herself had taken their toll on her body. As the family went home, there was every expectation that Grandma would no longer be with Grandad, Jess, Buddy, Alex, and Patrice in the next few days.

Grandma had been such an inspiring teacher, wonderful wife and mother of her children. Her husband, her children and grandchildren were the world to her. She would do anything for them. All she needed in her life was to feel happy for them. She loved spending time with the family and doing things for them. Buddy felt this unconditional love as she welcomed him into this wonderful and loving family.

CHOOSE TO PRIORITISE EXPERIENTIAL LEARNING

It was clear that Grandma would not be coming home again. At home, the family discussed their memories of Grandma. At Brig Royd, Jess and Buddy remember Grandma's seafood pancakes. On pancake day, Alex and Patrice would rush home knowing that Grandma would have the batter ready, with lemon and sugar available. The perfect pancakes would be for others. Grandma would always save the worst one for herself.

Patrice and Alex recalled the slow build-up of the atmosphere of an intense Football Monopoly game while listening to Grandma's conversations in the background. Grandma making cups of tea and crumpets by the fire were all lovely family memories. Jess recalled Grandma always being there to listen to her gossip about criminals and her day in court.

At Brig Royd and Luddenden Foot Chapel, what Grandma liked most were the regular trips to the Brambles' home, close by, to watch soaps and chat with Jess, Alex, and Patrice. Buddy often rang in, from someplace in the world, during the advertisement break to check on family news.

That night the Brambles went to bed fearing the worst. The family awoke the next day, and Grandma was still with them. Grandma's heart may not have been in tip-top condition, but she wasn't ready to go quite yet. The family regularly visited a motionless Grandma to give her company in these final hours.

As the hours went by, Grandma stabilised. Jess was with her, and after days of quietness, Grandma said, "Jess, can you get me a drink of water?" Jess wasn't expecting that and found some water for Grandma. It was a shock as the doctors had given the impression that Grandma wasn't going to talk again. For the next six weeks, Grandma slipped in and out of consciousness as she made a recovery of sorts. She was able to have many stilted conversations with the family. These conversations helped the family come to some closure. The Brambles knew that Grandma inspired many pupils when she was a teacher. They also had the benefit of her love and understanding.

A few days before Christmas 2008, she had a private word with Jess. "When I die, please look after your father." Even in her final moments, Grandma was still thinking of others.

Grandad visited Grandma daily, and the family discussed bringing Grandma home for her final days. Grandma never made it home in time for Christmas.

She died peacefully in Halifax Hospital on the 27th of December 2008.

CHOOSE TO PRIORITISE EXPERIENTIAL LEARNING

Learning the lessons from life stories

Buddy has often been inspired but he is not always consistent. During his life, he has learnt some of the skills to "be inspired". He is still learning.

The following actions helped him to be inspired, develop his character, and cultivate an experiential learning mindset. To apply "be inspired" in his life, he told himself to:

- Avoid thinking that inspiration and happiness is over there, somewhere in the future.
- Fire yourself up with a purpose you believe in and focus on activities you find rewarding.
- Take actions on your purpose, being inspired by your achievements and people around you.
- Enjoy the present moment and help others to make the most of their talents.

Is the "be inspired" habit important to you at this stage of your life? What actions might you be considering?

Learning to Be Inspired

Consider your answers to these four questions below when learning to be inspired. If being inspired is important to you, then what actions might you consider and in what timescale?

- Am I fixated on what inspires me and the people around me?

- Am I future-focused, applying myself to knowing what I want to be?

- Am I energised by what I can do to initiate change?

- Am I studying and learning from experts and successful people?

CHOOSE TO PRIORITISE EXPERIENTIAL LEARNING

BE ENCOURAGING

Giving someone the courage or confidence to do something

Be encouraging – take time to recognise others

"Be encouraging" is a key learning habit and essential to grow potential beyond initial thoughts. Encouragement means having the support, motivation, and positive reinforcement to pursue our goals, learn new things, and create positive change in yourself or others around you.

Encouragement helps us to tap into our inner strength, to see new possibilities and to push ourselves to reach our full potential. Take time to recognise others around you.

Being encouraged also helps us to stay motivated and engaged. Encouragement can come from many sources, it can be found in friends, family, mentors, or from within us.

Buddy had so little encouragement in his earlier life he decided to set about giving it to others as often as he could. It's a powerful tool that changed the lives of many who experienced Buddy's unique approach.

Is "be encouraging" a learning habit that you need to consider improving?

CHOOSE TO PRIORITISE EXPERIENTIAL LEARNING

"The leopard with blood all over its mouth"

In 1989, Buddy and Jess honeymooned in Kenya. It was a memorable holiday as it differed from what they had ever experienced. They often discussed the possibility of a similar trip with their children. Unsurprisingly, the Bramble family would visit Kenya when the children were old enough.

Buddy was concerned about the cost of this trip. He contacted a local provider in Nairobi. He was encouraged by their positivity about the delights of Kenya. They offered a guide and a full tour of the game parks for much less than a traditional travel agent in the UK. They received a half payment upfront. It was a nervous moment for Buddy as the Brambles walked through Jomo Kenyatta International Airport and into the car park looking for Alamini, the guide. Just as Buddy was becoming concerned about his upfront payment and the whereabouts of Alamini, he appeared. He was smiling and welcoming and calmed the initial concerns that Buddy might have had. He showed the young Brambles his rifle to reassure them that he was the man to be with on safari.

Alamini dropped them off at the inner-city hotel for a few days of relaxation before the safari.

CHOOSE TO BE RELENTLESS

Two days later, the family set off across the savannah on the bumpy roads arriving at the Lake Nakuru National Park just in time to see the flamingos. The seven-day safari took in the best of Kenya. Up early for the morning drive, back for breakfast, rest, and then out for the late afternoon drive. The Brambles were soon in a routine interspaced with long drives to other game lodges, including Meru National Park and Samburu Reserve. On the safari, the family saw all the animals you would expect and were not disappointed.

As one early morning drive ended, Alamini noticed another creche of young impalas. The Brambles had seen many of these on this trip, but Alamini seemed particularly excited this time. Through his binoculars, he had also noticed a leopard stalking the group of young impalas who were busily enjoying their freedom.

Alamini drove to a sheltered spot and waited, and waited a bit more. Eventually, the impala family spotted some movement in the grasses and panicked. A young impala had now broken away from the safety of the creche, and the leopard gave chase. It was over in minutes. The young impala had no chance. The short struggle occurred within twenty metres of the safari van. Patrice and Alex had witnessed a real-life killing. As the leopard settled down to its breakfast, Alamini, with his gun by his side, said, "Look at the leopard with blood all over its mouth." He seemed to be enjoying this entertainment. "It's not all over quite yet."

Within minutes, six hyenas had appeared, encouraged and full of confidence. They, too, were hungry. They didn't want to work for their breakfast. They were not frightened of leopards. They encircled the leopard and crept forward. They were only ten metres away when the leopard looked up, spotted them, and ran away. The hyenas didn't chase the leopard; they liked freshly killed impala. Within one minute, the hyenas had finished their breakfast.

The Brambles had witnessed the law of the jungle.

"Only you can get yourself out of this"

After the Brambles had eaten their breakfast, they set off for Treetops. Treetops is the famous Kenyan safari lodge where the late Elizabeth II learnt of her father's death in 1952. She was twenty-five. Treetops was certainly in Buddy's initial plan, but unfortunately, it was far too expensive. Buddy selected a cheaper alternative nearby.

The Red Monkey Lodge seemed perfect. It had a reputation for providing some of the best and most memorable monkey experiences in Kenya. The Brambles settled into their rooms.

The boys were in one and the adults in another. They each had a balcony to get a good view of the monkeys. Unfortunately, on this day, they seemed agitated. The monkeys didn't look friendly; thoughts of being "up-close and personal" were pushed to the back of their minds. Patrice was concerned about monkeys entering his room and locked the door to keep them out.

The Brambles should have been able to predict there were going to be problems. At lunch, out of nowhere, a monkey arrived at the table and helped itself to a crusty roll. "Welcome to Kenya," said a friendly American tourist on another table next to us.

It had already been a long day, so they all went off for a quiet time in their rooms. As the sun went down, the colours were perfect for photography. Buddy suggested that he should take some pictures of Patrice on the balcony. It was all a bit tight. It was clear that to get the best images, Buddy would need to be in his room next door, leaning over his balcony with Patrice in the corner of his balcony. Buddy left Patrice and Alex's room and went next door. As he lent over his balcony, the happy scene he expected was now one of deep concern. In the background of his room, Buddy could hear Alex explaining the situation to Jess. Jess was now in a state of panic. "We need to be calm; I'll sort it," said Buddy.

It didn't look good. Patrice was on his balcony in the corner, away from the door back into the room. Opposite Patrice on the balcony ledge, a family of monkeys had appeared. These didn't look friendly. Their teeth looked very sharp. They looked like they were ready to attack Patrice. Patrice was undoubtedly not keen on this "up-close and personal moment". He looked terrified. Buddy realised that he had to reassure, calm, and encourage Patrice. "Don't worry, Patrice. I will come round and save you. Don't move."

Buddy arrived in the boys' room and explained to Alex and Jess that he would open the door, frighten the monkeys, and save Patrice from what appeared to be a certain bloody death. Buddy looked through the window to check the scene. The monkeys were ready to leap towards Patrice. "Why is the door locked?" asked Buddy.

"Patrice was worried about the monkeys coming into our room, so he locked the door," said Alex.

"No problem," said Buddy. "Where is the key so I can open the door?"

"It's in Patrice's pocket," explained Alex. Patrice was so worried about monkeys coming into the room that he locked the door from the outside. There was no way of opening the door from the inside. Patrice was now locked outside with the monkeys. Patrice did all he could to avoid being near monkeys, but now he was unhappily and tearfully amongst them.

Buddy went next door and looked at the feasibility of climbing into the balcony. It didn't look good. It was a long drop, and Buddy didn't feel as confident as the monkeys. He certainly wasn't going to risk dying unless it was the only option. There was another option. He explained the plan to Patrice, who by now had already thought about the prospect of death in the hands and teeth of the monkeys. Buddy looked at a concerned and tearful Patrice and said, "Only you can get yourself out of this. You must be brave. Try not to cry. Crying will agitate the monkeys." Patrice wiped away a tear and listened to Buddy.

Buddy knew that looking into the eyes of brown bears was bad and quickly decided that monkeys didn't like eye contact. Unfortunately, Patrice was looking nervously at the monkeys. He was watching their every move as they prepared themselves to attack. "I know this is difficult for you, Patrice. You will need to be calm and courageous. Monkeys don't like you looking at them; it irritates them and makes them feel uncomfortable. You might frighten them," explained Buddy.

CHOOSE TO PRIORITISE EXPERIENTIAL LEARNING

In a highly agitated voice Patrice said, "They're frightened? I'm frightened!"

To encourage and build up Patrice's belief Buddy said, "They are probably more frightened than you. Whatever you do, don't look into the eyes of the monkeys. Slowly, very slowly, slide along the seat to the door." Jess and Alex were watching the event from the room.

It was a tense moment as Buddy encouraged a frightened Patrice to slide but not stare. In sixty seconds, Patrice was at the door of the balcony. The monkeys were on the other side and seemed more settled. They appeared to be much happier with sliding than staring. Patrice fumbled in his pocket for the key, put the key in the door, and clicked. The door was now ready to be opened. Patrice opened, ran through, and quickly shut the door. He ran into the protection and open arms of a relieved Jess.

Patrice was so brave that day.

"Introduce people using positive comments"

Buddy has attended many business conferences and has become well known in his industry. He can strike up a conversation quickly and enjoys meeting new people.

Buddy has noticed that when he is with others who know him, some have encouraging and motivational behaviour. On meeting people Buddy doesn't know, the selected few introduce him with some positive words. "Do you know Buddy? I've known him for years. He is an expert on culture change and has helped me so much."

Introducing people to others with positive comments is such a powerful, relationship-building approach. It makes such a difference to the conversation. It is also a great way to compliment and encourage someone.

"How did that happen? Do you want a diagram?"

Buddy and Jess's first home in West Yorkshire was a rented two-bedroomed cottage in Luddenden Foot. When they saw the property in early September, it looked delightful, full of character, alongside a river and nested amongst other similar properties, all built with traditional West Yorkshire stone. Johnny Flaggs, the owner, seemed to be a nice guy on the surface. He made it clear that the Brambles were not allowed to have pets in the home. "We don't plan to have any gerbils, rabbits, or mice, so you are okay there," said Buddy.

Johnny checked their background and was delighted that Jess was a lawyer, which made him feel safe that they would not cause him any problems. He was encouraged that this young, pleasant, trustworthy, and professional couple would not break the rules or try and get out of the rental contract early.

The trustworthy types discussed how they would sneak their young Labrador Jimmy into the home without being caught. They decided that Johnny would never know as he could not enter the property without their permission. This was the least of their problems. It was late autumn. The cottage was a perfect place for evening and weekend relaxation. As the nights closed in and the cold winter winds took hold, it became clear why the monthly rental was so cheap. Johnny had told the Brambles that the thick stone walls ensured the home was always warm and didn't need any heating. It seemed like sanctimonious Johnny hadn't been so trustworthy himself. They decided early to buy their own place and accelerated their search. They never slept upstairs at this place as it was far too cold. They slept on a sofa bed with a hot water bottle each, dreaming of their own place. Four months later, they escaped from the contract early and moved into their home in Stainland.

Jess was working for a solicitor firm in Brighouse and was making quite an impression. They loved her work and were delighted that they had chosen her from the list of candidates. She was building her reputation as an engaging lawyer with an incisive line of questioning not dissimilar to Perry Mason on steroids. She made good relationships with other solicitors in the courtroom and became very popular. One Bradford solicitor Roy took a shine to Jess. They enjoyed their conversations. Roy was hilarious, and Jess looked forward to his banter. It was clear that Roy recognised her talent and confidence. This had the potential to become an excellent professional relationship.

Jess and Buddy were busy creating their new home and being a young couple in love. They were delighted when Jess became pregnant. There was a rosy glow on Jess's face as the pregnancy progressed. Jess let her employer know that she would need time off for the baby. The conversation did not go well. They responded very badly. "How did that happen?"

"Do you want a diagram?" said an agitated Jess. They made it clear that Jess being pregnant was not what they expected. Jess was newly married. What did they expect? In those days, newly married couples would soon have children. It was just the natural order of events.

From being the star pupil, Jess immediately became public enemy number one. Jess came home and was so annoyed. She had worked so hard. It was so unfair. They longed for a Labour government to put fairness back into a broken Britain.

The Brambles discussed the situation and agreed that she should stick it out until the baby was born. It wasn't easy. The atmosphere in the office was no longer so welcoming. A few weeks before she went on maternity leave, they dumped her, and told her that she would not return after the baby was born. When Jess was in the hospital recovering from the birth, she was surprised to receive flowers from an admirer. They were not from Buddy. He doesn't understand flowers. They were from Roy. It was clear that when Jess was ready, Roy was prepared to employ her. What a lovely gesture from a considerate man. Roy became an excellent friend to Jess over the years. Jess and Roy have a manner that can touch people with their eyes, smile, words, actions, and little surprises. It's a great emotionally intelligent skill to have. Jess is a natural at it.

Buddy has some of these attributes but is still developing this side of his character.

"Always do the right thing"

Grandma was such a lovely human being. She took care of everyone. She loved unconditionally. Put others' needs before her own. She was compassionate, forgiving, and thoughtful. She was Jess's best friend. There are just too many heartwarming stories to show her love for the people in her life. Here is one.

The Brambles were in the Alpujarra region of Spain on holiday. They had a villa on the southern slopes of the Sierra Nevada. It was on top of a hill with a pool. It was a perfect location. Grandma took it upon herself to help Alex learn to swim. She was so patient with him as she helped him build his confidence. She was in the water daily, encouraging Alex to kick his legs and move his arms. She was teaching him the front crawl. Slowly but surely, Alex was learning to swim. Near the holiday's end, he realised he could swim without armbands.

Grandma was calm, a great communicator. If anyone needed advice, she was always good to talk with. She always gave Buddy great advice. Her best advice. "Always do the right thing." Her perspective and considered opinion always shined a new light on conversations.

CHOOSE TO PRIORITISE EXPERIENTIAL LEARNING

Learning the lessons from life stories

Buddy can be relied upon to "be encouraging". His life has been focused on ensuring that everyone has the confidence to shine a little brighter. He has seen so many watchers achieve more than they had ever thought possible because they had the opportunity.

The following actions helped him to develop an experiential learning mindset and encourage others to make the most of their potential. To apply "be encouraging" in his life, he told himself to:

- Recognise and appreciate people so that they feel good and value themselves.
- Show interest and enthusiasm for goals of others to help improve their motivation.
- Provide specific and constructive comments to help others improve their contribution to life.
- Stimulate others to have groundbreaking goals and make the most of their potential.

Is the "be encouraging" habit important to you at this stage of your life? What actions might you be considering?

Learning to Be Encouraging

Consider your answers to these four questions below when learning to be encouraging. If being encouraging is important to you, then what actions might you consider and in what timescale?

- Am I making time for and encouraging others, focusing on their strengths?

- Am I regularly noticing and acting on the little things as they happen?

- Am I introducing others with a few chosen words that highlight their abilities?

- Am I touching people with my eyes, smile, words, actions, and little surprises?

CHOOSE TO PRIORITISE EXPERIENTIAL LEARNING

BE MOTIVATED

Being very enthusiastic or determined because you really want to do something

Be motivated – surround yourself with winners

Being motivated is a key learning habit and essential for growing potential beyond initial thoughts. It means having the drive and determination to deliver on our aspirations and to make the most of the experiences in front of us.

Motivation helps us to stay focused, to overcome obstacles, and to reach our full potential. Being motivated also helps us to be more productive, resilient, and optimistic.

Motivation can come from anywhere. It can be found in our passions, our goals, our relationships, in the small daily wins, and our life achievements.

Keep your focus on what you really want to achieve and surround yourself with winners and people that inspire you. These people will help you achieve.

Is "be motivated" a learning habit that you need to consider improving?

CHOOSE TO PRIORITISE EXPERIENTIAL LEARNING

"I want to be alive to see my grandchildren"

Jess never took exercise and food consumption seriously. Jess had a stressful job and would grab unhealthy food on the move. She would arrive home shattered after a day on her feet. Food and its impact on the body was never a priority discussion in the Bramble family. There were many occasions when Buddy and Jess tried the latest fad to lose weight. Some provided early benefits, but all did not offer the long-lasting change that Buddy and Jess wanted. Their weight happily bounced up and down as they consumed what they liked, when they liked. They were enjoying life and happily squeezing into clothes that were always too tight for anyone to mention.

In March 2020, the Covid epidemic allowed everyone to reassess their lifestyle. More and more doctors suggested that overweight people were more likely to die from Covid. The Brambles knew they had bodies that were out of shape and very attractive to any coronavirus that might be nearby. They discussed what actions they could take to become fit and lean machines. They both agreed that they would need to lose 20kg.

Buddy stumbled across the keto diet that seemed to have immediate early benefits. He bought the books and read up about the benefits. Literature suggests keto diets help people lose weight quickly, particularly around the abdominal cavity. This visceral fat is lodged around the organs and is associated with inflammation disorders. When Buddy noticed that a keto regime also reduced blood sugar and insulin levels, he began to see that a lifestyle change was possible. They both decided to combine weight loss habits with an increased focus on fitness. Before starting this journey, they discussed why they were doing it – knowing the answer to why would help to focus their mind while changing their habits. They were a motivated couple with a changed mindset.

Jess explained that she remembered her mum struggling to walk and unable to be involved in the grandchildren's entertainment. Buddy's mum was on the heavy side and rarely exercised. Jess said she didn't want to die early. "I want to be alive to see and play with my grandchildren." This gave Jess her purpose.

It took a full eight months for Jess and Buddy to change their habits. In January 2021, they combined the keto principles and walked up to 8km daily. As lockdown was coming to an end, they both joined a swim and gym club. This accelerated their fitness levels.

Jess was adamant that she would not want to use the health features on her Apple Watch. Buddy explained how the watch measured the progress as fitness improved. "That sort of motivation might work for you, but it doesn't work for me," said an assertive Jess.

Buddy explained the measurements. It shows the heart rate, the number of steps a day, the number of minutes of exercise, and the kilocalories used. Attempting to influence Jess's behaviour, Buddy used a form of nudge theory, "It is trendy. It's the next big thing. Everyone will have one soon." Buddy's nudge words were not moving Jess an inch. "It′s not for me," she said as she finished her small bowl of cauliflower cheese with extra double cream.

Eight months later, Buddy and Jess had hit their targets. They both felt so much better for it. They were not fit and lean machines but were healthy and very happy with their achievement.

Jess has made fitness and health a habit. She is in the zone and puts energy into her day. She continues to swim and walk daily. She now has a skin-tight wetsuit to help her stay warm as she glides through the wintery waters. Pretty groundbreaking behaviour change for Jess. Jess wanted to achieve. She was now relentless.

CHOOSE TO BE RELENTLESS

"I will get the motorhome back to you tonight"

Buddy and Jess travelled back from Andalucía in their motorhome, chatting, and singing along to their favourite numbers. After years of family holidays, Patrice and Alex were no longer with them. Millie, the Labrador, was sleeping at the back of the motorhome. Not a care in the world as they all travelled through the Spanish countryside, near Valdepeñas, south of Madrid. They knew this route well, having completed it so many times. They were on track to arrive in Santander for the ferry to Plymouth. Just outside Bailén Jess pulled in, and Buddy took over the driving.

Buddy noticed oil residue on the back of the motorhome window. He had seen this problem before. The same problem led to the breakdown at the Traveller site in France. Buddy said he needed to find a garage that repaired an oil filter in a Fiat Ducato engine. This engine detail flew over the head of Jess, who had never been keen on car maintenance. They were in the middle of Spain. It didn't look promising. Just as Buddy was suggesting how difficult it would be, he couldn't believe his luck when a sign indicated that there was such a garage. Fiat trucks looked perfect.

Buddy whipped out his Google Translate and built a productive relationship with the bloke from Fiat Trucks. Google

311

CHOOSE TO PRIORITISE EXPERIENTIAL LEARNING

Translate was perfect. The conversation flowed back and forth as they discussed the problem and the potential solution. Manuel explained that they manufactured trucks but did not repair them. He knew a man in Bailén who could help the "in a rush" travellers. He started to explain the directions to Rafael's place but could see that Buddy wasn't taking them in detail. Manuel jumped in his car, and the Brambles followed him as he drove to meet a young super fit Rafael. Manuel and Rafael looked at the motorhome to assess what needed to be done. Cool-dude Rafael whipped out his mobile and explained the next steps using Google Translate. He understood that Jess and Buddy were required to get to Santander and needed the job completed today. It was 5 pm. The cool dude explained that they did not have the part needed to complete the repair. The part was in Jaén, forty-five minutes away by car. Rafael said he would drive to Jaén, "I will get the part today, work on it this evening and get the motorhome back to you tonight."

Jess and Buddy were blown away by this response. Rafael realised they needed somewhere to stay and telephoned his girlfriend, Gabriela, who worked in a hotel. He took Buddy and Jess to the hotel and set off to Jaén. A few hours later, there was a knock on the door. Rafael had finished the job, and the motorhome was now ready. Manuel, Rafael, and Gabriela showed the best of Spain that late summer evening. They were motivated and could feel the impact of their behaviour on these travellers. Rafael, really, really wanted to achieve.

"I will get this book finished by Christmas"

In September 2022, Buddy was developing his thoughts around his habits, one hundred questions, and the challenges faced by watchers, achievers, learners, and winners in life.

He knew successful people make choices. They choose to be something. What were the habits that informed their actions? Could Buddy identify these habits from his own experience? Buddy spent hours thinking and capturing his thoughts. Buddy remembered the relevant Bramble stories that would help to explain the importance of developing consistent habits. He discussed it with Jess, who helped to recall the stories.

As the rough notes became more organised, Buddy began to think about the book's design in detail. Near the end of September, Buddy had completed the groundwork and was ready to start the actual writing of the book. He explained to Jess that he had set himself a challenge. "I will get this book finished by Christmas. It will make a lovely gift for Alex and Patrice."

CHOOSE TO PRIORITISE EXPERIENTIAL LEARNING

Buddy was driven, internally motivated, and was on his purpose. He was committed and focused. He could see what the book would look like and began "chapter one". He had a clear vision and created a plan to finish the draft by the middle of November, ready for printing in December. He was up early most days and used any discretionary time working on crafting the stories.

Buddy was in the zone and focused. He hopes this will be impactful, fun, and meaningful to read. Buddy wanted to achieve. The family edition of this book was completed and under the tree at Christmas.

"Have I been a good girl?"

The Brambles have had three Labrador dogs in their life. Jimmy, Lucy, and Millie. Jimmy was chosen as Jess felt sorry for him. He was the runt of the litter. He wasn't very bright. He wasn't very motivated to learn. He died far too early. Lucy had a good and happy life but died early from a brain condition.

Unlike the others, Millie was bred by a top breeder in Hertford. Buddy and Jess had high hopes that this little puppy would last longer and be easier to train. Millie's emotional intelligence, spirit, and ability to learn quickly made her a family favourite.

CHOOSE TO BE RELENTLESS

Millie was motivated in lots of ways. Her tail would wag furiously at the sight of a lead, knowing it was time to go out and experience a fun activity. She had moments where fear was the motivator, and the need to get to a safe place was paramount in her mind. She loved all sorts of fetching games. Sometimes, she needed just the opportunity to sleep on the couch next to family members. She was, of course, motivated by food and would sit for a biscuit for many minutes.

Feeling safe was always a security goal for Millie. Jess took her along the canal in Hertford when she was eighteen weeks old. This had become a regular walk for Millie; as always, she was full of youthful energy. Suddenly a swan appeared, and this spooked her. She ran at speed away from the scene and kept running. Jess called her, but safety was on Millie's mind. As Jess walked home, unable to find Millie, she was distraught. She was fifty metres from home. She noticed a commotion in the doorway of the local chemist. As she passed the chemist, she spotted a petrified Millie surrounded by strangers. Millie recognised Jess straight away. The little puppy had run two kilometres and was nearly home to the safety of her basket when these strangers captured her. Millie doesn't like strangers. Buddy was out with Millie the next afternoon, and a resident spotted them. She explained that yesterday his dog was waiting for cars to pass so she could cross the road. She was eighteen weeks and knew all about safety. Jess taught Millie to fetch and drop. This game could be played for many minutes. Millie loved it. It combined the fun element with the intelligence of drop and stay. Millie was just so energetic when she was motivated and in the zone. She always gave her best.

Millie had learnt all the skills you need to be a perfect pet. She mastered "sit" and "stay" quickly, was house-trained in days, and always returned to her basket on command. She was no trouble in the Bramble house and promptly followed the rules whenever she visited other homes. She had excellent eyesight and hearing. She learnt more words than many dogs and quickly linked certain words before an action. If Buddy ever said "biscuits" in any sentence, she would immediately expect a biscuit, especially at night.

Millie was not a fan of loud noises, fireworks, aeroplanes, helicopters, or lorries. There have been many occasions when Millie has been away from the house and decided, quite at random, she needed to get home. Once, during a thunderstorm in France, she ran home and found the Brambles motorhome amongst the others. She hid under the motorhome. Buddy had to crawl under it in running water to get her. Like every good family member, she always knew where the love and safety of home were. Whenever she ran home, on every occasion, she would be found sitting and waiting at the back door. The Brambles never lost her.

Millie is now twelve, and when she looks back on her life, she will be proud of what she has achieved. She has travelled thousands of miles in the back of the Brambles' motorhome and car. She has walked the beautiful countryside of the UK. She has puffed and panted her way through many Andalucían summers. She was never complaining. Happy to be with her pack.

Millie is now facing her biggest challenge. One that does not have a happy ending. She has given so much to the family, but now the end is near.

Ten months ago, the Brambles were told that Millie had very aggressive cancer and would die in the next four months. She might last six months, but very unlikely. So, she has more than achieved her groundbreaking goal. Prior to Christmas 2022, the Brambles decided to have a last holiday with Millie in Derbyshire. She walked ten kilometres every day. She showed no sign of any health problems. Amazingly, Millie made it to Christmas. The Brambles are very proud of what the little puppy achieved. As of March 2023, Millie is still alive and still walking ten kilometres every day.

CHOOSE TO PRIORITISE EXPERIENTIAL LEARNING

Learning the lessons from life stories

Buddy learnt early in life that motivation had to come from within himself. When he trusted himself and avoided the distractions of drainers, he made progress with his achievements in life. Buddy can be relied upon to "be motivated".

The following actions helped him to develop an experiential learning mindset and motivate others to make the most of their potential. To apply "be motivated" in his life, he told himself to:

- Take responsibility for your motivation, seeing the recognition of others as a bonus.
- Create a positive approach to your life, focusing on progress not perfection.
- Be around achievers, learners, and winners; minimise time with drainers.
- Be with supportive and motivated people who will help you achieve beyond your thoughts.

Is the "be motivated" habit important to you at this stage of your life? What actions might you be considering?

Learning to Be Motivated

Consider your answers to the four questions below when learning to be motivated. If being motivated is important to you, then what actions might you consider and in what timescale?

- Am I concentrating on my planned achievements and why they matter to me?

- Am I focused on hitting the day with energy and being in the zone?

- Am I proud of my achievements and belief in my abilities?

- Am I ensuring that what I do is impactful, fun, and meaningful?

CHOOSE TO PRIORITISE EXPERIENTIAL LEARNING

BE CHALLENGED

Something that needs great mental or physical effort to be done successfully

Be challenged – step outside your comfort zone

Being challenged is a key learning habit and essential to grow potential beyond initial thoughts. It means stepping out of the comfort of what you know, trying things, and taking on new and difficult tasks. When we are challenged, we are pushed to learn new skills, to think differently, and to grow as individuals.

Being challenged helps us to be more resilient, to be more creative, and to find new solutions.

Challenges are opportunities for growth, they help us develop new perspectives, and learn from doing – experiential learning. Look for challenges and don't be afraid to take them on. It's what Buddy did. It helped him to become the best version of himself.

Don't wait for opportunities to come to you, be proactive and make them happen.

Is "be challenged" a learning habit that you need to consider improving?

CHOOSE TO PRIORITISE EXPERIENTIAL LEARNING

"With no one around, it was so quiet and peaceful"

The Andalucían countryside and mountainous terrain are beautiful. The Brambles have driven to many popular spots, enjoying long days out with Millie and any visitors. Some of the best walks are in Alhaurín el Grande, a popular destination for the Brambles. Many cyclists and hikers think highly of Pico de Mijas.

Once when Alex visited, he decided to walk the Pico de Mijas. It's a beautiful hike, 1,150 metres above sea level, with magnificent views of Málaga and the Costa del Sol. Alex set off at 6.30 am and walked up and down, returning at 11.50 am. He was gushing about the views and the relaxing nature when at the top. With no one around, it was so quiet and peaceful, he explained. When Alex first did this walk, Buddy was not in good shape and struggled due to a knee problem and excessive weight.

A few years later, Alex and Buddy did the 20km hike together. For Buddy, this was a physical challenge. He had walked many kilometres before the hike to ensure he was fit enough. It is a very safe zigzag route up to the top of the mountain. It can be challenging to climb parts of the hill, but Buddy is determined.

Alex was kind enough to wait on the route as Buddy made his way to the top. The stunning views of the mountains were indeed worth making an effort for. A year ago, Buddy did the walk on his own. Breakfast at 9 am at the top was a moment in his memories. Taking time to reflect on the beauty of nature in complete silence was such an experience. Everyone should, if they can, do this hike at least once, just for the occasion.

"I want to walk 195km by the end of September"

Jess is a changed woman with a newfound determination to be fit. The habit of being healthy and continually mobile has taken over her life. She has always been very anti any measurement of any progress. When Buddy gave her his Apple iWatch and explained the features, she was dismissive about the impact this measurement would have on her life. "These measurements might work for some but not me," she explained.

Jess didn't know herself. A few weeks later, she quite suddenly became hooked on the measurements. She set her daily targets and measured her progress. Achieving move, exercise, and stand goals became her focus. She also added in daily swim targets. From being sat on the couch, she is now focused on achieving daily goals. The iWatch app also sets monthly

CHOOSE TO PRIORITISE EXPERIENTIAL LEARNING

targets for Jess to aim for. It's been quite a turnaround in attitude.

In September 2022, Buddy noticed Jess swimming daily and suggested they walk more together. She was like a woman possessed. There was an urgency in her need to get moving. "Why are we walking all the time?" asked Buddy, recovering from the latest 8km walk. The "these types of measurement don't work for me" woman explained that she had been given a target by her fitness app of walking 195km by the end of September. Jess was treating this very seriously. This target seemed physically challenging, as Jess swam for an hour a day. It was doubly hard as Buddy and Jess would be driving through Spain for three of the available days. This would mean Jess had to achieve the target in fewer days.

Jess focused her mind. "I want to walk 195km by the end of September," was her mantra. It was no surprise when relentless Jess achieved her challenging target.

Jess continues to encourage and lead on family exercise and is much happier about it.

CHOOSE TO BE RELENTLESS

"One man. One run. One minute less"

When Buddy was younger, he could quickly run 5k in thirty minutes. Between the ages of thirty and sixty, he did not treat exercise seriously, which showed in his expanding waistline and inability to run for a bus. Buddy was slowly turning into a fatty slob. He challenged himself to change his habits, and health became a focus.

Since January 2021, Buddy has focused more on walking and exercising at the gym. This helped him regain his shape, and he began to move confidently as he knew that 20kg of fatty waste had been removed from his previous bulky self.

In September 2022, Buddy set the challenging goal of running 5k in thirty minutes by the end of December. The plan was to use the 5.5km York run that the laddies, Alex and Patrice, used on their trips to see retired parents. The laddie run has often finished with Alex throwing up, as he pushed to run faster than his brother. Buddy's target was not to throw up anywhere. He was happy to complete it within his maximum heart rate. "Can I run 5k in thirty minutes?" was his challenge to himself.

At the end of September, Buddy decided to find his base time of running and walking the laddie run. So off he set. He wanted to run within himself and steadily meet the target over twelve weeks. He completed his first run in forty-one minutes. At no time in the last thirty years had Buddy run this far, this fast. It was a personal best for Buddy. He could do better, and he knew it.

He continued to push himself. Through a bit more running and less walking, he achieved the 5.5km in thirty-eight minutes a few weeks later. He has eight weeks to go to meet his target. Buddy and Jess are on a Caribbean holiday in November, so Buddy will have plenty of time to build his fitness levels. Practice and more practice to improve himself.

Knocking a further eight minutes off his best time will be challenging. He will need to reduce his running time by one minute, weekly. Buddy will focus and will measure his progress on the Sunday run. One Man. One run. One minute less. Buddy likes to be challenged. This will be groundbreaking when achieved. Buddy didn't hit this target due to his illness. He is looking at achieving it in 2023.

"I wouldn't think you will be able to finish the pond"

The Brambles settled into Luddenden Foot Chapel and could design the garden as they wanted. They knew they wanted a pond at the bottom of the garden. It would provide a feature when viewing out of the large overlooking window.

CHOOSE TO BE RELENTLESS

Buddy was delighted when the family decided to get involved in the design and development of the pond. Jess and Alex were keen on plants and flowers, while Patrice was interested in digging and types of fish. Patrice threw himself into the project and worked hard to help Buddy shape the pond. The diggers must have been halfway through when Jess suggested Buddy should go with her and buy some plants. As Buddy left to buy plants, he said to Patrice, "I wouldn't think you will be able to finish the pond while we are away, but do your best."

Patrice saw this as motivation. While the senior Brambles were away from the hard digging, Patrice took on the challenge. He must have worked so hard. When they returned, Buddy could see Patrice's head over the top of the pond. Patrice, not for the first time, proved Buddy wrong. The pond was ready for preparation and lining. Patrice wore socks to not damage the pond lining as he placed the plants into position on ledges and the pond floor. Overnight, water was added, and a few weeks later, fish were swimming happily in the creation. The pond was now a home for the goldfish and a place for quiet contemplation for the Brambles.

A few years later, Buddy added some tadpoles. It was an educational experience watching them grow and become frogs.

CHOOSE TO PRIORITISE EXPERIENTIAL LEARNING

The Brambles often found the frogs in the garden enjoying their days out from the pond. The frogs became confident as they moved around the garden, finding areas where they could relax and hide from Lucy, the Labrador who didn't like them.

Eventually, the frogs decided that it was safer if they hopped into the next-door neighbour's garden. This caused havoc for the neighbours. They found hundreds of frogs lying about on top of their drain cover. Every week neighbours made trips to the local river to dispose of them. Another time, Buddy and Patrice emptied the pond as it was overgrown. They found over fifty full-sized live frogs at the bottom of the pond.

Lovely childhood memories.

Learning the lessons from life stories

Buddy has faced many challenges in his life and knows that the "be challenged" habit was one that he needed to prioritise and improve. He enjoys the challenge of the new and the uncertainty of outcomes. He knows with this habit he is still learning.

The following actions helped him to be challenged, develop an experiential learning mindset, and encourage others to make the most of their potential. To apply "be challenged" in his life, he told himself to:

- Stretch yourself with new experiences. Be unafraid of learning or fearful of any failure.
- Ask others for their honest thoughts on how you could improve your behaviour or skills.
- Look for opportunities to take on new responsibilities to activate your potential.
- Review your achievements, learn from successes, and take action on improvements.

Is the "be challenged" habit important to you at this stage of your life? What actions might you be considering?

CHOOSE TO PRIORITISE EXPERIENTIAL LEARNING

Learning to Be Challenged

Consider your answers to these four questions below when learning to be challenged. If being challenged is important to you, then what actions might you consider and in what timescale?

- Am I looking beyond my fears and setting myself groundbreaking challenges?

- Am I focused on practice and more practice to improve myself?

- Am I reflecting on, measuring, and improving my achievements?

- Am I challenging and influencing others to make the most of their potential?

BE ACTIVELY LEARNING

Acquiring new understanding, knowledge, behaviours, skills, values, attitudes, and preferences because of actual experience

CHOOSE TO PRIORITISE EXPERIENTIAL LEARNING

Be actively learning – connect concepts with actions

Experiential learning is a powerful way to gain knowledge and skills; it means actively learning through direct experience and hands-on activities.

It helps us to understand and retain information better, it helps us to develop problem-solving skills and critical thinking, and it helps us to apply what we learn in real-world scenarios. Experiential learning also helps us to be more engaged, motivated, and inspired to learn, as it allows us to make connections between the concepts and the real-world of action. When practised consistently it can transform mental fitness and emotional well-being.

Learning is not just about acquiring knowledge; it's about applying it and using it to make a positive impact in your community or even the world. Buddy embraced experiential learning and created concepts that were applied in several industries with huge success. Applying experiential learning, in this world of continuous change, will help you achieve more than you ever thought possible.

Is "be actively learning" a learning habit that you need to consider improving?

"It wasn't my fault Alex didn't turn"

Grandad walked the boys to school for years. Alex and Patrice were able to learn so much from these conversations. As adults, they now have so many happy memories of their time with Grandad and Grandma. Grandma was someone they could always talk with, and she was always there for them, offering sound advice whenever guidance was needed.

The young Bramble boys made the regular trip to the muffin shop in Oldham with Grandma and Grandad. On these trips, they would play legs using pub names as legs. The highwayman, for example, would have two legs, while the coach and horses would have ten legs, the maximum allowed in this game. They made the trip so often that they knew who would win the game as they knew what pub was coming next.

Every evening Jess arrived home to share her day with Grandma and Grandad. This was like many others. They would chat about her day, and the young laddies would play outside. This was not going to be a typical day.

Patrice was teaching Alex how to ride a bike. Patrice was confident on a bike and was a good trainer. As Alex built his confidence, it was time to ride the bike down a hill. Patrice showed him the training area. It was a short grassy slope, with

CHOOSE TO PRIORITISE EXPERIENTIAL LEARNING

a wall at the bottom, and beyond it, a fast-flowing river. Patrice showed Alex what to do. Patrice went down the hill and turned left into the safe area to avoid the wall. Patrice explained this route to Alex. "You must turn at the bottom of the hill to avoid the wall," said Patrice.

Alex climbed onto the bike and looked down the slope. He was confident and set off. He picked up speed as he arrived at the turning point. "Turn now!" said an urgent Patrice. Alex didn't leave it too late to turn; he didn't turn at all. Alex hit the wall at speed. It was a bloody mess. He was lucky that he didn't go over the wall into the river. Patrice ran into Grandma and Grandad's house, "There´s a problem; Alex has been injured. It wasn't my fault Alex didn't turn." Alex appeared at the door with a blood-covered face. Grandma and Jess set off to the hospital. Alex had his first stitches that day. It could have been much worse. Alex doesn't like bike riding. He learnt that day to consider the risks in day-to-day life.

"The key questions. What, need and how"

Buddy has spent his life action learning and taking on challenges. He is known for using unique phrases and words in their application. His day-to-day life is built around the use of these three questions.

- What do I want to do?
- What do I need to do it?
- How do we do it?

Buddy has encouraged Alex and Patrice to use these questions to save time in life. The very best build these three questions into their daily life. Daily activities such as getting out of bed in the morning, making breakfast, going to work, visiting the gym, or making an evening meal all require some thought. Even arranging a night out, planning a holiday, or your longer-term future must be thought about. Subconsciously, we all ask these three questions in our daily life. They are routines that make life easier.

Whenever Buddy has skipped one of these questions or failed to think them through thoroughly, it's a recipe for disappointment, delay, or frustration. Only yesterday, Buddy forgot his mask as he set off for an appointment at the chemist for his Covid vaccination. If only he had asked, what do I need to enter the chemists? Luckily, home was only a five-minute walk away.

It would be best if you had an up-to-date passport to go on a foreign holiday. Nothing is more frustrating than arriving at the airport and finding that you can't make the trip as your passport is not valid. This hasn't happened to Buddy, but it did

CHOOSE TO PRIORITISE EXPERIENTIAL LEARNING

happen recently to Bryn, one of Buddy's close friends. Bryn had a lovely caring family, full of fun and frolics. They always showed consideration for others in their small Welsh village. Sadly, the family waved Bryn goodbye on this occasion, as they had no choice but to go ahead without him. He missed the few days of the holiday and the animated conversation of family life as he rushed around Liverpool to obtain a new passport. If only Bryn had asked himself, "What do I need to go on holiday?"

Jess and Buddy love travelling. Many destinations were often out of reach during their life due to a lack of money to meet their dream. Flying from London to Australia for a holiday was a dream. They could make this happen only later in their pre-retirement life. On many occasions, in their early adult life, they could only afford a two-week camping holiday in France and a few weekend trips in the year. Jess and Buddy knew that if they wanted to go to Australia in the future or anywhere further afield, they needed money to make that happen. The money would give them the freedom to choose. Cutting back has always been the watchword in the Bramble family as Buddy juggled his family's daily needs, the love of travelling, and the future.

Always travel with a spare car key is Buddy's advice. Many years ago, Buddy and his family travelled in their car to

Bournemouth for a short holiday. While there, the car key was lost. Buddy needed a spare car key, but it was at their home 150 miles away. Alex was prepared to hop on a return train journey to solve the problem. Since then, Buddy has always added a spare key to his "What do I need to go on holiday list?" Never again will this situation occur. Buddy found out later that Alex was more than happy to make the trip to collect the key. He didn't much like his elder brother's new girlfriend. As it happens, Patrice wasn't too keen either as a few weeks later girlfriend was dumped.

"I would like to point out that I have not lost it"

Throughout Buddy's adult life, he always has focused on action learning. Action learning has been key to his progress in life. He has learnt so much from experience. He has a habit of asking two questions of himself every day and taking action from his thoughts. He doesn't always share his thoughts or actions with others but works to keep improving. Asking and reflecting on these two questions is a good habit.

The two questions are:

- What has not gone well that I can improve?
- What has gone well that I can learn from?

CHOOSE TO PRIORITISE EXPERIENTIAL LEARNING

These daily reflections have been so useful to Buddy. They have become a regular routine for him. Buddy has nearly always put his best into his contributions to life. When he has failed, he acts, and moves on. When he succeeds, he learns, and progresses.

Only recently, Buddy was at the O'Shaughnessys and was enjoying a few glasses of strong scrumpy cider. At some point, someone decided that Crème de cassis would be a good liqueur to add to the cider. He had been on the keto low carbohydrate diet for a few weeks and joined in the festivities, as he always did. It wasn't long before Buddy realised that he was becoming disconnected from the reality of any situation. As the alcoholic content was taking hold, Buddy decided to take control before he "lost it. "

Buddy announced to Alex and Patrice, "I would like to point out that I have not lost it." It was clear to Alex, Patrice, and anyone within earshot that Buddy had lost it. Buddy meandered about for a few more moments moving from room to room in an internal state of distress. He soon realised that standing was not helping. He decided that just maybe he might have lost it. He needed to make a further announcement. "Good evening again," he began. "A few minutes ago, I indicated to you all that I had not lost it. I want to announce that I have, in fact, now lost it."

It wasn't even ten o'clock, but for Buddy, it was bedtime. He needed to be horizontal. Swaying from side to side and unable to put one foot in front of the other, he looked at the stairs. They looked beyond his capability. He didn't want to embarrass himself by falling on the stairs. Buddy decided it would be less embarrassing if he crawled up the stairs. In no time, he was soon on all fours. "Do you need any help?" asked Jess.

"No, I'm making good progress," as he crawled along the corridor to his bedroom.

Jess checked on him a few minutes later. Buddy had managed only to remove one shoe. He had crashed out. He was now lying on the bed sleeping. Buddy had lost it. This is an excellent example of a not-gone-well for Buddy. He was sixty-two and still learning.

"Problems. I´ve never seen so many maggots"

The Brambles were returning from a family holiday in the USA. It had been an enjoyable holiday seeing the best of the deep Southeast of the states. It was educational, exciting, and relaxing. As they were getting closer to their home in Hertford, Buddy knew that there was a problem that he had put into the back of his mind.

CHOOSE TO PRIORITISE EXPERIENTIAL LEARNING

Two weeks before they set off on their holiday Buddy had forgotten to empty the black bin, the one with all the bin juice and decaying food. It wasn't a problem as the next bin collection day was before they left for the holiday. "No need to worry or get agitated," said Buddy. "I will put the bin out."

Jess had made it very clear that he needed not to forget "some of the food in the bin was now four weeks old. There are already a few maggots, and we will not want to leave the bins in that state." Despite Jess emphasising the importance, Buddy forgot to empty the bins. He learnt the importance of creating lists of the things that needed doing.

They were flying to Washington, DC, and Jess asked if Buddy had put the bins out. "Yes, no problem. I've sorted it." said a confident Buddy. Buddy knew it hadn't been sorted. His response just made the atmosphere on the plane much easier as a relived Jess settled into her *Hello* magazine and the celebrity news.

So, the Brambles were now on the way home, discussing the holiday they had shared. Patrice was soon off to university, and Alex joined the local sixth-form college. They all had much to look forward to. Not Buddy. He was thinking bin juice, maggots, and flies. He wasn't sure what the scene would be, but he knew he would need to sort it quietly.

CHOOSE TO BE RELENTLESS

The family were upstairs sorting their bags. Buddy grabbed his chance and was at the door to the cellar. Down the steps was the TV room, and across from that door was another entry into the enclosed private alley. This alley was where the unemptied bins were. As Buddy opened the first door, about thirty flies flew out into the hallway. Buddy quickly shut the door. Problems!

The rest of the family were still upstairs. Buddy found killer fly spray and set off like an excitable rat catcher. The plan was to open the first door and start spraying, keeping the mouth closed, and not breathing. Buddy opened the door, quickly shutting it behind him, and moved down the stairs spraying but not breathing. He sprayed for thirty seconds and then went back upstairs to the safety of the hallway and fresh air.

Ten minutes later, Buddy went back to the scene. Good News. All the flies were on the red carpet, dead. Buddy didn't count the flies, but the carpet was now black. There must have been two thousand flies or possibly more. Buddy found the Dyson and set about picking up the flies. It didn't take long. It was a complex job flicking the flies from the furniture.

Buddy was making good progress in covering the error of his ways. Out of the blue, Patrice arrived. "Dad, what are you doing?" He was at the bottom of the stairs admiring the red carpet and dad's commitment to housework.

"There was a problem with a few flies, but I have sorted it out now," said Buddy in a reassuring voice. "Don't mention it to mum; she's not keen on flies," said Buddy. They went back upstairs and enjoyed a cup of tea with the family.

A few hours later, after the fly fuss had calmed down, Buddy opened the door into the alley. It was like a scene out of a horror movie where the maggots took over the house. The wriggly maggots were two centimetres thick on the floor of the alley. Problems! Buddy shut the door to find a shovel and a few black bags. Jess was having a bath upstairs. Alex was recovering from opening his bedroom door and finding a pigeon had decamped in there while they were away. Alex hates birds. That's another story.

Buddy called in Patrice explaining, "We have a big problem here." Buddy explained the situation and needed his help. Patrice wanted to look at the scene for himself. Giving it a second look, it looked much worse.

"What has happened here?" asked Patrice. Unhelpfully, he wondered if Mum knew about it.

CHOOSE TO BE RELENTLESS

"No, no. Mum doesn't know about it. I'll tell her later. Let's sort it out first," said Buddy.

It was a messy job scooping up wriggly maggots and putting them in the black bags. As each bag was full, they were tied tightly to stop the maggots from escaping. Six or seven black bags later, Buddy and Patrice had transferred most of the maggots and rotting food into new bags. There was an awful smell that wafted around the situation. This, indeed, was a horrible job.

Buddy was now disinfecting the floor of the alley and the bins. He opened another door of the alley into the main street of Hertford and swept the last remaining maggots into a drain outside. Job done.

Patrice and Alex thought it was hilarious. Jess was furious about the whole thing.

CHOOSE TO PRIORITISE EXPERIENTIAL LEARNING

Learning the lessons from life stories

Buddy was an expert in applying action learning techniques but was not learning enough himself. The "be actively learning" habit was one that he needed to prioritise as he moved around different industries.

The following actions helped him to develop an experiential learning mindset and encouraged others to make the most of their potential. To apply "be actively learning" in his life, he told himself to:

- Apply everyday what has and has not gone well to build in daily learning.
- Be learning all the time. Find opportunities to learn new skills and gain new knowledge.
- See experiences as an opportunity to learn rather than allowing them to play on the fearful mind.
- Build learning from your experiences into your routine.

Is the "be actively learning" habit important to you at this stage of your life? What actions might you be considering?

Learning to Be Actively Learning

Consider your answers to the four questions below when learning to be actively learning. If actively learning is important to you, then what actions might you consider and in what timescale?

- Am I using positive and negative experiences to drive my continual learning?

- Am I trusted to take specific action to improve my behaviour?

- Am I saying sorry when I get it wrong, and people see a noticeable change?

- Am I surrounded by supportive and motivating learning environments?

CHOOSE TO PRIORITISE EXPERIENTIAL LEARNING

CHOOSE TO PRIORITISE PROGRESS & PROSPERITY

What do you want out of life, now and in the future, in terms of the progress and prosperity you need to enjoy your life?

CHOOSE TO PRIORITISE PROGRESS & PROSPERITY

CHOOSE TO BE RELENTLESS

The Progress, Prosperity and Winning Habits

So, you have mastered many of the previous habits. The winners in life consistently apply the following six habits.

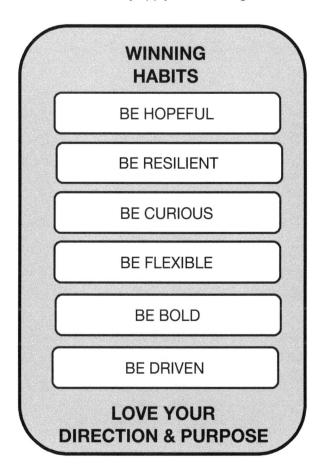

CHOOSE TO PRIORITISE PROGRESS & PROSPERITY

These winners have strong direction and purpose in their life. They are passionate and focused, often to the detriment of other habits. Buddy has been lucky enough to have met many winners in his life through his connections. Buddy has the approach of stepping forward and not back. Buddy stands up when others choose to sit down. He doesn't hide in the shadows of life.

These winning habits focus on people being inspired or optimistic about a future event. These winners recover quickly from setbacks or complex conditions. They always bounce back.

They are always eager to know or learn about new things. They adapt to changing situations as they occur. They are willing to be bold, courageous, and confident enough to take considered risks.

Winners fall in love with their plan. They are relentless in their goal, hard-working, and ambitious.

We can all learn from the winners. More could achieve beyond their initial thoughts with the right foundations and emotional support.

BE DRIVEN

Relentlessly compelled by the need to accomplish a goal, very hard-working and ambitious

CHOOSE TO PRIORITISE PROGRESS & PROSPERITY

Be driven – stay focused avoiding the distractions

Being driven is a key winning habit and essential for achieving groundbreaking goals beyond dreams. It means having a strong desire to succeed and to make the most of our abilities and opportunities. The winners are on this ground, full of purpose and direction.

Being driven helps us to stay focused, overcome obstacles, and reach our full potential. Being driven also helps us to be more productive, resilient, and optimistic. Winners avoid the distractions of the drainers – they just hold them back.

Winners know that motivation and drive come from within. It is the engine that fuels their ambition and desire to achieve.

Buddy kept his focus on what he wanted to achieve and always looked to improve himself. From a challenging start in life, he is content with the contribution he has made to the lives of many.

Is "be driven" a winning habit that you need to consider improving?

CHOOSE TO BE RELENTLESS

"It hit him in the face. There was blood"

Grandad was a very driven individual. Being the best and winning was important to him. It didn't matter your age. Grandad always competed to be at the top of any table.

Grandad was an excellent cricketer and used this knowledge to help Patrice become a high-scoring opening batsman and a good bowler. Grandad spent many hours assisting Patrice in perfecting his technique. Buddy would often come home and become involved in a cricket challenge. Grandad set up a cricket pitch for these everyday moments. Buddy did his best but was never good enough to defeat Grandad.

On one occasion, a six-year-old Patrice joined in as an additional fielder. He was doing very well, stopping certain fours from racing to the boundary. Patrice was enjoying it so much. Near the end of one game, Grandad mishit a cover drive, and the ball went high into the air towards Patrice. Patrice ran forward, watching the ball. There was a chance to catch the ball, and super Grandad would be out. The ball took ages to fall into Patrice's hand. Patrice stood there as the ball was coming towards him. Buddy was concerned that the ball might land on his head. Grandad looked on at the embarrassment of being potentially caught out by a primary school kid. Patrice cupped his hands and looked up for a memorable catch. He could visualise the achievement and be ready to celebrate. They all waited as the ball dropped into the little boy's area of the field. It was not a happy ending. Patrice missed the catch. The ball bounced just in front of him. Grandad lived to fight another day. Patrice was not so lucky. The rock-hard cricket ball was still in motion. After hitting the ground, it bounced up and hit Patrice in his eye. Game Over. Patrice had a black eye. Jess was furious that the grown-ups had allowed it to happen.

Just outside Grandad's house was another perfect area for cricket. The lawn was fantastic for quick games. It was alongside a river, so there were many occasions when Buddy was splashing about retrieving the ball after another wayward shot. If the ball went into the river, you were out. Buddy had a winning mentality and would work hard to bowl Grandad out, but it wasn't easy.

Alex rarely played cricket. He preferred playing quietly on his own in the sandpit. The sandpit was in another part of the garden, vaguely positioned at short third man. Buddy thundered in at speed, knowing that his best efforts could get Grandad out. On this occasion, it was not his best effort. The ball was wide, vast. Perfect length, but now the ball was on its way, at speed, towards the third man. The ball was just about to hit Alex on his head full on. Buddy could see the whole situation. If he called and Alex turned, Alex would be struck straight in the face. Time stood still as Buddy watched. Just as the ball was about to hit Alex, he leant forward to pick up a spade, and the ball flew past. Phew. Cricket came to an end that night. Jess was furious about that as well.

The Bramble family were on holiday in Austria. There was a table tennis table at the holiday cottage. Competitive Grandad loved table tennis. Patrice was challenged to a game. Grandad did not give an inch to the six-year-old Patrice. As defeat was near, Patrice was annoyed that he had lost again. He threw the bat at Grandad. The bat moved through the air at speed. Grandad saw it too late. It hit him in the face. There was blood. Patrice was embarrassed. He needed to learn to lose without resorting to anger.

"I'll chop your bollocks off"

The millennium was an exciting period to be alive, as there was so much hope for the future. We were at the beginning of a revolution in mobile and digital communication. One of the companies in the UK had a vacancy for a culture change expert.

Buddy was approached by the customer service director, Simon, to bring the company's values alive in front of customers. There was a view that the contact centre teams were not emotionally engaging with their customers. Simon wanted Buddy to use his solutions to help them differentiate the business.

Buddy joined the business in January 2000 as an interim manager responsible for the customer experience. He would be working with the senior management team across all the sites in the UK. It was an exciting opportunity. Buddy became very driven to succeed. He was a popular team member and very quickly made an impact with his unique ways of working.

It was clear early on that one of the senior managers, June, responsible for the consumer division, was not so keen on Buddy and his engaging ways. She avoided meeting Buddy and actively encouraged some of her team not to give Buddy any support. This game-playing was out of his control. Buddy made sure he was not distracted and concentrated on making a difference. June underestimated the power of a driven individual fired up with purpose.

Buddy worked with a pilot team in Durham and created a report that measured the results before and after his work. He measured employee engagement, customer satisfaction, and customer churn. In a short time, the pilot team proved that his methods would work. All the measurements were moving in a positive direction. Other groups wanted to use the techniques. June was busily trying to control Buddy while he was building relationships and making an impact. Soon Simon would pop by and add his motivational comments to the team effort. He indicated that he wanted this trial expanded across all UK sites.

Eventually, June called Buddy into her office. She made it clear that any new work he proposed must be shown to her before implementation. This was not to assist. This was to stop the momentum of the work from taking over her controlling methods. It was a very uncomfortable meeting. Buddy listened to understand her management style and could see why she was not popular.

June was uninspiring and full of conditional leadership. As the meeting ended, Buddy stood up and thought about his next step. He certainly knew he would need to tell Simon about this in his meeting with him later that week. As he turned to say goodbye, June appeared close to his face. "If you tell Simon about this meeting or bad-mouth me, I will chop your bollocks off."

"Okay, I'll bear that in mind," said a startled Buddy, unsure what to say. Buddy knew he would be telling Simon despite concern for his reproductive organs. Buddy had never been spoken to like that. He wasn't distracted by the threat; he just focused on the visual picture he had in his head of the future customer experience. He also thought how difficult it must be to be managed by someone with so much anger in their life.

A few days later, Buddy told Simon all about it. Simon motivated Buddy, saying he loved what he was doing, and so did many of the team. "Please carry on, and I will manage June," said Simon. Buddy worked successfully across all five sites for three years.

Buddy learnt the importance of having a senior sponsor when implementing change. A few years later, Buddy had a vasectomy; luckily, June was not in the operating theatre.

"Always a delight to return home"

Buddy was constantly tormented by the choices he made in his working life. His determination to do well and be successful meant he was often away from his home life. He was energised by the impact of his management style on the people within his work teams. He knows that he had a positive impact on so many people. Buddy put so much emotional energy into ensuring that individuals in his groups had the opportunity to make the most of their potential. He was driven and cared about making work life better.

Just when Buddy's career took off, a young family arrived. It is always a challenging time to ensure the work-life balance is correct. Like all successful people, sacrifices were made in his relationships.

It was always a delight for Buddy when he returned home at the weekends to see the love of his family. Jess, Alex, and Patrice shared Buddy with thousands. Their passion gave him the confidence to aim high and be ambitious. Buddy wasn't always around during the week but was always involved in holidays and family entertainment. Buddy's absence from daily life could have affected his children's progress in life. Buddy hoped it didn't.

It was so reassuring and emotional when in October 2022, Alex and Patrice said Buddy had been a great dad. "You have been motivating and gave us the passion to achieve in life." They went further and said, "Mum and you were great parents. You have always been there for us. We have so many happy memories of our time together." Clearly, Buddy and Jess achieved the right balance.

Buddy and Jess are so proud of Alex and Patrice. Watching them develop has been so rewarding. As responsible adults, they are making their way in life. Both different. Both talented.

Both still find reasons to be with Buddy and Jess. The Brambles are always at their happiest together.

"It's time to play the cherry game"

Christmas was always an enjoyable time with the Brambles and the extended family. When Alex and Patrice were younger, they were introduced to the Christmas games championship. A league table showing who was top and who was bottom. It was competitive throughout the holiday period. To some, it wasn't just taking part, winning mattered.

When the laddies were at junior school, the Brambles lived at Brig Royd. The conservatory was like Santa's grotto, covered in red berries and Christmas decorations. At night it looked spectacular. The Christmas games included monopoly, Connect 4, Jenga, Hungry Hippos and pick-up sticks. Simple games that everyone enjoyed. It was a long time ago, but Grandad probably won.

The Brambles moved to Luddenden Foot Chapel, and the red berries joined them. As a former chapel, this was a perfect place for Christmas. Buddy purchased some dancing white snowmen. The dancing was activated whenever anyone walked by the snowmen. Always popular with any younger ones that popped by.

CHOOSE TO BE RELENTLESS

Alex and Patrice were now at senior school, and so the intelligence of the games became more adult. Hungry Hippos and pick-up sticks were out, and cerebral games were in. Articulate, Cranium, and Trivial Pursuit were consistently popular, as was Psychologizer, an embarrassing game of life dilemmas. There was still space for Alex's favourites, Monopoly and Jenga. In the Chapel was a pool table that doubled as a table tennis table, and these games became part of the championship. In their other homes, as the family became young adults, other games such as crab football, indoor cricket, beer pong, and penalty kings were added. The winning was equally distributed around the family. Many felt the joy of being the best as they looked down on the disheartened family members who had fallen short. Buddy always did his best but never felt the pleasure of being top of the table.

One game always goes down well with Buddy, Alex, and Patrice. The chewing cherries game. Each player chooses three sweet Picota cherries from the Valle de Jerte region of Spain. The winner is the player who gobbles the three cherries with cleanliness. The game finishes with players looking at their cherry stones to assess cleanliness. Alex does his best. Patrice tries hard but laughs too much at the stupidity of the game. Laughing and chewing is not a good combination if you want to be a winner. Buddy was good at the cherries game. He always won. Sadly, for Buddy, it was never selected as a suitable game for the championship. It never appeared in the Christmas list of games. It was just a thing to pass the time between the serious business of being driven to win.

Learning the lessons from life stories

Buddy is a driven character with lots of vigour when fired up with purpose. He is rarely distracted and can easily bring people with him on the journey. "Be driven" is a dependable habit for Buddy.

The following actions helped Buddy to be driven, develop his character, and build the prosperity to enjoy his life on his terms. To apply "be driven" in his life, he told himself to:

- Know why you want to achieve, take responsibility, and avoid any distractions.
- Know what you want to achieve, what it looks like, and the measures of success.
- Create a plan to achieve, identifying the important steps to take and make a start.
- Identify the people who will encourage and guide you through any setbacks.

Is the "be driven" habit important to you at this stage of your life? What actions might you be considering?

Learning to Be Driven

Consider your answers to the four questions below when learning to be driven. If being driven is important to you, then what actions might you consider and in what timescale?

- Am I focused on not being distracted by events outside my control?

- Am I visualising the goal (I can, I will, I am) with a belief that I can achieve it?

- Am I climbing every mountain, achieving milestones, with a winning mentality?

- Am I focused on acquiring the capability to achieve what I want?

BE BOLD

Being able to show a willingness to take risks, confidence, and courageous

CHOOSE TO PRIORITISE PROGRESS & PROSPERITY

Be bold – spot the opportunities, consider, and act

Being bold is a key winning habit and essential for achieving groundbreaking goals beyond dreams. It means being willing to take considered risks, to step out of our comfort zone, and to try new things. The winners in life are regularly on this ground, full of purpose and direction.

Being bold helps us to pursue our passions, be more creative, and make the most of our potential. Being bold also helps us to be more resilient, be more adaptable, and find new solutions. Remember, life is short, and opportunities can be limited. Being bold allows us to make the most of them. Stand up. Be noticed.

Buddy wasn't afraid to take risks and to try totally new things. It's the way he discovered what he was truly capable of. Embrace your courage, be bold and make your mark in your part of the world.

Is "be bold" a winning habit that you need to consider improving?

"Please don't do it, he´s only eleven months old"

There was a period when the Brambles would often holiday in Italy. They loved the drive there, the friendliness of the Italians, the food made with so much love, the beautiful lakes and mountains, the magnificent scenery, the history, the coffee, and the wine. The reasons to love Italy are numerous.

In 1993, the Brambles were in Tuscany. They walked around a town full of cobblestone streets, reminding them of the historical nature of 15th-century street surfaces. They were outside an ice cream shop, looking at the numerous flavours of ice cream. Grandad's favourite was mint choc chip, Jess liked tutti frutti, and Buddy loved rum and raisin flavour. There was such a choice. Grandma looked at the flavours and went with the safe option, "I will have vanilla."

Alex was not born yet, but as an aside, Alex was not allowed ice cream in cornets. He just took too long looking at the shape of the ice cream allowing the melting ice cream to trickle over his hand. On far too many occasions, Buddy had to intervene with, "Alexander, get licking. The ice cream will go in the bin if you don't start licking." On one occasion, the ice cream was dribbling all over his Mickey Mouse sweatshirt. Alex was always a strong-willed and determined character. Once outside Disneyland in Paris, Alex insisted on wearing this sweatshirt even though it was thirty-three degrees.

They arrived at the top of the town and in front of them was a cobblestone hill. Grandad was already halfway down the hill admiring the ancient Roman architecture of the Renaissance period. He was sure to tell them later more about the mathematically precise ratios of height and width combined with symmetry, proportion, and harmony of the period. This history lesson would need to wait.

Patrice was sitting in his buggy, too tired to walk anymore. Buddy could see an opportunity that might be fun. Buddy always trusted his judgements when making decisions, but, on this occasion, he fell short. He could see Grandad fifty metres ahead. It was a cobblestone hill but flat with few bumps in the road. He asked Patrice if he would like to go on a ride towards Grandad in the buggy. The young Patrice said, "yes" straight away. A laddie with no fear. Buddy set the buggy wheels so that they would stay straight. Grandad was ready. Patrice was ready. Buddy was all set.

"What are you doing?" asked Jess pulling away from a conversation about pilgrims and churches with Grandma.

"We are having some fun. Patrice is going on a ride towards Grandad."

"Please don't do it; he's only eleven months old," pleaded an increasingly agitated Jess. Buddy assessed the risk – it looked safe. Jess assessed the risk, and it didn't look safe. It was a daft thing to do, but Buddy's decision-making was questionable that day in the hot sun.

As the sugar rush of the ice cream took over Buddy's brain, the buggy was off and was moving at speed down the hill. Patrice was screaming. The Italian mammas were looking on at the stupidity. Holidaymakers stopped looking at the architecture and were focused on the present day. Grandma was shaking her head, and Jess was shouting. It was a lively scene. Grandad had his hands out, ready to stop the buggy as it raced towards him. Jess looked at Buddy, "You are so stupid sometimes." It was over in seconds. Before Jess had time to get into the full-on angry mode, the buggy was safe with Grandad. He turned the buggy around. The only happy person was Patrice, who loved the whole experience. Buddy was bold but also lucky. It was a hazardous thing to do.

CHOOSE TO PRIORITISE PROGRESS & PROSPERITY

"My partner recommended you"

At one company, Buddy met many interesting people who were inspiring and fun to work with. He had a short meeting with an Australian guy called Hogan, who had been called in to add value to the customer experience team. Buddy was pleasant and built a professional relationship with someone he was unlikely to meet again.

During periods of unemployment Buddy had several opportunities but sometimes fell short at the final interview. In one discussion, his preparation involved dropping curry sauce onto the sleeve of his freshly ironed white shirt. He didn't take his jacket off in the interview. Not surprisingly, he didn't get that job.

Buddy was home in Luddenden Foot at the end of a week, where opportunities were drying up. He answered his phone and spoke with Denise, a customer sales director. She explained how she was looking for someone to work with her management team. She wanted someone different. Someone Bold. Someone who would help them differentiate. She explained, "My partner Hogan worked with you and recommended you. He says you are a great guy. Are you free to meet my team next week?"

CHOOSE TO BE RELENTLESS

That day Buddy realised the importance of building relationships with as many people as possible. His brief chat with Hogan gave him eighteen months of exciting work in West London and Europe.

"What are you doing? Why is Patrice up there?"

Buddy is bold but doesn't like heights. It's not the height. It's the fear of falling. When the Brambles moved into Luddenden Foot Chapel, there were always challenges, as the ceilings and ledges surrounding the sitting room were always out of reach.

On one occasion, the internet cable had become disconnected from the main socket. The central socket was on the far side of a high ledge. The only way anyone could reach the socket was to crawl along the ledge. It was a drop of three metres onto a hard wooden floor. The ledge width was relatively small and certainly smaller than the width of Buddy. There were also concerns about Buddy's weight on the ledge. Only one person could help – the fearless bold Patrice, who had recovered from the Italian buggy ride.

Buddy discussed the problem with Patrice, who was now a lot older and not so easily led by his dad's plans. "So, what you are saying is that you want someone to crawl very carefully

371

along a ledge with a cable, connect it, and then crawl back along the ledge, backwards without falling," said Patrice.

"Yes, that's about it. I thought that someone might be you," explained Buddy.

Patrice asked, "Have you thought about a ladder or finding an expert to help you?"

"A ladder is too expensive. It's not a job for an expert. We need someone light who can crawl along a ledge. You are light and can crawl."

"Looks like it's me then," said Patrice. "Where will you be?"

"I will wait at the bottom and catch you if you fall."

"I won't fall," said a confident and courageous Patrice. Very carefully, Patrice inched along sliding to maximise the load distribution on a ledge that had not been weight tested. All was going well. Calmly and bravely, Patrice made steady progress.

He was nearly at the cable connection point when they both were distracted, "What are you doing? Why is Patrice up there?"

It was Jess who had arrived to add extra stress where none was required. She had perfected worst-case-scenario thinking. By now, she had already envisaged a future where Patrice was on the floor with a broken rib or two. "It's not as bad as it looks," explained Buddy. Patrice must connect the cable and slide back along the ledge to safety. Patrice connected the cable and was ready to slide back.

"Would it be easier if I turned around?" asked Patrice. Jess was looking at a situation where her son contemplated turning around in a space where there was no space to turn.

"You will need to slide back along," said Jess.

"Be very careful, Patrice," said Jess as she looked up at the scene while shaking her head at Buddy. Patrice remained calm and relaxed on the ledge as he moved back to the safety of the flat ground. He was a bold and brave lad that day. No one was injured, and the internet connection was working. Family life right there.

"They went for a short holiday and bought a home"

The Brambles loved holidays together. There was so much to see. They rarely went to the same place twice. This was all about to change in the unlikely destination of Harrogate, North

CHOOSE TO PRIORITISE PROGRESS & PROSPERITY

Yorkshire. Buddy and Jess had just finished their afternoon tea at Bettys, the famous tearoom, and were walking towards the convention centre.

As they arrived at the convention centre, Jess noticed a Spanish holiday exhibition. So, in they went to wander about to fill some time. Thirty minutes later, they wandered out, having secured a free weekend to Andalucía to see a holiday home. Buddy had parted with a refundable thousand pounds, and the Brambles were off to sunny Spain for a free weekend. How did that happen?

Six weeks later, Buddy, Jess, Alex, and Patrice were in Alhaurín el Grande looking at plans for an unbuilt property on a piece of land 15km from the coast of southern Spain. This was just a free holiday, so there was nothing to worry about for Buddy, who was concerned about how he might get their money back. They would fly home tomorrow knowing more about a region they had only just visited.

When the Brambles set off from Manchester, there was never any intention of buying a property. They hadn't met Sarah yet. The estate agent listened, understood the Brambles' requirements, and matched their needs. She very expertly made an emotional connection with Buddy and Jess. She quickly manoeuvred her conversation away from the beach and the Costa del Sol benefits onto the countryside, mountains, and history. She blathered about charming white villages, cultural heritage, healthy living, round-the-year sunshine, and cheap weekend flights from the UK. She took the Brambles to Malaga to entice them into their decision.

On the Saturday night, Buddy and Jess spoke about what they had heard. The house looked perfect for them. The area was much better than they expected. They came for a short holiday and decided to buy a home. Quite unbelievable. They met Sarah and told her they were happy to proceed. It was a risk, but they seized the opportunity.

The Brambles have had sixteen happy years at the property. They were so bold in this decision.

CHOOSE TO PRIORITISE PROGRESS & PROSPERITY

Learning the lessons from life stories

Throughout his life, Buddy has made bold decisions as he reached out for the opportunities that the digital age presented. Being bold has given Alex and Patrice a life so much better than Buddy's sad start in life. Buddy is consistently bold.

The following actions helped Buddy to be bold, develop his character, and build the prosperity to enjoy his life on his terms. To apply "be bold" in his life, he told himself to:

- Take considered risks to make the most of your potential and the opportunities you see.
- Challenge your limiting thoughts; try new approaches not allowing fear to hold you back.
- Speak up: Share your ideas and opinions, even if they may be different from those of others.
- Believe in your abilities; however, seek advice and guidance from a supportive network.

Is the "be bold" habit important to you at this stage of your life? What actions might you be considering?

Learning to Be Bold

Consider your answers to the four questions below when learning to be bold. If being bold is important to you, then what actions might you consider and in what timescale?

- Am I fixated on knowing that at the end of each day I gave it my best?

- Am I trusting my own judgements when I am making decisions?

- Am I taking considered risk as I reach out to seize the opportunities?

- Am I building relationships with as many interesting people as possible?

CHOOSE TO PRIORITISE PROGRESS & PROSPERITY

BE FLEXIBLE

Being able to change easily and adapt to different conditions and circumstances as they occur

Be flexible – learn to adapt to the surprises in life

Being flexible is a key winning habit and essential for achieving the groundbreaking goals beyond dreams. It means being able to adapt to new situations, to change course when necessary, and to embrace new opportunities. The ground of winners, full of purpose and direction.

Being flexible helps us to be more resilient, more open to new experiences, and find new solutions. Being flexible also helps us to be more efficient and effective in our work, it helps us to manage our time and energy more effectively, and it helps us to build stronger relationships.

Buddy knows only too well that life is full of surprises. Being flexible allowed him to navigate through them with ease.

Being flexible will help you to be more successful, fulfilled, and happy in all aspects of your life.

Is "be flexible" a winning habit that you need to consider improving?

CHOOSE TO PRIORITISE PROGRESS & PROSPERITY

"I´ll slit your throat"

Buddy has learnt to adapt to many different circumstances in his life. In his sixty-three years, he has faced a few near-death experiences. Many have involved driving, while others have been more direct and in his face.

Buddy was waiting at King's Cross to meet a work colleague for an evening meal before jumping on the train north. It was a busy scene with commuters running around to catch their trains. Lovers were embracing one another as they met again. Others were waiting for their train to be announced. It was a typical scene.

Running and embracing seemed more purposeful than waiting, especially for Buddy, when out of the blue, a dishevelled guy appeared in front of him. How Buddy wished he was one of those running. Dishevelled didn't look like a guy that had been embraced recently. Before Buddy could move away, Dishevelled moved in closer and whipped out a knife and stuck it near Buddy´s throat. Flexibility and choice were no longer an option.

"If you don´t give me some money, I´ll slit your throat." Buddy had to think with his feet fixed firmly to the floor. In those short few moments, Buddy was out of his comfort zone. He had

CHOOSE TO BE RELENTLESS

never been threatened in this way. It was a new situation. He had to think quickly and act spontaneously.

Sensible people may have reached for the money, but Buddy decided on a different course of action for some reason. As Dishevelled waited to see what Buddy would do, he could see Buddy's mind working overtime. Blood surged into Buddy's brain to maximise his decision-making.

It was all over in a flash. Buddy looked at Dishevelled and said, "No, I'm not giving you any money" Dishevelled didn't know what to do in this situation. He would now need to slit Buddy's throat or do something else. There was a nervous moment when the emotions were high on both sides. Buddy thought maybe money was the answer, but it was too late. Dishevelled had already decided his next action. Dishevelled looked at Buddy, opened his mouth, and said, "Fuck You."

Dishevelled took away the knife and walked off to terrorise his neighbourhood. Buddy was shaking at the delayed response. A few moments later, the Police picked up Dishevelled and took him away.

Buddy was spontaneous and stupid on that day. He should have been flexible and not allowed emotion to influence his decision making.

CHOOSE TO PRIORITISE PROGRESS & PROSPERITY

"I have some bad news for you"

In 1988, Buddy and Jess had been back together for a few months and decided to take a holiday in Turkey. A few months earlier, Buddy's sister Joanne had been flexible, given up her hairdressing job in Middleton and joined a tour company as a tour representative. Joanne was based in Rhodes, so it would be easy for Buddy and Jess to visit her while on their holiday. Buddy's other sister Susan, her husband, and her children would be in Rhodes simultaneously. Buddy and Jess thought it would be good to tell them all that Buddy and Jess were back together again, this time forever.

So, Buddy and Jess set off on the one-hour ferry from Marmaris to Rhodes. It was an early morning boat. They arrived at 11 am and found their way to the hotel. They planned to meet Joanne at lunchtime and were looking forward to a family meal in the evening. They arrived in reception and waited for Joanne's happy face to appear at any moment. She was an enthusiastic, driven young girl who would stand out as she walked into reception. They waited, but there was no sign of her.

Buddy went to reception. He explained the situation, who he was, and that he was there to meet his sister. Did they know how he could get in touch with her? Oddly, after a short conversation, Athena arrived and said that Buddy would need to ring his mother in the UK. This was a time before mobile phones were in consumers' hands, so there was no way for anyone to contact Buddy and Jess while on the move. Buddy thought this request was odd but wasn't prepared for what he heard. Doris answered, "Hello, Buddy; I have bad news for you. Joanne is dead." Buddy broke down and cried, as this was such a shock. Jess took over the call.

It seemed there had been an accident the day before. Joanne had died on her moped after being hit by a car. Athena, the manager at the hotel, and the holiday company were so flexible, compassionate and helpful to Jess and Buddy on that day. They allowed them free use of the hotel while they waited for a flight home. A distressed young Greek boy came over to them. He explained in perfect English how upset he was. Joanne was a lovely young person. Susan and her family had already flown home. A few hours later, Jess and Buddy caught the flight to Athens and the trip back to Heathrow. Buddy thought how awful it would be to lose a son or daughter this way. How would Doris and Jack react to this shock?

Within four hours Buddy and Jess were at Doris and Jack's house. Jack was quiet. Very quiet. Doris was very matter of fact as she spoke. She showed no emotion as she explained what she knew. Susan and her family had just had a meal with

Joanne. They were all waving her goodbye, and she was hit by a car as she set off on her moped. All of them, including the three young children, saw the incident. Susan rushed to Joanne. She encouraged her to hold on for the ambulance to arrive. Joanne was too severely injured. She died in Susan's arms. She was only twenty-one. In a family with little love, Susan and Joanne loved one another. Buddy knows that his elder sister never recovered from losing her sister in that way. She didn't cope. She was distraught for years. Buddy cried. Buddy saw his father cry. His mother, Doris, never cried. Just so, so sad.

"Should your car be rolling backwards?"

Travelling through France over the last thirty years has been a regular occurrence for Buddy and Jess. Many times, with Patrice and Alex. Sometimes on their own and sometimes with the broader family group. Once, they were in rural France when they were joined by Jess's brother Daniel and his family.

They often decided that a family picnic would be a good idea as they travelled from place to place. They stocked baguettes, Camembert, Roquefort, ham, and drinks. They pulled off the road in the Rhône Valley, famous for the Châteauneuf-du-Pap appellation, and set up the camping spot. All was going well as they sat amongst the vineyards enjoying family time and the views.

Just as Buddy bit into a fresh baguette, Daniel said very calmly, "Should your car be rolling backwards?" Buddy looked around and saw that the vehicle was indeed moving back. Daniel was relaxed, highlighting what he could see. The car was twenty metres from the road, and beyond that, a sharp drop into the valley below. With a full mouth of baguette and Camembert, Buddy jumped up and flexibly responded quickly to this situation. He ran at speed towards the vehicle ten metres away, unsure if he would get there in time.

It was touch and go as Buddy ran to get alongside the moving vehicle. He grabbed the wing mirror and held on as the car moved backwards. Buddy knew that there might be a time when he would need to let go. He was sure he had no intention of holding on to a vehicle about to drop into the valley below.

As he became concerned that his efforts were to no avail, the vehicle started to slow. Buddy brought the vehicle to a stop five metres from the road. He went inside the car and put the handbrake on. Panic over.

CHOOSE TO PRIORITISE PROGRESS & PROSPERITY

"I want to give your sons a better start in life"

Buddy continued to visit his mother and father in Middleton as they entered the final stages of their life. Jack looked after Doris for years as she struggled with vascular dementia. When Doris died, Jack found a new lease of life and flexibly threw all his enthusiasm into his fitness. He walked every day and ate healthily.

On one of Buddy's visits, Jack explained how bad he felt about how Buddy was treated when he was younger. He said that Doris and himself were proud of what Buddy had achieved. "You have a lovely, kind wife, and a thoughtful couple of children. You made your life a success, and it's great that you have done so well."

Jack then started talking about his will and asked Buddy if Jess and himself would be executors. Jack explained, "I want to give your sons a better start in life than we gave you. Your mother and I agreed that we should split the inheritance three ways between you, Patrice, and Alex. We know they will spend it wisely. You must be so proud of them."

In his final years, Jack became unsteady on his feet, his hearing was deteriorating, and his sight was causing him many problems. A set of private guys employed by the local authority arrived to assess Jack's capability. Their methods were designed to prove that Jack did need private home help.

After the six-weeks assessment, it was no surprise when they suggested that Jack needed medical visits three times a day. Jack's financial situation meant that he would be paying for this help. After they left the property, Jack, a keen supporter of the NHS, said to Buddy, "There is no way that I am paying any money to a private concern. I will find a way to ensure this doesn't happen." They were the last words that his dad said to Buddy.

Within two days, Jack was rushed into hospital with liver disease. The doctor phoned Buddy and told him his father would not recover as his vital organs were too damaged. The organs were not responding to the drugs Jack was given. They were going to make him comfortable, but he had to prepare himself for his dad's death. They could not predict the actual date but told Buddy to be flexible about his whereabouts the next few days.

When Buddy arrived at the hospital, Jack was sleeping. There were occasions when his eyes were open, but he was not talking. He was in this sleepy state for a couple of days. Buddy had a call from the hospital, and the nurse said they expected

Jack to die in the next four hours. Buddy drove the eight miles to the hospital.

The nurse said, "Your father will probably be able to hear you."

Buddy chatted about sea fishing at West Bay and watching Bristol Rovers games together. He thanked him for the financial help he had given Patrice and Alex. "You can be very proud of how you looked after mum all those years. You have had a meaningful life. You can go now, happy about how you made a difference." A few minutes later, Jack took one last gasp and died.

The inheritance from Jack gave Alex and Patrice some financial freedom. It has given them a better financial start in life than Buddy had. They both invested the money in property enabling them to have a more relaxed and flexible life.

Buddy knew that Jack would have been so happy about that.

Learning the lessons from life stories

Buddy's life has always required flexibility as opportunities required the Brambles to be permanently on the move. As a preferred state, Buddy does value the steadiness of routine and so the "be flexible" habit is one that he is continually improving.

The following actions helped Buddy to be flexible, develop his character, and build the prosperity to enjoy his life on his terms. To apply "be flexible" in his life, he told himself to:

- Be open-minded and learn to adapt to any new situation, seeking to understand, not judge.
- Consider many perspectives and be open to change your mind based on new information.
- Spot the opportunities around you and take responsibility to make things happen.
- Walk away from any toxic circumstances, negative thoughts, and relationships.

Is the "be flexible" habit important to you at this stage of your life? What actions might you be considering?

CHOOSE TO PRIORITISE PROGRESS & PROSPERITY

Learning to Be Flexible

Consider your answers to the four questions below when learning to be flexible. If being flexible is important to you, then what actions might you consider and in what timescale?

- Am I remaining positive and acting spontaneously to the opportunities ahead?

- Am I embracing changing situations, and am I flexible where I work?

- Am I looking and contributing outside my comfort zone?

- Am I coping well with change, uncertainty, and lack of clarity?

BE CURIOUS

Eager to know or learn about people or things around you

CHOOSE TO PRIORITISE PROGRESS & PROSPERITY

Be curious – be open-minded and adaptable

Being curious is a key winning habit and essential for achieving the groundbreaking goals beyond dreams. It means having a desire to learn, explore and discover new things. Winners are on this ground, full of purpose and direction.

Being curious helps us to stay engaged, be open-minded, and think differently. Additionally, being curious also helps us to be more creative, more adaptable, and find new solutions.

Curiosity is the spark that ignites our imagination; it drives us to learn, explore and discover new things. Buddy looked for new knowledge and experiences, and wasn't afraid to ask questions and try the new.

Being curious helped Buddy become a better person. He achieved more than he ever thought possible.

Is "be curious" a winning habit that you need to consider improving?

"He's a pleasure to teach"

During his early life, Patrice loved geography. His grandad Bob had taught him so much about physical and human geography. From a very young age, the laddies had played rivers, mountains, countries, and capitals. Patrice was all set to shine in the subject.

When he started at his comprehensive, Patrice threw himself into geography, curious to learn more. He had a brilliant teacher. Mr Smith was full of enthusiasm. He made his lessons fun, educational, and interesting. At a parents' evening, Mr Smith said, "He loves geography. He is a pleasure to teach."

Patrice continued to be eager to learn as much as he could. He loved the subject, asked questions, and continued to stretch his knowledge. If only Mr Smith had continued to be his teacher. Motivated teachers are so crucial to the education of the world. Mr Smith made a lasting impression on Patrice.

Meanwhile, Alex was interested in stargazing and planets and became very curious about the wonder of the skies. He was always asking questions to stretch his thinking. The Brambles hadn't spent much time talking about space and stars, but now they had an expert to inform them if they were ever short on astronomical knowledge. He was full of interesting facts, such as that every star in the night sky is bigger and brighter than our sun. They are just a long way away from us.

On one occasion, the Brambles were walking back to their Andalucían home. Alex looked up and pointed to the brightest light in the sky, Jupiter. Alex then spoke for twenty minutes about stars and the mystery of the universe. Who knew that NASA was still identifying planets outside our solar system? It seemed like Alex knew. Fascinating stuff from the laddie that the Brambles sometimes call Stars.

"Buddy walked tall in the kitchen"

The Covid lockdown of 2020 changed so much. Suddenly, all the things that took ages could easily be accomplished. Working from home became an easily achievable activity. Many companies continued in business with an army of homeworkers contributing happily.

Buddy decided to use this time to learn all about cooking. He enjoyed cooking and was particularly proud of his cottage pie, bolognese, rice pudding, and omelettes. With work responsibilities and being away, Buddy never really focused on learning about cooking beyond his favourites. Now that he had time, he decided to concentrate not on improving the dishes he knew about but on discovering new skills and knowledge. Buddy was curious about the new and rocket-fuelled on purpose and, as always, threw himself into the learning.

Buddy made a start by understanding how to make a curry paste. He built his confidence by throwing cumin, paprika, chillies, ginger, garlic, coconut oil, and tomato puree into a blender. The chicken was sizzling in the coconut oil and browning off nicely. Soon this would be mixed with the curry paste and the coconut milk, but before then, Buddy had to learn an essential skill.

Buddy had always enjoyed cauliflower cheese made by Jess, but now he was to learn a new skill. He read about how to make cauliflower rice. This has been a revelation to Buddy. Finely chopped, mixed with spring onion, a sprinkle of garlic granules, all drizzled with olive oil. Twenty minutes in the oven. Perfect to complement the creamy curried chicken above.

With a spring in his step and his chest pushed out a little further, the new confident Buddy walked tall into the kitchen. He now made a move into ice cream production. He bought an ice-cream maker and made the creamiest homemade ice cream you could imagine. Raspberry ripple was popular with some. Buddy preferred strawberry, drizzled with hot chocolate sauce and covered in nuts. Another culinary delight mastered

CHOOSE TO PRIORITISE PROGRESS & PROSPERITY

by Buddy. Next up was homemade yoghurt. That was more difficult. Buddy is still learning about how to master yoghurt production. It's fair to say that Buddy is not opening a yogurt factory anytime soon.

"His wife of twenty-five years on a blind date"

Buddy and Jess love travelling. If they can, they get away for short trips either in the UK or Europe. This time they were ticking off a European capital they still needed to visit. As they flew into Berlin Brandenburg Airport, they were looking forward to seeing the rich culture of this fascinating and vibrant capital city. They visited the Brandenburg Gate, the Reichstag Palace, and various museums and churches.

They knew the Berlin Wall fell in November 1989, three months after their marriage, so Buddy wanted to make this a romantic weekend. He had a secret plan to take Jess to a dark place. A place where they could reconnect with life without distraction. A place where they could use all their non-visual senses.

Buddy was taking Jess, his wife of twenty-five years, on a blind date. Buddy had been to the famous Dans le Noir in Clerkenwell on a work visit and had enjoyed the experience of eating a meal in complete darkness. He knew this would be something new for Jess. She was curious as she had never dined in the dark. Buddy had booked up the Dunkel restaurant in Berlin.

The Senior Brambles were given a menu to choose their meals from and were soon being guided down a corridor. They were quickly, in complete darkness, shown to their table by a blind guide, Franz. Buddy had his hand on Franz's shoulder, and Jess was just behind with her hand on Buddy's shoulder. They could not see a thing. It was completely black. They were close together but had to rely on other senses.

Franz helped them individually as they settled into their table. They heard other diners but could not see them. Franz pointed out where the knife and fork were. Jess felt for her glass of wine. Buddy reached out and felt his hand on Jess. It was an odd experience relying on touch as a communication tool.

It was a trouble-free evening for the accident-prone Buddy. They could hear glasses being knocked over on other tables, but they were perfect students. Franz appeared every so often to top up wine and bring new meals. Unable to see, they marvelled at the explosion of their taste buds enjoying the texture of food with no idea what was entering their mouths. It was over too quickly.

CHOOSE TO PRIORITISE PROGRESS & PROSPERITY

Buddy and Jess left the restaurant's darkness and hit the Berlin nightclubs hard, dancing till dawn and enjoying a night to remember. As the sun rose, they walked back to their hotel in one another's arms with all their senses intact. What a night to remember!

Anyone who knows Buddy will know that the night to remember didn't happen. Buddy and Jess left the restaurant at 10 pm and were back at the hotel by 10.30 pm, sleeping by 11 pm.

"Having the fingers chopped off, one at a time"

Buddy and Jess loved new experiences and valued the education they gained from their travels worldwide. They appreciated the different voices and perspectives of the people they met. Some have become friends that they can always talk to. Buddy and Jess have not got any friends in Moscow.

After many years of thinking about it, Buddy and Jess decided to visit Russia. It seemed a perfect time to go. They organised their visa and were ready to enjoy the architecture of St Petersburg and Moscow. Around the same time, a couple of Russian guys were planning a trip to the trendy tourist destination of Salisbury. The Russians packed what they needed for their trip. They packed light, double-checking that their Novichok nerve agent was primed and ready. They flew in and out of the UK but not before poisoning Sergei and Yulia Skripal in Salisbury. This was six weeks before the Brambles trip.

The British government accused the Russian government of attempted murder and expelled diplomats. The Russians blamed the British for the poisoning and expelled some British diplomats. Other countries expelled diplomats. It was a diplomatic nightmare.

The Brambles felt sure their cruise between St Petersburg and Moscow would be cancelled. It wasn't. The trip they thought was perfectly timed was now a few days away. It was not the time to visit Russia, but oddly, they sat in 27A and 27B on the flight to Moscow. They were about to learn about visiting a country when diplomatic relations were strained.

Buddy and Jess enjoyed their Moscow and St Petersburg visit. Both cities were architecturally a delight; the history was always worth seeing up-close. They felt safe with the tour guides, but there was always tension when meeting authority.

On entering their boat for the river cruise, Olga, the receptionist, said, "We need your passports so that we can allocate your internet connection to you personally." It was told in such a terrifying way. Buddy and Jess loved sharing their world with their family and commenting on what was happening. On this trip, they decided that digital communication was kept to a minimum. Buddy and Jess had witnessed prisons in Lithuania. They didn't want to be pulled aside at passport control for some inappropriate messaging and find themselves part of a diplomatic negotiation. It was the only holiday where they felt thoroughly scrutinised by the authorities.

Buddy and Jess arrived at Pulkovo Airport in St Petersburg for the flight home, knowing they had done nothing wrong. They were, however, English, and this was not the time to be English at that moment. They checked in, dumped their bags, and made their way to passport control. At the control, they were immediately separated. They were made to wait as other nationalities calmly breezed through, whistling and humming, relaxed, knowing they were not English.

After ten minutes of nervous tension, reflection, and waiting, Buddy and Jess were individually called to their passport office cubicles. As Buddy entered the small space, shutters appeared from both sides. Claustrophobic Buddy was now in a tight area looking at Grigori. Buddy was also in a tight spot. Grigori looked at his passport seriously, flicking through the pages. Buddy wasn't so concerned about his claustrophobia; he was now catastrophising. Jess had always encouraged him to think of the worst when facing a problem. The worst was right now. Grigori looked like he knew how to frighten nervous British passengers. Just as Buddy ramped up his worst-case scenario of having his fingers cut off, one at a time in a St Petersburg torture unit, Grigori gave him his passport. The shutters went up, and Buddy was now through passport control.

Buddy waited to see where Jess was. Five minutes passed as Buddy held his passport and bag of essential items. Eventually, the shutters went up, and he waited to see Jess appear. It wasn't Jess, however. It was someone else. *Where was Jess?* She is now missing. Just as Buddy was about to check out the Russian lost person service, another shutter came up, and relief, it was Jess.

The Brambles flew home with great memories of the friendly Russian people and the country's history. They feared the authorities, however. They knew they would not be revisiting Russia, ever.

CHOOSE TO PRIORITISE PROGRESS & PROSPERITY

Learning the lessons from life stories

When Buddy was younger, he sought the new and embraced curiosity. As he reaches his pre-retirement years, the buzz of the new is being replaced by other habits that are important at this stage of his life. Buddy is less curious but still learning more than most his age.

The following actions helped Buddy to develop his character, be curious, and build the prosperity to enjoy his life on his terms. To apply "be curious" in his life, he told himself to:

- Find new experiences and make learning something new every day a habit.
- Learn from people with different cultures, backgrounds, and experiences.
- Reflect on your thoughts, feelings, and actions; understand the motivations behind them.
- Become up to date with the latest trends and developments in your area of interest.

Is the "be curious" habit important to you at this stage of your life? What actions might you be considering?

Learning to Be Curious

Consider your answers to the four questions below when learning to be curious. If being curious is important to you, then what actions might you consider and in what timescale?

- Am I asking questions to stretch my thinking and to test my assumptions?

- Am I discovering new experiences with a desire to grow my knowledge?

- Am I aware of what I need to learn more about to achieve my purpose?

- Am I learning from different voices and valuing perspectives?

CHOOSE TO PRIORITISE PROGRESS & PROSPERITY

BE RESILIENT

The ability to withstand or recover quickly from difficult conditions

Be resilient – when knocked down, get back up

Being resilient is a key winning habit and essential for achieving the groundbreaking goals beyond your dreams. It means being able to bounce back from disappointment to navigate through challenges and overcome obstacles. Winners are always on this ground, full of direction and purpose.

Being resilient helps us to maintain a positive mindset, learn from our experiences, and grow as individuals. Being resilient also helps us to be more adaptable, more efficient and effective in our work, and to build stronger relationships.

Buddy found his inner strength, learnt from his experiences, and was not afraid to ask for help as he aimed to be personally groundbreaking in life.

Is "be resilient" a winning habit that you need to consider improving?

CHOOSE TO PRIORITISE PROGRESS & PROSPERITY

"Does my arm still smell?"

In 1991, the wider Bramble family travelled to the West Coast of the USA en route to Chicago. They were met by the newly married Daniel and Jean in their campervan. The rest of the remaining family hired a motorhome and visited well-known tourist attractions. They squeezed so much into the holiday: Fisherman's Wharf and Golden Gate Bridge in San Francisco, the Pacific Highway to Los Angeles, the heat of the Badwater Basin in Death Valley, and Old Faithful and Bryce Canyon in Yellowstone National Park all stood out.

The Brambles' group arrived in Yellowstone late afternoon and hooked up the motorhome to the facilities. They were in a rush as they had booked a restaurant in West Yellowstone for early evening. The plan was to jump in the campervan and set off together. There were signs all around about smells attracting grizzly bears. Everyone was on their best behaviour to avoid attracting the grizzlies.

We had five minutes to spare, so Buddy thought it would be a good time to empty the toilet waste. He just needed to attach a pipe to the waste unit. Jess asked, "Do you need to do it now?"

CHOOSE TO BE RELENTLESS

Buddy replied, "It will be dark later. So yes, I should do it now. It will not take long." No one else in the family was keen on the job. Grandad called Buddy "Dan the Man" as he set off to investigate what needed doing.

The family jumped in the campervan and were ready to go as Buddy prepared to fix the sewerage facility pipe. There were two parts to the job. Firstly, setting one part of the pipe to the external sewerage facility alongside the motorhome. That bit was easy. Buddy attached the line in seconds, ensuring it was a tight seal as to not attract any grizzly bears. Grandad turned up to check progress and was at the front of the vehicle, watching. The second part of the job should have been easy, but Buddy was in for a surprise.

The toilet waste in the motorhome tank was protected from escaping by a small sluice gate. This sliding gate would be opened once the pipe had been attached to the motorhome, allowing the waste to flow cleanly into the park sewerage facility. This gate should never be opened without the pipe attached, as untreated sewerage would escape onto the floor. A plastic cap covered the motorhome pipe connection area. All Buddy had to do is remove the lid, connect the pipe, and open the sluice gate. He was unequivocal about what needed to be done.

Buddy bent down. The plastic cap was difficult to remove, but when he pulled the cap, he was showered in urine, poo, and paper towels. He stank of sewerage. He looked up, and there was Grandad with tears of laughter running down his face. Buddy had the stench of urine all over himself. He wasn't laughing but knew he would need to be resilient if the job was to be completed.

Buddy investigated the situation. It might have been marginally better if the sewerage was from his own family, but it became clear that this was from a previous rental. Other family sewerage had been collected between the sluice gate and the plastic cap. It was an accident waiting to happen. It was also a hot sunny afternoon, and the smell was likely to attract the grizzlies. The scent was also on the move, as it was all over Buddy.

Buddy went to explain the situation to the rest family in the campervan. They were all laughing at "Dan the Man". As Dan moved towards the vehicle, the family were not laughing quite as much. The intensity of the smell increased as Dan approached the opened back door. Looking to add some humour to the situation, Dan asked, "Do I smell?"

Buddy returned to the sewerage area, fixed the sewerage pipe to the motorhome, and opened the sluice gate. Bramble sewerage flowed into the camp sewerage unit. It was working as it should. Technically, it had been a success.

Buddy took responsibility and recovered quickly. He walked the smell to the camp showers. The scent was passing perfectly clean Americans. Their look of disgust as smelly Buddy walked past was a picture.

Buddy had a shower and changed his clothes. When he jumped into the campervan, he pushed his arm in Jean's direction and asked, "Does my arm still smell?"

Buddy was forever known as "Dan the Man". He learnt a lot that day about motorhome sewerage systems.

"There is water coming through the ceiling"

The Brambles loved Brig Royd. With Grandma and Grandad living next door, it was the perfect set-up for a growing family. Slowly, bit by bit, Jess and Buddy got themselves debt-free. Never again would they allow themselves to have debt holding them back from their dreams.

Buddy was keeping a tight grip on the finances, and expenditure was scrutinised regularly. However, he knew they would soon need to paint the wooden conservatory as the elements would attack the wood, adding more damage.

Buddy called in three decorators who discussed the job. Two of them sent written proposals with detailed descriptions of what they would do. Both were very professional but also very expensive. The third guy was a bloke from Dublin called Danny. He was personable and showed Buddy written evidence from delighted customers. He seemed genuine, was keen on the work, and was "on the cheap". He could also start next week. Within two weeks, Danny had completed the conservatory. He rubbed down, replaced any rot, undercoated, and repainted twice. Danny was a success.

Danny asked if there was any more work that needed to be done. From Buddy's point of view, the facts suggested that Danny was good at painting, but could he do plumbing?

Buddy asked, "Are you any good at plumbing?"

"Oh Yes, I've done lots of plumbing. I prefer plumbing," said Danny. Danny's confident reply reassured Buddy. Buddy explained that he wanted a new shower, and could he do tiling? It seemed that Danny could tile as well. Buddy had found the perfect handyman.

Danny started the job, and all was going well, with no complaints from Buddy. Danny only had a few days to go to the job's completion. On the surface, all looked good in the bathroom. Buddy was upstairs admiring Danny's work when he heard Jess shout, "There is water coming through the ceiling!" Buddy rushed downstairs, and yes, water was gushing through one of the light fittings onto the floor below. It became clear that the water was coming from an area where Danny had been working. Buddy switched off the water to the house and telephoned Danny.

Danny visited and noticed an error in his plumbing work. A small leak in one of the pipes led to water build-up on the ceiling below. It was a tiny leak. Danny had isolated the leak so they could turn the water back on. Buddy remained resilient as Jess spent the evening berating Buddy about why he employs people on the cheap. She pointed out, "Time and time again they let you down. Will you not learn." It was a long night.

Danny would return on Monday and complete the job. Jess didn't like the quality of Danny's work. They didn't use him again. It was an example of how being good at one thing does not necessarily mean being good at other related skills. Buddy has tried to notice when his pattern of thought affects his judgements. He is still working on it.

CHOOSE TO PRIORITISE PROGRESS & PROSPERITY

"Can't really see how you can add value now"

Buddy has had a lifetime of bouncing back from difficult situations. He is super resilient and has built a solid interior that enables him to withstand setbacks, remaining persistent and patient when following dreams. When all seems bleak, Buddy often receives a call from unexpected people looking for his advice and guidance.

In May 2019, Buddy seriously thought of retirement and discussed the options with Jess. He was pleased with his career achievements but now wanted to spend more time with Jess after years apart. An unexpected call came from someone he had worked with eighteen years previously and who now directly worked in her family business. She now needed his help.

Retirement plans were put on hold as Buddy gave advice and guidance to a hi-tech company's owners and senior managers through 2019 and into early 2020. Before their cruise starting in February 2020 around the South China Sea, Buddy had agreed on a one-year contract with the owners into 2021.

The impact of Covid on business and personal life was immense. At the end of March, Buddy received an email from the hi-tech company explaining that they could not see how he could add value to their business due to the impact of Covid. This was understandable as Covid would mean their employees would be working from home, and it was unclear how company revenue would be affected. Buddy fully understood the situation. It was difficult for everyone. Buddy held onto his emotions and looked at ways to contribute during this difficult time. He remained resilient, and they are still customers today.

"What is that noise?" Bang!

The Bramble family travelled through France on their way home from a lovely holiday in Provence and the Côte d'Azur. It's a delightful region with Roman remains, monuments, structures, architecture, and some of France's best dry, crisp, bright rosé wine. They purchased a few bottles for their cellar at home. They also stopped off in Burgundy and added to the car's weight with some of the region's best Premier and Grand Cru. They were delighted when they stumbled across bottles of Aloxe-Corton wine, famously used by Basil Fawlty in a sketch in *Fawlty Towers*.

They were on a tight timescale as they had plans to take in a Lionel Richie concert in Newcastle, so there was little leeway in the travel arrangements. They stopped off in Beaune, had an evening meal with Grandma and Grandad, and slept well.

CHOOSE TO PRIORITISE PROGRESS & PROSPERITY

Grandma and Grandad were in their vehicle and were later making their way home separately. The Brambles were up early, as always, to catch the 4 pm ferry to the UK. It was dark and wet. Buddy saw this as a chance to sleep more as Jess took over the driving.

French motorways are excellent. There was not too much traffic as Jess motored along, overtaking any slow Renault vehicles in her way. While chatting with Alex, she noticed a strange sound from the car. She pulled over to the slow lane. She was about to wake Buddy to take his view on the noise when there was a huge bang. Jess knew she had not hit anything, but now, Jess was left to control the vehicle. It was unclear what had happened, but the car was tilting. It was scary as Jess used all her skill to own an out-of-control car. Buddy woke up as the vehicle was weaving around the A6. Buddy couldn't see a thing as his glasses had fallen off, so he wasn't much help. As the car hit the central reservation with an even louder bang, Patrice shouted, "I love you all!" Patrice was now in the worst-case scenario, believing that if they were to die, they would all know he loved them.

Jess continued to wrestle with slowing the vehicle down while avoiding any cars around at the time. Using all her driving abilities, somehow Jess managed to bring the car to a stop. Buddy asked if everyone was okay. No one had died. There were no injuries. The Brambles left the vehicle and made their way to the safety of the edge of the motorway. The vehicle was now across two lanes, and cars were queuing behind. Jess said it looked like a wheel had come off the vehicle. Buddy couldn't confirm as he did not have his glasses with him. He needed to get them. He set off towards the car. It was dark. Buddy opened the door and fumbled around to feel for his glasses. Eventually, Buddy found them. He picked up his bag of essential items, bereft without it, and left the vehicle. Buddy knew the days travel arrangements would need to be flexible. Another occasion when the Brambles would need to recover from a difficult situation.

As he looked back, the vehicle was a mess. A wheel was missing, the front badly damaged, the side badly scratched, and a few windows smashed. Many boxes of wine were broken. The vehicle was towed away. It was a write-off. Luckily, they were insured.

Jess phoned her father, who came to the garage to offer help. They continued their journey north. The delay meant that they did not see Lionel that year. Most of the wine supplies were dribbling all over the French motorway. Sadly, the Aloxe-Corton wine didn't survive. All the bottles were smashed. However, they were all alive due to the driving skills of Jess that morning.

CHOOSE TO PRIORITISE PROGRESS & PROSPERITY

Learning the lessons from life stories

Buddy's life experiences helped him learn about the benefits of learning to "be resilient". These experiences gave him a bank of memories to calibrate the severity of any situation he faced. During his life he has learnt many of the skills to be resilient.

The following actions helped Buddy to be resilient, develop his character, and build the prosperity to enjoy his life on his terms. To apply "be resilient" in his life, he told himself to:

- Reflect on the limiting thoughts that hold you back from making the most of your potential.
- When you have been knocked down, get up and go again.
- Ask others for help when struggling with the challenges of life.
- Associate with winning characters as often as you can, as they will keep you on the right track.

Is the "be resilient" habit important to you at this stage of your life? What actions might you be considering?

Learning to Be Resilient

Consider your answers to the four questions below when learning to be resilient. If being resilient is important to you, then what actions might you consider and in what timescale?

- Am I quickly learning from my mistakes, taking positive action?

- Am I patient and persistent in following my hopes and dreams?

- Am I noticing when my pattern of thought is not focused on facts?

- Am I receiving advice and guidance from the trusted network around me?

CHOOSE TO PRIORITISE PROGRESS & PROSPERITY

BE HOPEFUL

Feeling or inspiring optimism about a future event

Be hopeful – a positive and optimistic attitude helps

Being hopeful is a key winning habit and essential for achieving the groundbreaking goals beyond your dreams. It means having a positive outlook, to see the possibilities, and believe in, and sometimes see, a much better future of joy.

Being hopeful helps us to maintain a positive mindset, find solutions, and persevere through some very difficult times. Being hopeful also helps us to be more resilient, more optimistic, and build stronger relationships.

Often when things are difficult and seemingly impossible, hope is the fuel that keeps us going. It gives us the strength to keep moving forward, even when things are tough. Step forward in life, not back. Hope allows us to learn and grow.

Buddy found hope when he most needed it. His positive and optimistic outlook helped him achieve more than he ever thought possible.

Is "be hopeful" a winning habit that you need to consider improving?

CHOOSE TO PRIORITISE PROGRESS & PROSPERITY

"How do you feel about my mum and dad living with us?"

In 1992, Jess and Buddy were three years into married life. With a baby on the way, all was well. They were so happy to be in one another's company. Jess had shown Buddy a different life, and they were enjoying every single moment.

Jess's mum and dad were enjoying their life in Sandwich, Cape Cod, Massachusetts, although it was clear that Jess's nana was in poor health. It was clear that she would need to come home to the UK very shortly. Jess and Buddy discussed how they could help. They had a spare couple of bedrooms and agreed that it made sense for Nana and Grandma to return to the UK at the earliest possible moment. Four weeks before Patrice was born, Nana and Grandma arrived. Both settled quickly into the routines and rituals in the home. It was a lovely time together. Buddy could see how close Jess was with her mum and how much they enjoyed one another's company. After Nana died and Patrice was born, Grandma flew back to the States.

One evening Jess was talking about the future and how much she had enjoyed Grandma being around. She was so used to the closeness of family life, with generations living harmoniously in the same house. It was so far away from Buddy's view of family life. As they chatted further, Jess explained that her mum and dad would return to the UK. Her dad had suggested that they could buy a house and all live together. "How do you feel about my mum and dad living with us?"

This was a step too far for Buddy. Bob was a strong character and was sure to interfere with the upbringing of their children. "I'm not sure I can live in the same house as someone with such strong views," explained Buddy. It was a critical conversation as they discussed how it might work. Jess was hopeful and discussed the benefits. She was very optimistic it could work. Buddy could see his long-term future with Jess slipping away but continued to understand the situation. Could they make an impossible situation possible? Could they find a way to make it work? Buddy loved Bob. They got on so well. Buddy knew he would be a good influence on his children. They talked about how it could work. They began to agree on some ground rules about how Bob would need to behave if this was to occur.

Over the next few days, these ground rules were finalised. Jess wrote to Grandad explaining how this new family arrangement would work. Upon receipt of the letter, Grandad phoned and explained how he understood the situation from Buddy's point of view. He was sure they could agree on a good way forward.

CHOOSE TO PRIORITISE PROGRESS & PROSPERITY

"I will send you a letter later today to share my thoughts," he explained to Jess.

When the letter arrived, the contents calmed the situation. Bob was so understanding and agreed to all the ground rules. Buddy was hopeful of a good future. A few months later, Bob and Pat joined Buddy and Jess in Stainland, West Yorkshire. They lived with them for seventeen happy years. To this day, Buddy cannot remember the ground rules. They didn't matter. Bob had built the trust, understanding, and belief in the future that was so important in family life.

After Grandma died, Grandad didn't cope that well and, for some unknown reason, decided to move on his own to Hastings. After many years of extended family life, it was odd that he would now choose to live independently. During a holiday in France in 2010, he had a stroke that affected his thought process. His health was suffering. It cannot have been easy for a proud man.

The family had a lovely Christmas together in Hertford in 2010. Grandad had a bad cough and explained that he had an appointment to see a doctor in Hastings after Christmas. Jess and Buddy agreed with him that in the New Year, he would come home and live in Hertfordshire. He was surrounded by family again. Patrice had a lovely conversation with Grandad as he drove him home. Patrice helped him up the stairs to his cold flat overlooking the sea.

Grandad never did get to Hertford. Grandad never got to see his doctor. He died early in January 2011. He was found in his flat, in a chair overlooking the sea. He had just completed a bowl of mint choc chip ice cream. He had inspired Alex and Patrice to reach beyond the average and bring their best to each moment. He made an impact on thousands of children as a teacher. As a grandfather, he saved his best result for his grandchildren, whom he adored.

Grandad and Grandma had a significant impact on the extended family. They all miss them. Their influence lives on in their children and their grandchildren.

"Have you seen a little boy on his own?"

The Brambles were off travelling again. This time around the UK. They stopped off at Hilton Park for a bite to eat. On the way out, they stopped in WHSmiths, the newsagents, when Jess looked round and said, "Where is Patrice?"

Buddy replied, "I thought you had him. He will be in this shop."

Buddy rushed around the shop, but there was no sign of Patrice. They checked out the place where they had eaten. No sign of him there. They believed they were responsible parents, but they had let him down. Patrice was on his own somewhere, and they were not with him. Jess feared the worst as child abduction was in the news, and she began catastrophising. Buddy explained that few children are abducted in the UK. That is most unlikely. "No need to worry yourself quite yet. He will be here somewhere. We need to keep looking," said Buddy.

Buddy was always calm in these situations as he always remained hopeful. They began asking anyone, "Have you seen a little boy on this own? We have lost our boy." No one had seen him. He was nowhere to be seen. Jess suggested that he might have gone outside. It was getting desperate as he wasn't responding to their shouts.

As they moved urgently to check outside, they could see a little boy holding the hand of a woman. As they got closer, they could see it was Patrice. He spotted Jess. "Mummy! Mummy!" he shouted out. Patrice let go of the woman's hand and ran towards Jess. They embraced one another. Both were crying. Patrice was now safe in the arms of his mother.

The lady explained that Patrice was walking around outside in the car park crying. He came up to me and said, "My name is Patrice. I have lost my mum and dad. Could you help me find them?" More tears, but relief as well. The lady was so lovely as she comforted these parents. That day the senior Brambles understood what it was like to have a child go missing.

Patrice later explained that when he couldn't find Jess in the shop, he went outside as he knew the family were on their way to the car. When he got outside, he looked up. He knew he had lost his parents and now he couldn't find the car. "There were too many cars," he explained.

Jess said, "Why did you choose that lady?"

"She had a beautiful smile, like you mum." Even at that age, he understood the power of empathy. He was a slime.

"Ringo went into the old belfry and started praying"

Liverpool Football Club has always been integral to Alex and Patrice's life. Watching live matches with Grandad and Buddy was always memorable, as they were huge fans. Ringo O'Shaughnessy and his family sometimes joined them if the game was important.

When Liverpool won their Champions League semi-final against Chelsea, it was clear that the final would be an important match. The O'Shaughnessys were invited to Luddenden Foot, and the night could not come quickly enough. Drinks were purchased and snacks were prepared as they settled for the match.

Ringo was born in Merseyside and had supported Liverpool from when he was in short trousers. He was excited as he climbed the stairs and took his seat for the match on the 25th of May 2005. As the teams came out, the atmosphere was electric in the Olympic Stadium in Istanbul. Red-hot favourites AC Milan looked determined, while Liverpool just looked hopeful. Early enthusiasm was cooled when AC Milan took an early lead; by halftime, it was 3–0 to AC Milan. Liverpool had been blown away. They looked lost as they ran about but didn't make an impact.

The AC Milan team were super confident, and it didn't look good for Liverpool. One of the TV pundits said that if Liverpool could get an early goal, then who knows what might happen. It was desperate stuff. Ringo went into the old round belfry and started praying. They were now in wing and prayer territory. Ringo settled back into his seat, inspiring optimism around the room. He was all set for the comeback. Hope was alive and kicking.

Amazingly, Liverpool scored three goals in six minutes in the second half. AC Milan were shell-shocked. They had one hand on the trophy, and now they were done. They all looked shattered when Shevchenko missed a penalty for AC Milan at 3–2. Extra time could not separate the teams. Divine intervention was needed, so Ringo went into the belfry again for more inspiration.

The Liverpool team took action that night to make the impossible, possible. Liverpool won on penalties, and the blokes all ran outside, cheering, and running about like madmen. Liverpool Football Club had won the European Cup for the fifth time and were allowed to keep the trophy. What a final. The miracle of Istanbul. Ringo went home happy that night.

"You could die in ten, twenty or thirty years"

It was 2016, and Buddy thought he had a few weight problems. He did. Further tests showed that he had a minor disease in his bone marrow. The Exeter consultant at the haematology unit said it was slow growing. He could die in ten, twenty, or thirty years, depending on what type of lymphoma it is. Buddy's blood has been checked every year since then. Six years later and Buddy is still with us. He lives with hope every day.

He has received a further diagnosis, and the new consultant in York has indicated that he has a low-grade non-Hodgkin lymphoma. He likely has marginal zone lymphoma, although it could also be Waldenstrom macroglobulinemia.

Buddy also has low iron in his blood, indicating active bone marrow disease. Lymphoma cells in the bone marrow take up space usually used to make healthy blood cells. This lowers the number of red blood cells the bone marrow makes, meaning Buddy has less haemoglobin and is becoming anaemic. This means that Buddy has spells where he has extreme tiredness, can be irritable, lacks energy, and has headaches for no reason. Sometimes he has a shortage of breath.

The consultant indicated that Buddy should prepare himself for the next stage. For the time being, Buddy is on watch and wait. Buddy explained his thoughts about the future to Jess, "I am going to take an active approach to life and control what I am responsible for. I am hopeful about the future."

The cancer is highly treatable and so Buddy is relaxed about it but sometimes does worry, especially when tired through no reason other than lymphoma. Buddy is still with us and still learning.

"Hopeful that victory is round the corner"

The Brambles have been lifelong Labour Party supporters, knowing they only win when they combine aspiration with social justice. For far too many years, the party have forgotten this combination. They seem to have preferred the purity of the socialist alternative to the capitalist system.

The Conservatives always win whenever Labour has vacated the centre ground of politics.

Since 2010 there has been a lack of belief that Labour could win any election. The Labour Party are now well ahead in the recent polls, and many supporters are hopeful that victory is around the corner.

The last time Labour won a national election was in 2005. It has been a long time. It's time for Labour to make this part of the world a better place. The Bramble family will need to wait a little longer for that happy day. They remain hopeful.

CHOOSE TO PRIORITISE PROGRESS & PROSPERITY

Learning the lessons from life stories

Whatever the situation, Buddy is always a hopeful character. There have been many occasions when the circumstances of his life have called upon Buddy to be hopeful. When the chips are down, Buddy can be relied upon to lift his and others' spirits.

The following actions helped Buddy to be hopeful, develop his character, and build the prosperity to enjoy his life on his terms. To apply "be hopeful" in his life, he told himself to:

- Have a realistic belief that with your own effort, a positive outcome could be possible.
- Build and maintain relationships with friends and family, reaching out to professionals if necessary.
- Hold on to your memories where your negative thoughts turned out not to be true.
- Stay connected with current affairs and news but don't get overwhelmed by the negativity.

Is the "be hopeful" habit important to you at this stage of your life? What actions might you be considering?

Learning to Be Hopeful

Consider your answers to the four questions below when learning to be hopeful. If being hopeful is important to you, then what actions might you consider and in what timescale?

- Am I looking forward to and hopeful about my long-term future?

- Am I taking action to make the impossible, possible?

- Am I reaching beyond average, bringing my best to each moment?

- Am I proactively making my part of the world a better place?

CHOOSE TO PRIORITISE PROGRESS & PROSPERITY

CHOOSE TO BUILD LOVE INTO EVERYTHING YOU DO

CHOOSE TO BUILD LOVE INTO EVERYTHING YOU DO

Sprinkling love into every bit of your life

Buddy's life stories have encouraged him to believe that whatever the question, love is the answer. In 1965 the American record producer Burt Bacharach, who died on February 8th, 2023, composed *What the world needs now is love, sweet love*. Love was key to Buddy's life. These stories show the challenging journey that Buddy took to find someone to love, find something he loved to do, and find something he looked forward to.

Throughout these life stories, Buddy found that when the "be loving" habit was sprinkled into his contributions, he was motivated to achieve his goals. At his very best, he was a winner. He was surrounded by talented people and was not distracted by the watchers or drainers that hindered his early life.

When he moved to Carshalton in 1986 and rebuilt his confidence, his persona attracted like-minded individuals who shared his enthusiasm, passion, and commitment. He met the winners in life, and this gave him inspiration to aspire to be better.

As Buddy began his management career, he realised that his drive energised the people around him and encouraged them to be creative and release their potential. He was focused on his purpose and loved what he was doing.

Buddy learnt to love himself so that he could love his partner and his family. With Jess in his life, Buddy had a strong individual that was not going to distract him with the drama that some watchers somehow attract. She was an achiever. They were individually confident. As a team, each comfortable in their own skin, but much stronger together.

Buddy never underestimated the power that confidence and a strong relationship gives the winners in life. Distractions in their home life affect the contribution that anyone can make to their life. These emotional situations can occur in any aspect of life. They affect close relationships and the mental health of many. Buddy knows all about the impact of home-life distractions and the positive impact when there are none.

With Jess he learnt about building trust and understanding with others. As he felt the power of emotional support and unconditional love at home, he felt he could love the company of his friends and network.

From the stories, you will know that Buddy built strong relationships in his career, and these opened so many opportunities for advancement. These strong relationships helped him find meaning and purpose and gave him a belief that he could achieve more in his life.

When Buddy loved his workplace and the leaders around him, his positive attitude, energy levels, and engagement were noticeable to all. The high levels of emotional connection enabled him to work with executive boards and design in action-learning environments that were fit for the digital age ahead.

Buddy had an ability to fire teams up with passion. He cared about helping the people in his teams make the most of their potential. He loved working with many of them and many are still friends. He learnt so much from many of them.

There are four components to the love ingredient. Buddy has needed to prioritise these at various aspects of his life. Winners in life, often work on all four, at the same time. The four components are explained in the next few pages.

Build the healthy foundations – love yourself

Adults raised to feel good about themselves are in a much better position to love another. These people have an advantage when it comes to love. They are confident and value themselves. They are comfortable in their own skin. They are already in a good place when they face the world.

Until you love yourself and your many talents it is difficult to be totally committed to others. When love is within yourself, you can use it to reach out, love others, and help them feel valued. Whatever your circumstances, applying the foundation habits in *Choose to Be Relentless* will help.

Build relationships – love your partner and family

Reaching out and showing vulnerability is not easy when in a new relationship. When people switch on the commitment factor in a growing relationship, it builds the hope of something stronger.

As younger adults build closeness, trust, and understanding with their partner, they give themselves a solid foundation to develop their relationship further. A trusting, solid relationship as equals creates a good environment for their children to be the best they can.

Not everyone has the good fortune of these home circumstances. Buddy knows this only too well. Often children from these homes need to dig deep, take responsibility, and find solutions for themselves. A few find sustainable solutions.

Many do not. Many are held back by the circumstances of the past and their fearful mind.

Build learning – love friends and networks

Building belief and commitment with friends and a work network is vital. It helps people contribute, be in the right place, and know the right people when opportunities present themselves. Meeting the right manager in his business life helped to put Buddy's life on track. She gave him a chance in a new industry. She believed in his potential. Buddy is so grateful for the opportunity and pleased that he was bold and stood up. He was noticed in the crowd and Buddy has not looked back. She believed in him.

Build your life – love your purpose and direction

So be loving to your partner, children, friends, and work colleagues. This love will energise you to love your goals and passions and the dreams you share.

With love in your heart and good habits in your life, you can build the confidence to achieve groundbreaking goals beyond your dreams. Be consistent and you can be a winner in the life you have chosen.

CHOOSE TO BUILD LOVE INTO EVERYTHING YOU DO

Don't wait to be loved, be loving

So, Alex and Patrice, don't wait to be loved. Be loving. It fires up the passion and encourages a level of effort in life that is beyond the bare minimum. When discretionary effort flows into everything you do, it makes all the difference to your work, relationships, and home life.

Put love into what you are doing. Watch people that love what they do. They are often happy and a pleasure to be around. They are having so much fun that love finds them.

Find your passion and enjoy your life

Apply the habits and enjoy the learning experiences that will inform your life. You will:

> Find yourself and your talents.
>
> Find someone to love you.
>
> Find something to love.
>
> Find the power of daily improvement.
>
> Find your purpose and passion in life.

LEARNING FROM THE LIFE STORIES

LEARNING FROM THE LIFE STORIES

Reflections, learning, and be ready for the future

There are so many people that Buddy would want to thank for his life. Thank you for your love and surviving the highs and lows. So many have influenced him and helped him learn and achieve. He has been inspired by so many talented people who trusted him to make things a whole lot better. To those that had lost their way Buddy hopes that he had inspired them and given them direction. Buddy can now look back and be proud of his work and life achievements. He gave many a platform to achieve.

Buddy now looks forward to a future with Jess, focused on health, relationships, learning, and prosperity and success on their terms. He intends to be relentless as he attacks each day. For Buddy every moment will matter. He takes the approach that life is for living and he is going to live it for as long as he can. He hopes to be around to support any grandchildren as they progress in the world. He remains inspired by life and the hope for a better future.

Buddy's life has always been about making choices at the key moments. He knows that he is responsible for his choices. The habits reflect many of those choices and have driven much of his day-to-day behaviour.

He is still on his learning journey knowing that he is human, and his emotions can get in the way of his progress. For this reason, Buddy is reluctant to offer advice and guidance, but annoyingly for some in the family, he will. He hopes readers find these useful as they reflect on their present situation.

Every individual moment informs learning for all of us. We are all unique with so much untapped potential. Many could shine brighter if they take control of their own situations, take responsibility, and take action to improve. Every single day.

The following are Buddy's thoughts, reflections and learning from life that he hopes are worth considering.

Take personal control with positive energy

Focus on taking control of happiness and health. Successful people have a positive attitude with high levels of energy. This attitude helps them to cope with life challenges, the complexities, and the changes ahead.

They surround themselves with winners, learners, and achievers.

When disappointment or failure occurs the very best bounce back. They have spotted the immense power of taking personal responsibility even when it is not their fault. They look to find a solution. If they cannot, then they move on. They don't get distracted from their progress with negative thinking and looking back on what might have been. They learn and move on.

The very best people are totally relentless on how they attack their day. They value their free time and use it wisely.

They often benefit from the love and kindness of the supportive people around them. This network gives them a balanced perspective and feedback to keep them grounded and self-aware. Most of all, this network are inspiring to the people in the network.

Value your life and work relationships

The best focus on developing a supportive family life and many strong relationships to help them achieve. They actively listen and understand, showing they care. They set out to have a positive impact on the lives of others. Having a supportive family who believe in you and want you to succeed is so important.

Buddy knows he is lucky. He is respected by people that matter. He is loved by Jess, Patrice, and Alex. This gives him

LEARNING FROM THE LIFE STORIES

security when some in the world judge too quickly or are unkind.

Take time to understand and not judge

Seeing things through the eyes of others is the key enabler of strong relationships. Buddy has needed to accept the daily difficulty of seeking to understand others consistently.

Judging people is so easy. Seeking to understand people is a lifelong challenge for many. Suspending judgement is so very hard when listening to others. Seeking to understand others is a habit worth cultivating.

Behind every voice is a story yet to be told.

Be with winners, achievers, and learners

No matter the circumstances in life, whatever age, keep pushing forward. If you can.

Life can be competitive; however, Buddy focused on achieving his personal best as often as he could. For him this was progress.

We all move at different paces in our life. Behind, alongside, and in front of us are others. The best way for many to achieve is to avoid comparing accomplishments with others, as this can be toxic and dangerous to mental health. It really can. Be relentless. Focus on doing your very best, aim high and keep on improving.

Choose the habits important to you and do your best every day. Make the most of your unique talents. Buddy's biggest fear was always setting the bar too low and achieving it.

Buddy identified the destructive nature of negative, judgemental conversations about his potential achievements. Buddy knows that negativity has had a huge impact on his mental health. For that reason, he always avoids people who rain on his parade. Drainers and negative influencers are just hard work. Buddy prefers achievers, learners, and winners.

Find your passion and be relentless

Find interesting and high-quality work and be a role model if you can. Find what you are most passionate about. Do it as often as you can. Your enthusiasm and love for your passion will drive you to do your best work. Others will see your best, and that is where the future opportunities will be.

Buddy also recognised that his happiness is when his realistic expectations meet the reality of the achievement.

Hitting realistic goals is the always the aim. When he has focused on improving and doing his best, he has been groundbreaking. Only yesterday he swam for twenty-two minutes – a personal best for Buddy. Celebrate your achievements and be grateful for what you already have.

Know what you want out of life

Buddy's vision for 2030 is for him to have hit his life with a focus and an energy. He decided to be relentless, as often as he was physically and mentally able. In September 2022, Buddy spent time thinking about what he wanted out of life, now, and over the next eight years. He wanted to:

- Be personally fit and healthy
- Be able to build strong work/life relationships
- Be able to learn to keep his mind sharp
- Have the finances to enjoy his life

Buddy's direction and purpose has been so powerful as he begins his journey of change. Buddy has a plan and is remaining flexible to seize the opportunities as they present themselves. Buddy has found that his motivation has increased when he has defined his own life success. It has been decreased when others have set the target. When Buddy is connected to a purpose and can see the bigger picture he is energised and a much happier person.

Winners define their own targets and are relentless. Buddy learnt that the most successful people tend to know what they want out of life, now, and in the future. Buddy has found this focus very useful as he chartered his progress over the last few months.

Take responsibility for learning and improving

Buddy realised years ago that if he was going to be successful on his terms he would need to stop comparing and charter his own course. He recognised that he had learnt more from the disappointment, pain, and error in his life than he had from the successes.

He realised the motivational impact of learning from what happened and moving on to the future and not looking back. He is daily motivated by the continual use of "What has gone well and what has not gone well." This inspires him to look forward without revisiting life's failures.

Make a start and keep on learning and improving. Get better every day. Attack the unknown, look for the higher ground and continually learn about the new. Life is not a race but a series of steady improvements.

You will be surprised where your potential will take you if you do your best and keep improving.

Avoid comparison with others in your life

Recognise that comparing or judging yourself against others who think differently, have different values, or come from a different background can be exhausting and dispiriting. Choose your field of expertise and be a better version of yourself and keep on improving.

Of course, comparing is good for identifying learning opportunities and can be a motivator for some confident people. Clearly it can be a huge motivator when used appropriately. Unfortunately, for many it can lead to low self-esteem and demotivation, as the comparable is unachievable. When Buddy was at school, he recalled a teacher saying, "you are clever" to a student. On hearing this Buddy thought, *the real learning for all the students would have been to discuss why the student was clever*. Never once did they discuss or understand why this student was clever. It was a private moment but even the individual student didn't understand why he was clever.

Buddy realises that competing against himself gives him a healthy measure of success as the measures are focused on his goals not the goals of others. This approach enables him not to be demotivated by the people who are better than him. He just focuses on improving. Often this approach has enabled Buddy to achieve more than he thought possible.

Accepting that many other people are better allows him to celebrate their accomplishments. Buddy noticed years ago that when competing with others it stopped him from learning from, and appreciating, their achievements.

Buddy understood that when he focused on doing the right thing and not worry about what people thought, he released himself from the controlling judgements of others. Breaking his own records was more satisfying and rewarding than breaking someone else's record.

Learning about the impact of fear on life

In the last few years, Buddy has come to realise the negative impact of fear in the day-to-day decisions in life. Often news is not history but a comment on a future that has not occurred. Career progress can be held back by the fear of the unknown with many choosing to play it safe.

For example, in November 2022, at the end of the Caribbean cruise, guests were told that there were very few taxis outside. It would be safer if all guests allowed the shore excursion team to arrange the taxi to the beach and subsequently the airport.

Buddy and Jess were more hopeful about the availability of taxis. They happily walked out of the terminal and there were lots. They arrived at the beach early and settled into their day. Three hours later the shore excursion group arrived having spent twice as much for the same service.

There is money to be made peddling fear. Always be happy and hopeful about the future. Be Relentless. Don't let fear hold you back from your dreams. Push past the negative noises in your head or from those around you. Find your passion and hit the day hard.

Take time to make the habits stick

Habits are powerful because they are automatic and unconscious behaviours that we repeat regularly. Making habits stick is the challenge for so many. Making the habit fun, enjoyable, and regular seems to be key. Jess and Buddy have shared this life journey, and regular application of habits has helped them remain consistent.

Buddy found the gym incredibly boring and gave up. Buddy feels that boredom is one of the main reasons for habits not sticking. When he is passionate about something he is relentless. His new passion is running, as he loves the buzz following the routine. He also knows that being fit will keep him stay alive.

Buddy noticed that Jess has made exercise a habit. She has built the focus into her daily routine. It has become a habit. Jess completed her fitness habit as she did not want to die early and more importantly wanted to be able to play with these non-existent grandchildren. She has a passion and there is no stopping her. Jess was consistent in turning up at the gym. Every day at the same time. This regularity helps the habit stick.

Buddy has focused on this book for days. Every day for seven weeks. It has become a habit. This continual focus helped to make the behaviour a habit.

Buddy was really fired up with purpose when writing this book. He set a deadline with Jess. Agreed to complete by Christmas. He visualised what the book would look like under the tree. He was energised by giving back his knowledge to his children for their benefit.

LEARNING FROM THE LIFE STORIES

Buddy realised early in life that to avoid bad habits he had to understand the triggers and temptations in life. He always asked himself what precedes a bad habit. In simple terms, to give up smoking, it's a really good idea not to be anywhere near cigarettes or situations that might encourage reaching for a cigarette. Find the trigger and change your life.

Create your short-term plan – make a start

Focus on why you want to make a change. Buddy found it useful to review the 100 questions and consider what steps he might take to make improvements in his life. The questions act as a stimuli to help him think about potential actions to improve his life in the future.

He applied the "Stop, Start, continue" approach, identifying actions that he could choose to take.

What do I need to **Stop**?	By When?
What do I need to **Start**?	By When?
What do I need to **Continue**?	By When?

WHAT ARE THE STORIES THAT INSPIRED YOU?

WHAT ARE THE STORIES THAT INSPIRED YOU?

CHOOSE TO BE RELENTLESS

Forty years ago, New Year 1982/83, Buddy met Jess. Buddy only knew the back streets of a Somerset town and a few local villages. He had friends whom he enjoyed being with. Forty years later, Buddy has learnt so much about life and the world. It has been a relentless journey, creating a caring family, enjoying the love of an extended family life, and making a success of his life on his terms. The family have relentlessly focused on travelling, learning so much from other cultures. The more they understand about other cultures the less they fear. Education must be the key to creating a world community that reaches out to others with love and not fear and hate. Working collaboratively with the EU with so many common causes and interests would be a good start. As committed Europeans and people of the world, the Brambles can only hope for a brighter future.

The last words Buddy wrote to Jess were thirty-five years ago. The words were on the postcard from Paris offering an all-expenses paid trip to the capital of Indonesia, Jakarta. She has visited many countries in her married life, but she is still waiting for Jakarta. She remains hopeful.

The words in this book have been thirty-five years in the making. There is no doubt that Jess changed Buddy's life beyond his wildest dreams. Jess and Buddy look forward to seeing how the next thirty-five years treat Patrice and Alex.

WHAT ARE THE STORIES THAT INSPIRED YOU?

Patrice and Alex know that Jess offers the unconditional love that Buddy never had from his mother. Buddy is so happy that Patrice and Alex, only a few weeks ago, told him what a great supportive, motivational, and caring dad he has been. At the end of life, being important to the life of a child and inspiring others is surely a key measure of success.

Buddy and Jess may not be around when Patrice and Alex look back on their life in years to come. Will Patrice and Alex be happy about the way they have lived their life? Will they have seized the opportunities in this world full of uncertainties?

Unconditionally, Jess and Buddy will always be there to love the young Brambles. More importantly, they both like the young Brambles and enjoy their company.

Hope this book resonates with you and your circumstances. It has been written with love. Buddy hopes that the stories will inspire you to examine and question your own life. You could reflect on which stories touched you and instigate the changes to make the most of your life and the people around you.

Don't wait for others to recognise or notice you – put yourself out there and make an impact with your unique talents.

You are the future now. Make the most of it.

CHOOSE TO BE RELENTLESS

HOW TO PLAN FOR SUCCESS

HOW TO PLAN FOR SUCCESS

How to apply the habits in your life

There are six steps to creating a high-level plan of action. The key questions to consider are in this diagram below:

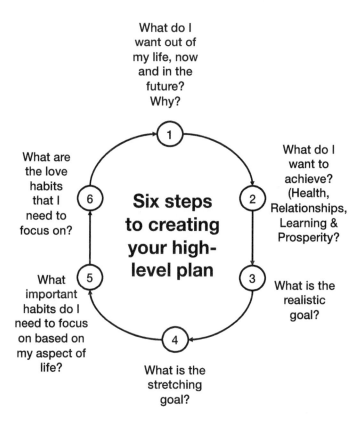

HOW TO PLAN FOR SUCCESS

Step One

Take time to consider what you want from life now and in the future. *It can help by asking why you want to do this. Knowing the why does give additional emotion to achieving the goal.*

The plan can be over any period you choose. You may select a five-year plan or a 100-day plan. Once you have thought about what you want out of life and why, move on to the next step.

Step Two

Decide what this would look like in terms of Physical and Mental Health, Fulfilling Relationships, Experiential Learning, and Prosperity on your Terms.

Putting your thoughts onto paper helps you to visualise them. Visualisation is a powerful technique. It involves imagining that what you want to achieve has already occurred in your own mind. Think about what you will be. I will be…

Step Three

Agree to the realistic goal. This measurable goal is achievable with a bit of focus and determination. Buddy found that writing his goals down increased the probability of him achieving it.

Step Four

Agree to the stretching goal. This will be more difficult but possible with the consistent application of habits and personal drive. Find your purpose and intention and go for it.

This step can also include a groundbreaking goal if you want to aim beyond your present thoughts.

Step Five

Decide what specific foundation, relationship, learning, and winning habits you will need to focus on to achieve your goals.

Check out each of the habits in this book to help you create detailed plans. Try to select no more than eight.

Choose the ones that are important for you, at this stage of your life, to achieve your goal.

Step Six

Finally, love is a crucial ingredient to any success. Choose up to two love behaviours you will need to focus on during the period you have chosen .

HOW TO PLAN FOR SUCCESS

Example of a blank high-level charter

1. What do I want out of my life, now and in the future? Why do I want it?

2. What do I want to achieve? (Health, Relationships, Learning & Prosperity?)

| Physical & Mental Health | Fulfilling Relationships | Experiential Learning | Prosperity on your terms |

3. What is the realistic goal?

4. What is the stretching goal?

5. What important habits do I need to focus on?

HEALTHY	OPTIMISTIC	PASSIONATE	DRIVEN
PURPOSEFUL	HAPPY	INSPIRED	BOLD
CARING	PROACTIVE	ENCOURAGING	FLEXIBLE
CONFIDENT	RESPECTFUL	MOTIVATED	CURIOUS
RESPONSIBLE	COMMITTED	CHALLENGED	RESILIENT
ORGANISED	EMPATHETIC	ACTIVELY LEARNING	HOPEFUL
Foundation Habits	**Relationship Habits**	**Learning Habits**	**Winning Habits**

6. What are the love habits that I need to focus on?

| Love Yourself | Love Partner & Family | Love Friends & Work Network | Love Purpose & Direction |

464

CHOOSE TO BE RELENTLESS

Example of a high-level charter

What do I want out of my life, now and in the future? Why do I want it?

1. Be fit and healthy so I can put energy into my future passions

2. What do I want to achieve? (Health, Relationships, Learning & Prosperity)

Physical & Mental Health	Fulfilling Relationships	Experiential Learning	Prosperity on your terms
Be personally fit & healthy	Be building strong work/life relationships	Be an author of my second book	Have the finances to enjoy our life

3. What is the realistic goal? (December 2022)

Achieve a weight of 80kg; Run 5k in 32min	Succeed in NED role	Second book created in time for Christmas	Enjoyed and totally focused on family Holiday

4. What is the stretching goal? (December 2022)

Achieve a weight of 79kg; Run 5k in 30 mins	Know my work plans	Identified how to amend the book for full publication	Know where future income is coming from

5. What important habits do I need to focus on?

Foundation Habits	Relationship Habits	Learning Habits	Winning Habits
HEALTHY ●	OPTIMISTIC ○	PASSIONATE ●	DRIVEN ○
PURPOSEFUL ○	HAPPY ○	INSPIRED ○	BOLD ●
CARING ○	PROACTIVE ●	ENCOURAGING ○	FLEXIBLE ○
CONFIDENT ○	RESPECTFUL ○	MOTIVATED ●	CURIOUS ●
RESPONSIBLE ○	COMMITTED ●	CHALLENGED ○	RESILIENT ○
ORGANISED ●	EMPATHETIC ○	ACTIVELY LEARNING ○	HOPEFUL ○

6. What are the love habits that I need to focus on?

Love Yourself ○	Love Partner & Family ●	Love Friends & Work Network ●	Love Purpose & Direction ○

465

HOW TO PLAN FOR SUCCESS

Example of a Sunray Plan of Action

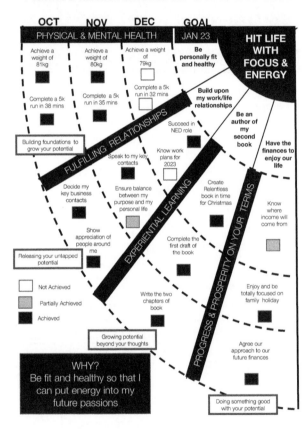

Achieving ground-breaking goals

Buddy studied winners in life and noticed that they had incredible belief and confidence that enabled them to aim high.

They worked hard to achieve their seemingly unachievable goals. What separated them out from many others was the ability to fail, learn from the experience, get up and carry on. A resilience that is not felt by the many.

Buddy developed a framework and an approach to goal setting in life that enabled him to achieve more than he thought possible.

He visioned an impossible goal and then asked questions about what would need to change to achieve this dream. This method was applied in many companies as they grew their business. This method is included here.

Buddy began to see life achievements as a series of four goals. Security, realistic, stretching, and groundbreaking goals.

For many years, he has used this method to set goals knowing that when he sets off to achieve there are four targets to aim at.

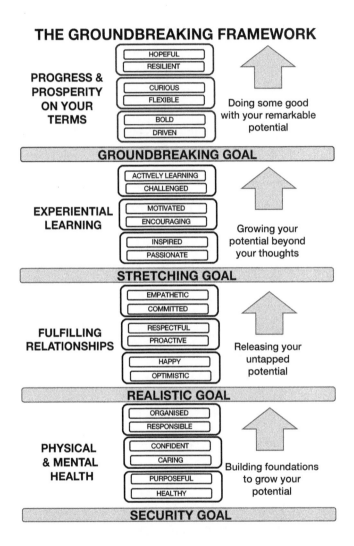

Buddy always aims at groundbreaking as this encourages innovative thoughts that move him outside his comfort zone.

He hasn't always achieved groundbreaking results; many times, he has fell short of his goal. Buddy bounces back stronger.

His approach is to do his best and if he has done that then he is relaxed in his outcomes. In life, all you can do is your best.

Buddy describes the four goals here so that readers can understand the method that has helped him achieve on his terms. Buddy concluded that:

Security Goals

Security goals re easily achieved with little effort. They are expected.

They don't require much creativity or innovation. Security goals are the lowest goal. This is often the minimal level of achievement. This is the home ground for watchers in life. They feel safe here.

To build the foundations to grow their potential, the watchers in life are to be healthy, purposeful, caring, confident, responsible, and organised. These attributes give them self-respect.

Realistic Goals

Realistic goals are expected. It requires a little more extra effort.

These are achievable by most with helpful and encouraging parents, teachers, or friends. Short-term coaching and a focus can help achieve this goal. With a consistent contribution, this is undoubtedly achievable for many. This is the home ground for the achievers.

Achievers must be optimistic, happy, proactive, respectful, committed, and empathetic to release their untapped potential. These attributes help them develop fulfilling relationships with a trusted network.

Stretching Goals

Stretching Goals are difficult to sustain with the current capability.

People are on the very edge of their ability to achieve this goal. They need to learn new skills and apply them to their day-to-day contribution. It requires focus and dedication to maintain this level of achievement. This is more challenging but can be achieved. This is the home ground for the learners.

To grow potential beyond their thoughts, learners are passionate, inspired, encouraging, motivated, challenged, and able to learn. These attributes help them learn, develop their capability, and build a work-life network.

Groundbreaking Goals

Groundbreaking Goals are usually impossible to achieve with the current capability. There will be many barriers to overcome to achieve it. It requires a level of focus, determination, and belief beyond many. Only dedicated winners can maintain the consistency of habits to make this happen. They have hope, and this sustains them as they build the belief that it might be possible. This is the home ground of the winners.

To do something seemingly impossible, winners are driven, bold, flexible, curious, resilient, and hopeful. These attributes help winners to build a prosperous life on their terms and hopefully do some good with their remarkable potential.

HOW TO PLAN FOR SUCCESS

Are you setting your own Groundbreaking Goal?

When considering an opportunity to make the most of your potential, consider the questions below as you create your groundbreaking plan.

1. What is my groundbreaking personal goal?
2. Do I want to achieve the goal?
3. Am I passionate about it?
4. Why am I doing it?
5. Is it achievable for me?
6. Can I do it?
7. Will people around me support me when the going gets tough?
8. What specific steps do I need to take to make it happen?

Your goals can be developed around the four themes in *Choose to Be Relentless*.

So, find your purpose and direction, and be driven and focused. Take control of your circumstances and daily, be the best you can be. Put love into everything you do.

Step out of the shade and into the sunshine of life.

CHOOSE TO BE RELENTLESS
Step out of the shade into the sunshine

PRIORITIES FOR A BETTER YOU

HOW TO PLAN FOR SUCCESS

ACKNOWLEDGEMENTS

In the preparation of *Choose to Be Relentless* I have been supported, assisted, and encouraged by so many people as I refined my thoughts.

I would like to express my deep appreciation to the many readers who took the time to read the draft copies of the book and offer insightful feedback. This intelligent, independent, opiniated reading group were so important to me. Their suggestions on the structure and content were diverse and very helpful in shaping the look and feel of the final product. They were both critical friends and inspiring.

I am grateful for the support of Paul Smedley, the founder and chair of the Forum, for his unwavering support and guidance to me personally as I looked to improve this book.

I would like to thank my editor, Nikki Shanahan, at Tall House Editing for all her expert advice and guidance on the production, layout, and design of this book. She was patient and recognised that the essence of the stories contained the character of Buddy and his family.

ACKNOWLEDGEMENTS

The front cover has been expertly designed by Sarah from Hight Design. Her warmth, ideas, and creativity delivered a finished product that reflects the content of this book.

I feel that the stories expose the strengths and weaknesses of Buddy's character. I hope that the honesty and reflections will provide learning to help others make the most of their life.

Finally, I would like to thank all the readers who have taken the time to read this book.

I hope that you found *Choose to Be Relentless* informative, engaging, and thought-provoking. A valuable guide to assist as you choose to step out of the shade into the sunshine and transform your life.

Richard Brimble – April 2023

RECOMMENDATIONS

"Buddy writes with humour and honesty about rising beyond a difficult childhood, to give himself new choices and build success in life. Working with him over fifteen years, I've seen the difference he has made, by his distinctive, relentless focus on learning, and the relationships that make this possible. This book won't leave you untouched. I love that we learn about the framework of habits and attitudes that have helped him to be what he wants to be, with stories that were comforting and inspiring.

Read *Choose to Be Relentless* if you want to feed your imagination, consider how your own life could be different, or build love into everything that you do."

Paul Smedley, Director & Founder, The Forum, UK

"*Choose to Be Relentless* is an honest view of what it's like, both personally and professionally, to grow from relative humble beginnings to the challenges of executive leadership. It is funny, serious, and practical, recounting the story of an award-winning leader that has led teams of thousands.

The story of Buddy's family is truly inspiring and the openness, trust, drive, and love within the family unit is distilled into every story. Most importantly, it makes you think about your own life and what you should be doing to be the best you can be and have some fun along the way.

It is a powerful guide for anyone looking for motivation, inspiration, and practical advice on how to live a fulfilling life."

Chris Cope, father of two, Digital Innovation Manager, Gloucestershire, UK

RECOMMENDATIONS

Choose to Be Relentless is a powerful, must-read book and story of what it takes to take control of your life.

"Buddy demonstrates an abundance of humour, sharing his own personal journey along with his failures, successes, and lessons learnt. An open and honest book about how to make healthy choices and habits and how to recover when things don't go as planned.

I found myself reflecting on my own journey, personally and professionally, whilst immersed in the stories and relating to the easy-to-understand habits and behaviours the stories bring to life of love, family, travel, music, and teamwork.

The book is an easy-to-read guide to helping anyone live a happy, healthy, and fun-filled life regardless of their starting point."

Anita Yandell Jones, mother of two, Chief Customer Officer, Somerset, UK

"I loved reading *Choose to be Relentless*. It is a fantastic book with many moments that made me smile and countless opportunities for me to reflect and consider my own life.

If you're lucky, at some point in your career you will meet a leader that has such a significant impact on your career that you never forget the lessons that you learned with them. For me, that was Buddy and reading *Choosing to Be Relentless* took me back to those times of introspection, passion, focus and achieving ground-breaking goals. I've experienced the benefits of the thinking and tools first hand, and now I'm ready to go through the process again. Thanks Buddy, for your inspiration."

Richard Bench, married, Technology Leader UK & Ireland, Warwickshire, UK

CHOOSE TO BE RELENTLESS

"*Choose to Be Relentless* is a wonderful example of bringing real life experiences and the journey of building relationships into the business world.

Buddy's honest and heartfelt stories provide a real authenticity to a very clever book bringing autobiography together with business models for behaviours for the first time.

The behaviours for life are brilliant. A model to help set yourself real aspirational goals that drive growth and release your true potential.

Having worked with Buddy I can honestly say he's one of the most inspirational leaders I've ever come across who truly cares about the people he works with and the culture he wants to create. His legacy lives on in any organisation he works in.

He has certainly shaped the leader I am today and the one I aspire to be tomorrow."

Laura Gillson, mother of two, Digital Product Director, Hertfordshire, UK.

"Sprinkled with both heart-felt anecdotes and humorous reflections on the ups and downs that life can bring. *Choose to Be Relentless* provides a genuine perspective into how to identify and work on what is important in life."

Paul Shingler, Teacher, West Yorkshire, UK

"Moving, funny, and self-reflective, Buddy Bramble and his family had me in stitches and shedding a tear while digging deep into life's lessons."

Nikki Shanahan, Editor, North Yorkshire, UK

RECOMMENDATIONS

"As a recent graduate and politically involved 23-year-old, I found Buddy's story to be both extraordinarily comforting and motivational. His encouragement to take control and assess your life's direction will stay with me forever. His words have transformed any fear at what potentially lies ahead into excitement. I urge every young person starting out in the world of work to give it a read.

Choose to Be Relentless appeared in my life at the perfect time – the book I never knew I needed but now I can't imagine having never read! It is such an inspiring read for anyone.

Buddy makes it clear that to live a fulfilling life you must be hard working and impassioned – and to not take yourself too seriously! His journey will resonate with people of all ages, in all stages of life. His recollections of life, work and family are illuminating and insightful.

A moving tale of determination and self-reflection, *Choose to Be Relentless* is a must read for anyone looking to unleash their true potential."

Isabelle Poulter, graduate, Anglesey, Wales

"Most leadership books are academic and theoretical with some practical examples. They don't work for me. They are hard to read as they are not personal. Leadership is about people and you learn and improve by feeling their experiences.

Choosing to Be Relentless is a refreshing alternative to the standard leadership book. You get to understand Buddy's journey as he lets you into his life and you feel part of his career and family. Buddy's failures and successes come to life so that it is easier to apply the lessons learned to your own future journey. Well done on a refreshing alternative."

Guy Chalkley, CEO, New South Wales, Australia

CHOOSE TO BE RELENTLESS

"I loved Relentless because it lifted my spirits and refired my passion.

An inspirational read with laugh out loud stories and emotional anecdotes coupled with deeply engaging questions. It is this mix that left me more and more refreshed and energised as I read on, and then kept me invigorated."

John Maddocks, Global Portfolio Director, Essex, UK

"Buddy is undoubtedly the most inspirational leader that I have worked with. He is also, despite his self-confessed flaws, a thoroughly decent human being.

Buddy genuinely cares about making the human connections, which puts him in a different class to most."

Kathryn Betts, mother of two, Lincolnshire, UK

"I highly recommend *Choose to Be Relentless*. Having known Buddy for over a decade, I have seen first-hand his ability to turn an underperforming company into a success. His book is not just a corporate career guide filled with tips on navigating the workplace, but a comprehensive mantra for living, working, and prioritizing what truly matters in life.

Buddy raises important questions that will challenge readers to make the most of their time on this planet."

Helen Parton, Journalist, London, UK

RECOMMENDATIONS

"It's easy to feel disconnected from self-help and motivational books, but that is not the case with *Choose to Be Relentless*.

The steps shared to help live a well-rounded and fulfilling life are grounded in so much humanity that it becomes impossible not to make connections to your own personal experiences and to identify areas of growth.

It's a truly personal account from the author that is written with care, humility and honesty and is delivered without a hint of judgement or condescension. I can honestly say it's one of the best books I've ever had the pleasure of reading and one I'll definitely be re-reading for years to come."

Leanne Merrill, living with long term partner, Marketing Leader, North Wales

"Buddy's life lessons are an inspiration to many. This book brings them to life, in a funny, jaw dropping and relentless manner.

The life lessons provided me the opportunity and life journey that I am sure other readers can utilise to accelerate their careers using the framework, habits and questions that are thought provoking and enabling us all to keep learning and become winners.

I learnt these having worked with Richard in the 1990's and think it's fantastic to see them available for all."

Kees van Ek, coach to two grown boys, Director, Harrogate, UK

THE AUTHOR

Richard Brimble is a renowned leader with a passion for unlocking the full potential of a team's power when working together as one. His inclusive, collaborative style and inspiring approach have earned him recognition as a top thought leader. He is married, with two adult children and lives in York, North Yorkshire.

With a Lifetime Achievement Award from the European Contact Centre, he has a reputation for designing organisations that drive transformation, sustain exceptional customer experiences and increase profitability.

In the last twenty-five years, he has trailblazed the design of organisations, embedding experiential learning into the heart of their culture. His unique thinking, tools, and frameworks have had a significant impact on the careers of many and facilitated companies to be groundbreaking in their industry.

In 2006 he co-authored *Understanding & Learning: keeping the human factor alive in the digital age.*

With a background in multi-channel contact, digital technologies, and change management, Richard is a master at creating high-performing digital and social teams that drive improved learning, productivity, and commercial performance.

He is the managing director of Understanding & Learning Limited, based in the United Kingdom. He is a non-executive director and delivers advice and guidance to chief executives and their teams to improve the culture, people, and customer experience across different sectors and countries. He continues to be relentless in his passion for helping people find their purpose in life and designing companies fit for the future. A future where the power of teams, collaboration and experiential learning will be the differentiator in any customer experience transformation.